Kościuszko, We Are Here!

Kościuszko, We Are Here!

American Pilots of the Kościuszko Squadron in Defense of Poland, 1919–1921

Janusz Cisek

McFarland & Company, Inc., Publishers
Jefferson, North Carolina, and London

A grant supporting publication of this work has been provided
by the Kosciuszko Foundation, an American center for Polish culture,
promoting educational and cultural exchanges and
relations between the United States and Poland since 1925.

LIBRARY OF CONGRESS CATALOGUING-IN-PUBLICATION DATA

Cisek, Janusz.
    Kościuszko, we are here! : American pilots of the Kościuszko
Squadron in defense of Poland, 1919–1921 / Janusz Cisek.
        p.   cm.
    Includes bibliographical references and index.

    ISBN-13: 978-0-7864-1240-2
    (softcover : 50# alkaline paper) ∞

    1. Poland. Armia. Eskadra Myśliwska imienia Kościuszki, 7.
2. Russo-Polish War, 1919–1920 — Regimental histories — Poland.
3. Russo-Polish War, 1919–1920 — Participation, American.
4. Russo-Polish War, 1919–1920 — Aerial operations, Polish.
I. Title.
DK4406.3.C57   2002   2002008137

British Library cataloguing data are available

©2002 Janusz Cisek. All rights reserved

*No part of this book may be reproduced or transmitted in any form
or by any means, electronic or mechanical, including photocopying
or recording, or by any information storage and retrieval system,
without permission in writing from the publisher.*

Cover image: Kościuszko Squadron's flying equipment at the
Lewandowka aerodrome in the winter of 1919-1920. (Dr. Tomasz
Kopanski, Warsaw)

Manufactured in the United States of America

*McFarland & Company, Inc., Publishers
  Box 611, Jefferson, North Carolina 28640
    www.mcfarlandpub.com*

Acknowledgments

First and foremost I am indebted to the Kosciuszko Foundation in New York City and its president, Mr. Joseph Gore, for providing the publisher with a grant toward this publication.

I would like to thank all of the institutions and persons who have supported me in research and who have allowed me to use archival material. Individually, I would like to thank Mr. Hugh Ahman, Oral History Program, Historical Research Agency, Maxwell Air Force Base; Maria Christian, Pilsudski Memorial Committee, Cracow; Colonel Jon Lewis Allen, USAF (Ret.); Lt. Col. Aleksandra Rhode, United States Army; Maciej Siekierski, Ph.D., Hoover Institution; Tomasz Kopański, Ph.D., Institute on Military History, Warsaw; Richard Kaleta, New York; Paul Konys, Rocky River, OH; Andrzej Krawczak, Ph.D., Executive Director of the Archive of Modern History (AAN), Warsaw; Andrzej K. Kunert, Ph.D., Director of the Archive of the Underground Poland, 1939–1956; Andrzej Suchcitz, Ph.D., Polish Museum and General Sikorski Institute, London; Colonel Zygmunt Kozak, Central Military Archives (CAW), Warsaw; Krystyna Piórkowska, New York; Jan Adler, Ph.D., Professor Emeritus, New York University; Wanda Wyporski, Ph.D. Candidate, Oxford and Warsaw University.

TABLE OF CONTENTS

Acknowledgments	vii
Preface	1
1. Legion or Squadron	5
2. Spiritus Movens	18
3. Motives	43
4. Paris — Warsaw — Lwów	51
5. Objectives of Piłsudski	87
6. In the Kiev Offensive	96
7. An American Legion Again?	130
8. In Defense of the City of the Lion	140
9. Captain Cooper's Odyssey	165
10. Wartime Air Force Experiences	174
11. The Squadron's Odyssey	183
12. The Defenders of Lwów Cemetery	192
Appendix: Service Histories and Commendations of U.S. Airmen in the Polish Military	199
Notes	209
Resources	237
Geographical Index	239
General Index	243

Preface

When reviewing the history of the United States, it is not difficult to list military missions the nation has entered into outside its own borders in the defense of democratic ideals or the safety of American allies. The great majority of these missions have found their deserved place in history books and the general historical consciousness of the American people. However, some missions, entered into almost single-handedly, are glossed over in the larger historical overview, and even people with a serious interest in history know little about them.

Among such events one can list the expedition organized in the fall of 1919 by a small group of American flyers who decided to form the Kościuszko Squadron for the defense of Poland. The departure of these flyers to Poland was in no way related to the official policy of the Department of State. In fact, it occurred against the guidelines of the State Department and without the official concurrence of the American Expeditionary Force in Europe. Not one of the pilots was bound to Poland in any way, neither by blood nor by any other link, and only one, Merian Cooper, had any emotional links with the homeland of two American soldiers, Generals Kościuszko and Pulaski. Further, it was difficult for them to count on receiving honors, fame or financial rewards for this action. Instead, what awaited them on the Polish-Bolshevik front line were dangers unknown in Western Europe. Their equipment was in poor condition; there was a severe shortage of medical services; and when captured by the Bolshevik forces, these pilots faced the prospect of immediate execution.

It was extremely difficult for their story to break through to the front pages of any newspapers. There were but a few reporters in Warsaw transmitting information on the progress of the war. Aside from this, one must remember that these pilots served in the Polish Army; hence it was impossible for them to count on automatic advance or promotion upon their return to the United States.

Most Western politicians and military leaders, as well as most of the public, underestimated the military significance of the Polish-Bolshevik war and showed no comprehension of its political importance. Few wanted to subscribe to the opinion that Western civilization was being defended near Warsaw and that the war was in fact a prelude to Russia's plans to occupy central Europe, if not the whole continent. Only a few of the most attentive observers unhesitatingly described the war and the battle of Warsaw as crucial events in world history. It was only possible to fully appreciate these farsighted fighter pilots from abroad after World War II.

Therefore there arise questions of a more general nature:

- What were the goals of these idealists who arrived at the very edges of Europe?
- Was the debt of honor owed to Poland for the services of General Kościuszko and General Pulaski enough to risk one's life?
- Could an aversion to communism be so fully developed as to face down the armies set upon Europe by Lenin and Trotsky?
- Could the presence of around a dozen pilots on the Polish front have any effect on the outcome of the war? Could it even leave the slightest mark on the efforts of hundreds of thousands of people?
- What was their knowledge about the political imbroglio of the Polish-Bolshevik conflict, or about the farsighted goals of the war against Bolshevism?

To answer all of these fascinating questions is the goal of this volume. It is based on archival materials stored in the United States, Great Britain and Poland. Access to some of these materials was, during the years of communist domination of Poland, totally precluded. In fact, the very Polish-Bolshevik War of 1919–1920, in essence the only military defeat of the Red Army in its entire history, was a forbidden subject. Since Poland is now a member of NATO, it has become perfectly natural to open archives and seek out the roots of joint cooperation.

This book documents Americans' participation in and emphasizes their influence on the events on the Polish southern front. Their achievements were fully appreciated during the course of and after the war. Even later when Eastern Europe had fallen under the control of Stalinist Russia, memory of these pilots had not died. Poles living in Lwów and other cities continued believing that joint Polish-American military operations would yet occur. None of the American participants of the 1920 aerial operations survived to see such a day. Perhaps they were left with the belief that someone would someday stand and report: "Kościuszko — We are here!"

1 | Legion or Squadron

The presence of American airmen in the Polish army was preceded by a series of efforts between the individual enlistment of officers, soldiers and citizens of the United States and the drafting of a separate American legion to fight in Poland. Endeavors in this field lasted as long as the Polish–Bolshevik war itself. Their one tangible result was the establishment of the Kościuszko Squadron, a military unit unique in being the sole representative of the Western Hemisphere in this war, since in 1920 the only regular military forces helping Poland were the army of the Ukrainian People's Republic under Ataman Semen Petlura and a small Belorussian Army under the command of General Stanisław Bułak Bałachowicz. Unlike the American volunteers, both of these formations fought primarily for the independence of their own nations.

The efforts of representatives of the Polish Republic were based on a variety of factors. The main one was the threat of German and Russian revolution and the continuation of the war in Eastern Europe. When Poland regained her independence in 1918, her borders were not yet defined. Her administration was based mainly on the dedication of civil servants of Polish descent, who remained on their jobs after the fall of the three occupying powers, Germany, Russia and Austria-Hungary. The Army comprised barely a few tens of thousands of veterans of the Polish Military Organization, the Polish Legions, and officers and soldiers who gradually flowed in from the armies of the partitioning powers. After four years of war, during which enemy armies plundered everything that could be of any use, there was nothing left in Poland. The infrastructure of roads, railways, bridges, water-supply systems and power-plants was almost completely destroyed. One must remember that the front rolled through some areas several times.

Józef Piłsudski, Commander-in-Chief and Head of the Polish State, and the entire nation faced an enormous challenge. Confronted by shortages, many Polish politicians turned towards the West. It was not only about delivering aid to a suffering population. It was also of primary importance to repel the Bolshevik armies approaching from the east and to prevent the communist revolution in Russia from uniting with the German "Spartakus" movement. However, the young Polish state did not possess enough military might.

Thus Pilsudski's attention concentrated on bringing to Poland the 80,000 strong army of General Józef Haller, which included a significant number of Polish residents of the United States and which was still stationed in France after November 1918. In fact, it remained there until April 1919, and became the pivot of many plans both political and military within the Polish National Committee, and also in French, British, and American circles. Haller's Army was officially chartered in France by a decree of the French president on June 4, 1917. Following insistent appeals by the famous pianist Ignacy Jan Paderewski to President Woodrow Wilson, permission was given also to recruit Poles living in America. Up until the end of the war, 24,260 American Poles served in the army's ranks. The rest were recruited from prisoners of war, Poles living in western Europe, and Polish volunteers from other countries. That superbly trained and equipped army was no mere bagatelle in November 1918, when Poland reappeared on the European map. For both the Americans and the Poles, it had already set a precedent — as reborn Poland's first army recruited from beyond her national territory and as the first American contingent to fight beyond its own national boundries in the sole interests of a foreign state.

The hope given by the existence of this precedent was rekindled when some of the hundreds of thousands of demobilized soldiers and officers of the American Expeditionary Force (AEF), who were mainly based in France, indicated their readiness to serve, even under a foreign flag. It did not only affect Poland.

Among the important factors, it is also worth mentioning that as a consequence of the partitions, a significant group of Polish officers served in the armies of other states, which obviously influenced organization of the Polish army after over a century of occupation. In November and December 1918, the cadre of officers, at first derived from the Polish Legions of Józef Piłsudski, began to fill with Poles who, lacking other opportunities, had trained and become officers in the Austro-Hungarian, Russian, or to a lesser extent German armies. One can assume that in the Polish Army there was a conducive atmosphere for the transfer of officers and soldiers from other armies. We already mentioned here the consistent threat to the Republic, prevalent from the very beginning of its independent existence. Polish politicians and the military thought that a foreign military contingent would have a restraining influence on the appetites of both her large and small neighbors. On the assumptions made above, Ignacy Jan Paderewski, a few days after the signing of the armistice in November 1918, asked the American Secretary of War Newton D. Baker for permission to discharge all soldiers and officers of Polish extraction from the American Army to enable them to serve in the Polish Army. According to various estimates — independently of Haller's army, which was not a part of the American Armed Forces — there were approximately 200,000–230,000 officers and soldiers "of Polish extraction" who were serving under the Star Spangled Banner. It needs to be stressed that in the aforementioned appeal to Baker, Paderewski was only concerned with Polish "resident aliens," excluding American citizens. Baker, who had been considered a friend to Poland, refused, fearing that the officers and soldiers would serve a nationalistic cause, which he suspected Poland of propagating. This argument managed to convince Wilson, thanks to which the project failed.[1]

Equally doomed to failure in the United States were the efforts in this direction of John Smulski, a Chicago banker, who worked closely with the Parisian Polish National Committee. Even worse, the cessation of hostilities in Europe led to the prohibition of the continuation of enlistment into the Haller Army on U.S. territory. As a result of various pressures, on January 25, 1919, Roman Dmowski, in the name of the Polish National Committee, informed the American Charge d'Affaires in Paris of the cessation of recruitment to the Haller Army on U.S. territory. At the end of February, recruitment was ceased.

During the first few weeks after Poland regained independence, the scope of the search was broadened beyond the Haller Army. At the turn of the years 1918–1919 a project was discussed in Paris which entailed sending a corps of Allied Forces, most preferably made up of Americans, to Poland to form a *cordon sanitaire* from Riga to the Dniepr River. Even a railway line linking the port of Gdansk (Danzig) with Toruń (Thorn) and Warsaw was considered. Irrespective of the fact that the project turned out to be ephemeral, yet again, it entertained the idea of the use of foreign military forces, in this case American, on the Vistula River.[2]

Exactly at the same moment, precisely during the last days of December 1918, Paderewski returned to Poland. The observations he made on the spot were alarming, the Bolshevik threat was more than tangible. In a January 4, 1919, dispatch to President Wilson's adviser Col. Edward M. House, Paderewski wrote:

> Conditions most critical. Former Polish territories are still being invaded by the Bolsheviks. ... There are no arms, munitions, equipment, but human material still considerable. Imminent disaster. My country appeal to the best, most generous friend asking for help, for salvation in this tragic hour. This barbarous movement will certainly be stopped in its further progress if fifty thousand Americans, one division of British troops and one French are sent immediately with necessary material for large Polish Army. Our entire civilization may cease to exist if action is delayed. The establishment of barbarism all over Europe may result from the war.[3]

It turned out that not all the appeals reached House. On January 12, Paderewski lamented, "I shall not be able to fully describe [to] you the situation which is simply tragic." He emphatically stressed the danger of the German-Bolshevik alliance:

> There is also not the slightest doubt that the present Spartacus movement in Germany and the Bolshevik revolution in Russia are most closely connected. They simply intend to meet on our soil.... Poland cannot defend itself. We have no food, no uniforms, no arms, no munitions. ... I have been asked to form a new cabinet, but what could I do with the moral support of the country alone, without the material assistance of the Allies and the United States.[4]

These appeals provoked no tangible results. The issue of the Allied Forces providing direct help to Poland came to a standstill. The U.S. Administration and President Wilson's entourage were against intervention in Russia or sending the army there. In a dispatch of February 23, 1919, Col. House wrote to the President:

> No foreign intervention in Soviet Russia and no foreign troops to be sent to aid of non–Bolshevik Russia unless volunteers choose to go of their own accord, but material assistance to be supplied to these Governments to enable them to hold their own in the territories which are not anxious to submit to Bolshevik rule. ... We are bound to give moral, material and if necessary military support to protect Poland, Finland and other states against Bolshevik invasion.[5]

The date of the dispatch coincided with the final suspension of recruitment to the Haller Army in the U.S. One can therefore regard this as the closure of the first stage of Poland's efforts to obtain American military help. It did not, however, mean that the issue had been abandoned. The next stage began a few months later. Its main protagonists were now General Tadeusz Rozwadowski and two American officers, Colonel Harry S. Howland and General A.W. Bjornstad. Rozwadowski had become head of the Polish Military Mission in Paris as of March 21, 1919. In June of that year, on Paderewski's initiative, he became the official representative of the Polish Armed Forces in Paris. Of course, the nature of his assignment and his position were far greater than the Military Purchasing Mission, which operated there first under the orders of General Jan Romer, and then General Józef Pomiankowski. Rozwadowski, in the midst of efforts to build a foreign legion, did not enjoy the best of relations with General Romer. Due to this fact he failed to exploit certain incentives to purchase more American equipment, which could have promoted the idea of an American Legion for Poland.[6]

Aside from his military credentials based on his achievements and heroic service during World War One, Rozwadowski was a man of significant political ambitions and much initiative. He was more than ready to take up and put into action every available plan for strengthening the military potential of Poland. The favorable atmosphere for the advancement of the plan for the Legion was tied in to the approaching date of the signing of the peace treaty. It was feared that after this date, there would be mass demobilization and the departure of potential volunteers. Halfway through the year, signals appeared of a change in attitude towards Polish matters by the American side. On July 3, 1919, Jan Ciechanowski, Paderewski's secretary and later Ambassador of the Republic of Poland in Washington, reported to the Minister of Foreign Affairs on the approval by President Wilson and Secretary of State Robert Lansing to Poland's advancement and seizure of territory beyond the line of the River Zbrucz on the East. Rozwadowski also tried to take advantage of the more favorable attitude towards the purchase of American equipment from the supplies remaining in Europe. He also wanted to take advantage of American officers volunteering for service in the Polish Army. Such was the background of his sincere friendship with Colonel Harry Howland, an American Military Attache accredited to the Polish Military Mission in France on the orders of General John Pershing, the Commander-in-Chief of the AEF. In his report to Piłsudski on the subject of Polish policy towards Germany and Russia dated June 10, 1919, he considered the possibility of taking advantage of this potential:

One ought to approach this, at the same time involving the Americans, who are extremely interested in us. Among them, there is a mania for signing up to the ranks of our army. Not having yet obtained fundamental guidelines about our position in this respect, I then replied that at this time, we could only accept officers who speak Polish. However, I know that a strong agitation is developing now in the American army, which is still in Europe, for whole units to enlist in the Polish forces in the event that we face battle against the Germans. It would be a great shrine of ready and organized strength, but I doubt that the American government itself currently wants to allow this. It has constantly sent back and systematically demobilized the forces, because it did not want to allow America to be dragged into any further military action in Europe. These are fears that ought to be seen clearly, so as not to yield to dangerous illusions.

Not all of those who were discharged wanted to return to America. Some of them tried to remain in Europe as instructors, advisers, and even, if such occasions arose, as regular officers contracted by foreign armies. The armed forces of the newly established states showed particularly great interest, and the most sought-after were officers with experience in technical weapons, and among those, of course, the Air Force. The authenticity of Rozwadowski's reports on this matter is confirmed by a memorandum by Lieutenant Colonel Robert J. Halpin from the Headquarters of the American Embarcation Center, AEF, to General Colonel Arnold on the subject of voluntary American legions. Taking advantage of the interest of the AEF personnel in serving Poland, Halpen asked about the conditions, the remuneration standards, the relationship of the U.S. government to the undertaking, conditions of transfer from U.S. service, and entry into the ranks of the Legion.[7] Foreseeing that the most valuable element would simply leave Europe, on June 15, 1919, Rozwadowski reported to Warsaw in a very pressing tone:

> Yesterday, a Canadian colonel reported to me again, declaring that many officers and at least a few thousand soldiers would volunteer now to go to Poland, merely in order to fight against the Germans. The enthusiasm of the American and English officers, who are reporting every day, is ceaseless. ... Since at the moment the pertinent governments responsible for the greater part of these volunteers are sending them abroad and their redirection would cost both a lot of time and money, therefore it would only be possible to consider those who are already in Europe.[8]

It can be concluded that there was a discrepancy between U.S. politicians and the military. Policy makers and high-ranking officers were reluctant to commit American forces, voluntary or otherwise, for Eastern Europe. On the other hand the lower echelons of the AEF were apparently eager to continue their service, this time against the Bolsheviks or a German-Bolshevik alliance. These inconsistencies were to accompany the project right to the very end. Pershing's aversion to involving the military, even the forces that remained in Europe, was noted by Colonel House. "We discussed the return of our troops to America. ... Pershing is not enthusiastic over any of our troops remaining for occupation purposes."[9]

Another obstacle was that the Polish High Command did not, at this stage, develop a cohesive approach to this problem. It was Gen. Rozwadowski, who was forcing his views and tried to influence a change of approach in the matter. He expressed the coviction that the situation in Silesia, where a German-Polish conflict had arisen concerning the question of Silesia's future, would force the Allies to send their troops to monitor the situation. He still thought that the very presence of Americans in Poland would be advantageous and that this situation would improve the chances of establishing the legion. In addition, Paderewski appealed for a presence in Silesia in a somewhat later letter to Secretary of State Lansing:

> Considering the ties of closest friendship which bind my people to the American nation, nothing would better please Silesian population, than to see their country, during the hours of trial, occupied and protected by the U.S. troops.[10]

Taking advantage of the somewhat favorable atmosphere invoked by the imminent signing of a peace treaty with the Germans, Rozwadowski decided to address General John Pershing directly. On June 27th with Rozwadowski's authorization, John Smulski relayed to Pershing the question of the possibility of organizing an American legion for Poland.[11]

This idea most clearly landed on fertile ground, because already by July 5, 1919, there was a meeting between Howland and Pershing, at which the establishment of the legion was discussed. On July 7 Howland committed to paper the results of this discussion and his own thoughts. His memo was the first written definition of the legion organization, although there was still no officially expressed approval for the legion from the AEF. Howland wrote that as regards the large number of those reporting for service in the Polish Army, their individual enlistment would be impracticable, especially because of the language barrier:

> It would be possible therefore only to admit these volunteer American officers and soldiers into the Polish service by organizing them into special legions which can be formed most easily in France by attaching them temporarily to certain Polish troops that remain here for the time being. ... It is proposed to utilize the services of American volunteers: (a) Combatants to be enrolled in an American Legion, to be commanded by American officers, to be organized in France, to consist of as many tactical units as numbers enrolled permit.
>
> (b) Medical, sanitary, technical and service personnel to be organized for services with the Legion and with other units of the Polish Army. ... Combatants (i.e., the Legion) will be employed exclusively in operations against the Bolsheviks on the Russian frontier, not against Germans unless the latter attack Poland, then with the consent of the American Government.[12]

The behind-the-scenes plans at last took the form of a memo written by a high ranking American officer, with Pershing's permission, which meant that the matter had been moved up a notch. Not surprisingly, Rozwadowski was extremely happy. On the same day, he informed Warsaw of the basics of Howland's position:

> The continuous reporting of officers and soldiers for duty in the Polish Army, has forced me, since there are no relevant guidelines, to take a basic position. According to an understanding with the Prime Minister, I declared to Colonel Howland, General Pershing's special delegate, that the enlistment of native American officers and soldiers in our army, would, for a variety of reasons, present many problems. If, however, these volunteers wanted to create a separate legion, using the [French] Foreign Legion as an example and according to French law, our Government and High Command undoubtedly should to accept America's help for Poland in the fight against Bolshevism with only gratitude. I report on this briefly, adding that according to Colonel Howland's project, the Americans would like to organize such a volunteer legion here in France, from our units. Apart from chosen officers and soldiers, specialists in particular would be admitted, but one of the most famous military aviators undertook to immediately create a whole air wing. The matter reached such a stage that it would not have behoved us to refuse American help, as Monsieur Pichon, the French Minister of Foreign Affairs stated to me yesterday.[13]

This document confirmed interest in a U.S. legion, and also the advancement of the matter from a stage of initial considerations to the level of the AEF HQ. It proves at last precise personal cooperation between Pershing's representative and Rozwadowski. No less important was Pichon's agreement, noted in the last of the quoted reports. It was a valuable achievement, considering the sensitivity of the French military to its special status in Poland. There is finally the mention of a project to create a group of airmen by an unnamed American officer. At this stage, Rozwadowski certainly knew Merian Cooper. It is less likely, although not out of the question, that he was already in contact with Major Cedric Fauntleroy. The latter said that General Mason Matthews Patrick, Chief of the AEF's Air Service, made his acquaintance with Rozwadowski. Fauntleroy, later the Commander of the Kościuszko Squadron, did not, however, specify the date of that meeting. In any case, in a 1962 interview he said that he did not intend to serve in Europe, that ultimately it was the lucrative financial incentive by the Polish Army Purchasing Mission that induced him to it.[14]

One can allege that the architect of the squadron, of whom Rozwadowski wrote, was Captain Merian Cooper, known to him from Lwów. His project was then still treated as an integral part of the volunteer legion, and most certainly in Rozwadowski's mind the success of the whole venture depended upon it. Nevertheless, it is worth noting that the concept of an air unit comprising American volunteers appeared at this time.

The attitude of the Polish authorities in Warsaw at this stage requires a commentary. Historians writing on the subject emphasize the indifference of Piłsudski and the Polish military authorities. This may be corroborated by several documents. For instance, on July 3, 1919, the Polish Minister of Military Affairs issued an instruction which confirmed that the enlistment of a large number of officers abroad could cause relations with the French Military Mission in Poland to deteriorate. Shortly after, however, the Ministry, the General Staff, and the Commander-in-Chief treated this matter equally favorably. In his commentary on Rozwadowski's next report, the Chief of the General Staff, Colonel Stanisław Haller (not to be mistaken with Gen. Józef Haller) wrote to Piłsudski: "as far as the use of a whole volunteer legion in the fight against the Germans and Bolsheviks, the High Command insisted on an opinion from the Ministry of Foreign Affairs, stressing that eventually it would be advantageous to deploy these troops in Upper Silesia, during the plebiscite."[15]

On July 14, Colonel Haller sent Rozwadowski's next report to Piłsudski's General Adjutancy, together with an outline of the official position:

> The High Command in consultation with the relevant ministries and according to the opinion received from the Commander-in-Chief, consider it possible to accept the opinion of Colonel Howland in principle, with the intention of utilizing one unit consisting of American officers and soldiers, only for the occupation of Upper Silesia.[16]

Therefore it is difficult to say that there was complete lack of interest. Furthermore on this basis, one can dismiss the thesis of those historians who wanted to see the presence of Americans as an anti–Bolshevik tool. The Polish General Staff considered the deployment of volunteers in the west to be an efficient instrument to counterbalance the Germans in Silesia and more politically opportune. The concern that the U.S. would improvidentially be drawn into a conflict in the east is also clear. Politically, it was significantly more advantageous for Warsaw. As a matter of fact, in the quoted documents, there was no commentary whatsoever on the subject of financing the venture, therefore one can suppose that the High Command of the Polish Armed Forces thought that the Americans would also provide assistance in this matter. The newly reborn Republic certainly could not afford to allocate greater financial resources.

This time Howland's memo of July 7 did not wait long for a reply. On July 10 Major General J.G. Habard, Chief of Staff, AEF General HQ, told Howland of the opinions of General Pershing:

> If such persons after their discharge desire to enroll for Polish Service, it is a matter with which our military authorities have nothing to do. Such officers and soldiers, if their desire discharge, should make it a subject of an application in the same way as those desiring discharge in Europe for any other reason.[17]

As a matter of fact it was not unconditional support, but nevertheless Rozwadowski and Howland considered that Pershing's answer was encouraging. The General appeared to show the way, mainly in the organization of a legion, following individual discharge from the ranks of the AEF. Howland and Rozwadowski considered that, having tacit approval from Pershing's side, they ought to obtain agreement from the political authorities even if it was conditional. They also attempted to widen the recruitment base. In correspondence to the High Command of the Polish Armed Forces on July 13, Rozwadowski wrote:

> It seems to me, however, that all these (officers) should be rather encouraged to create a separate legion consisting of their own American people. They could be re-formed most easily in France, and transferred to the country as an equipped and compact unit, which would

immediately strengthen our fighting force. If the American and Canadian governments want to agree to this, it would be the best way out, because it simply built up our forces.... The strengthening of our forces by an American-Canadian auxiliary volunteer corps, according to the proposition of the American Colonel Howland and General Bjornstad, and recruitment in America and organization in France, could be exceptionally advantageous and desirable. Therefore, the rather affluent and enthusiastic General Townsend needed to be pushed in this direction and encouraged to create English legions.[18]

It turned out, however, that there were also Canadians and even Britons by the side of the American officers. Additionally, Rozwadowski and Howland succeeded in persuading an eminent officer at Pershing's HQ, General A.W. Björnstad (who had on behalf on Pershing established the War College in France), to cooperate. His task was to prepare specific guidelines for the organization of the legion. It was a project, which forged ahead in terms of priority, in relation to Howland's memo of July 7. Bjornstad had already prepared his memo on July 16. He assumed that recruitment to the legion would be conducted similarly in France as in the U.S. Enlistment for North America was to be based in New York under its own leadership. After the completion of the enlistment and preparation of the cadre, Bjornstad was to return to Europe to head the legion personally. In addition, he sought Washington's permission, though in a veiled form, as "tacit approval ... or that no objection will be made." The project assumed the following organization:

> (a) Battalions, with experts in infantry, machine guns, small cannon and tanks. (b) Air service units — day bombers, reconnaissance and chasse [fighter], (c) Sanitary [medical] units, especially hospitals rather than ambulance companies.[19]

Björnstad wrote that the organization of the legion would be identical to American standards in the level of remuneration, conditions of service, and promotion. Howland explained this in a letter sent on the very same day to Paderewski on the guidelines and benefits to be gained by the acceptance of Björnstad's project by the Polish Government. The letter magnified the General's profile informing the Polish Prime Minister that Björnstad was on his way back to the U.S. on board the same ship as Secretary of State Lansing. It was expected that the time would be used to obtain the sought-after political approval of the plan.[20] There are reasons indicating that indeed Lansing tended to agree that the establishment of the legion would be advantageous to American interests, and that he promised to make an effort in the State Department.[21]

In the search for allies for his plans, Rozwadowski, together with Howland, solicited the support of Major General Tasker H. Bliss, one of the members of the American Commission to Negotiate Peace and the Supreme War Council. He, however, evaded granting a guarantee to the project. His stance towards Polish matters at the Peace conference was negative in many aspects. He thought that Poland was developing into a militaristic and aggressive state, and because of this he refused support for Polish territorial demands and even attempts to buy American military equipment in Europe.[22]

Therefore, it was unlikely he would support the idea of the legion. He had earlier expressed a negative opinion about the French plan of General Belin, the Chairman of the Allied Military Representatives. In a report from the beginning of July 1919, Belin suggested that following the definition of Poland's military needs, all of the countries of the Big Four should diligently act to support them. On July 11, Colonel S. D. Embick gave a negative reply on behalf of General Bliss.[23] Equally unsuccessful was the attempt to gain Lansing's support despite his well-publicized pro–Polish attitude. The expected agreement by neither the Department of State nor by the President was forthcoming — precisely the opposite. In August 1919, the War Department, at the request of the Department of State, refused permission for Major Allen W. Pollit (who the Polish Government intended to employ in the capacity of an instructor and advisor in motorized units) to leave for Poland.[24]

General Björnstad's talks in the War Department in Washington were equally unsuccessful. He also did not manage to ensure cooperation from John Smulski, who was influential among Polish Americans, and who was counted on for financial support for the project.

The plan to establish an American volunteer legion failed. Among the reasons, the most important were a lack of political will and coordination between the AEF, War Department and State Department. The lack of a clearly defined U.S. policy towards Poland was apparent at this stage and manifested itself both in the politicians' mutually conflicting stances and in specific military factors. Rozwadowski, like his American collaborators, acted in isolation from the decision-making center. Neither the Polish Consulate in New York, where volunteers reported, nor the U.S. Military Attache in Warsaw, was aware of plans to establish the legion. They had received no guidelines in this matter. Anyway, Pollit's case and the completion in the middle of August 1919 of the basic phase of evacuation of the AEF personnel from Europe to the U.S. ultimately buried the idea of the legion. The chances of its establishment faded also due to President Wilson's failing health and because at the end of the year Lansing ceased to be Secretary of State. They were both considered to be favorably disposed towards Poland. The project itself brought valuable experience, which the Polish side used in the organization of the Kościuszko Squadron, especially in attracting volunteers and handling their contracts and other legal matters.

2 | Spiritus Movens

The officer mentioned in Rozwadowski's report who offered his services for Poland was most probably Merian Cooper. Rozwadowski did not name him, but Cooper himself managed to go to Paris at the time with the more or less crystallized intention of organizing a voluntary air squadron consisting of American airman. Cooper's idea lacked the momentum of Howland or Björnstad, and he did not expect comfortable conditions of service. He was driven by a more idealistic motivation when he left for Lwów, where for two months he had been the head of Herbert Hoover's Food Mission. His family tradition had led him to that town. General Casimir Pulaski had fought together with the regiment of the Continental Army whose commanding officer was John Cooper, a direct ancestor of Merian Cooper. According to family history, John Cooper transported the mortally wounded Pulaski from the battlefield at Savannah on October 9, 1779, to the *Wasp* moored in a nearby bay. It was on board this ship that Pulaski died. This family tradition was upheld so strongly that it had passed to Merian Cooper's generation.[1]

Merian Coldwell Cooper was born on October 24, 1893, in Jacksonville, Florida, into a family with old military traditions. He studied, for three years and eight months, until 1915, at the Naval Academy in Annapolis. However, his interests reached far beyond the obligatory curriculum. In one of his later letters to a friend, he wrote:

> I learned nothing from books there. When I was supposing to be studying Physics and Chemistry, and Engineering, I visited the Academy Library and read Plato, Aristotle, Spinoza, Darwin, Russel and the very great geographer who wrote "The Effect of Climate on Civilization" Professor Huntington of Yale. More that any man in the Naval Academy,

2. Spiritus Movens

I studied long and hard the Military Tactics and Strategy as taught by Admiral Mahan and by Alexander the Great, Julius Caesar, Moltke and Jomini. I learned one thing, which I believe in: in War, only a simple plan can succeed. This is how Napoleon beat everyone untill he fought Wellington at Waterloo. Wellington had even a simpler plan. But the greatest of all strategists was Nelson. Admiral Nelson said: "Morale is to the Physical as Three to One."[2]

This motto inspired Cooper throughout his entire life. Merian Cooper did not graduate from the Academy. Before his graduation, he transferred to the National Guard, with whom he took part in the campaign against Pancho Villa at the Mexican border. He was assigned to the 2nd Georgia Infantry stationed at Camp Cotton, El Paso, Texas. During his service in this unit he rejected several times promotion to 1st Sergeant and declined his chance of a commission in order to remain with his own company. It was not to be the last time. In fact, Cooper twice turned down commissions in favor of aviation training as a private first class.[3]

The opinions of his superiors testify significantly to the young officer's character. His superior in the National Guard wrote: "Sergeant Cooper is an excellent soldier, far above the average of enlisted men of the National Guard. I believe that he possesses the necessary qualifications for the aviation service."[4]

His application in 1917 for permission to transfer to the Air Service was the third in a row. The second one was refused by the Secretary of State on November 23, 1916. However, the worsening military situation in Europe helped Cooper to accomplish his aim. On July 7, 1917, his application to train in aviation was accepted. Neither the future hero's father nor his superiors were convinced that his decision was the right one. In a letter to John Cooper, the young Merian's father, Walter Harris wrote:

> I wanted to keep Merian with me more than I have wanted anything else since I have been in the military service, but his heart was set on flying and I am glad that he has at last got what he wanted. All that I have said of him is shown in his record in this command; he was considered the best soldier in the Second Georgia and that this made him the best in the brigade I believed and acted upon to the extent of asking for his commission as my aid.[5]

On September 26, 1917, Cooper finally received his wings as a Reserve Military Aviator. The very next day he submitted an application to the Chief Signal Officer of the Army to be posted to Europe with immediate effect. His superiors strongly favored his application. One of them, James Murray, who was Commander of the 200th and 201st Squadrons, was assigned for training service in England at the end of December. Prior to his departure, he gave his opinion about Cooper, whom he described as the most gifted officer that he had met in his 20 years of service in the Armed Forces. Captain H.H.C. Richards, Aviation Section, S.C. Department Aeronautical Officer, expressed a similar opinion.[6]

In France Cooper was originally sent to Issoudon aviation training center. After having completed the course, where he met many of his later friends, he was transferred to the 20th Squadron of the First Day Bombardment Group, which fought within the 1st Army. Besides purely military assignments, he was also in charge of a Movie Picture unit, which documented the service of American pilots. Newsreels with his footage were shown in France and the United States.[7] Together with his squadron he distinguished himself during the offensive at St. Mihiel from September 12 to 16, 1918, and the offensive on Meuse-Argonne, September 26 to November 11, 1918, in which the Air Force efficiently prevented a concentration of the enemy forces.[8] Cooper himself followed the displacement of the army and fought against the German Air Force. On September 26th during a bombing expedition over Dun-sur-Meuse, he came under fire from four German planes. His plane caught fire and he himself sustained heavy burns. A description of the action from this day can be gathered from the Cooper's promotion application:

> In the course of a bombing mission on Dun-sur-Meuse on September 26th, 1918, the formation was attacked far behind the German lines and at an altitude of 15000 feet by a formation of enemy scout planes three times the size of our own formation. In the course of the fight which followed five of the seven planes were shot down. In attempting to protect a plane below the formation, Lieutenant Cooper took a very exposed position against overwhelming odds, and by skillfully maneuvering his plane he enabled his Observer, Lieutenant Edmund C. Leonard, to bring down one enemy aircraft and assist in bringing down another. Lieutenant Cooper held his position until his observer was severely wounded and his motor burst in flames. The plane then started down out of control. Thinking his observer dead, Lieutenant Cooper climbed from his cockpit, intending to jump from the plane. Upon seeing that his Observer was still alive, Lieutenant Cooper showed great courage and determination, despite the flames in the cockpit, climbed back and succeeded in cutting off the gas supply to

2. Spiritus Movens

the motor and managed to extinguish the flames. In doing so, Lieutenant Cooper was severely burned on the hands and on face. Despite the fact that his hands were practically useless as a result of the burns, and the great pain he suffered, he succeeded in regaining control of the plane and brought it down without injury to himself or his Observer.[9]

Cooper saved his own life but lost his freedom, since he found himself in German hands.

His superiors recognized his behavior in action and recommended him for decoration with the Distinguished Service Cross. When he heard that the six other pilots who had perished in the same bombing raid had not been recommended for a similar distinction, he did not accept it. Telling proof of his attitude was a letter, now deposited in the Hoover Institution. His only "decoration" was the lasting burns that he sustained to his face and hands. Treatment in a hospital accessible to prisoners of war near Wrocław (Breslau) did not manage to get rid of them. In any case, months later the scars saved his life.

During the above mentioned interlude near Wrocław, Cooper had a chance to get to know prisoners of war from the eastern front. Here for the first time, as he later wrote, he encountered Russian officers from whom he learnt his first lessons in Communism. His aversion to the ideology and desire to fight it dates from this time. His incarceration did not last long. The cease-fire signed on November 11, 1918, in Compiegne meant a swift return to France. Not long afterwards Cooper was transferred to the Red Cross hospital in Neuilly.

Despite his harrowing experiences and incomplete recovery, Cooper had no intention of returning to the U.S., nor of indulging in a more than well-earned rest. He quickly discovered another passion, service in the American Food Administration, which had started its activities also in Poland. Its chairman Herbert Hoover, had already visited Polish territory in 1913 and in November 1915 sent Vernon Kellogg there. He was to evaluate the situation of those in Poland who had been affected by the war. The situation was tragic. Right until the end of the war, the country had been pillaged by the German, Russian, and Austro-Hungarian armies. According to Hoover's findings, the front rolled across some parts of territories populated by Poles seven times, causing death and enormous destruction to the infrastructure.[10] Agriculture was particularly badly hit and due to this fact the food situation deteriorated. Many areas had not been sown for several years, others had fallen into neglect because of the death of the owner, lack of machinery or an epidemic. The worst disasters affected the poorest layers of society and children. When Poland again roused herself to an independent existence she not only faced military threats from East and West, but was forced into battle against hunger and epidemics, which attacked her together with the Bolshevik armies advancing westward.[11] The prices of basic articles increased repeatedly several-fold. Even firewood was rationed due to lack of coal. The tragic food situation was reflected in the reports of the U.S. Military Attache to Warsaw.[12] Herbert Hoover had already drawn attention to the suffering in Poland in his speech entitled "An Appeal to World Conscience," enumerating it along with the suffering in Belgium, northern France, Serbia, Romania, Montenegro, Armenia, and Russia.

At Hoover's initiative on January 24, 1919, Congress passed an appropriation bill of $100,000,000 to finance appropriate aid. In a later period, the financial aid was significantly increased. Prior to this resolution, Hoover, in December 1918, before the official recognition of the Polish government by the U.S., sent Kellogg to Warsaw to ascertain Poland's needs and to examine the possibilities of providing effective help. Kellogg together with Colonel William R. Grove and others arrived in Warsaw on January 3, 1919, almost at the same time as Paderewski.[13] After a tour of most of the centers, Hoover's envoys estimated that from a general population of 27 million who were under the control of the Warsaw government, at least four million were famine stricken, and another million were in need of additional nourishment. Shortly after, food distribution stations run by Americans appeared in many Polish towns. In May 1920, at the height of the operation, 1,315,490 Polish children were being fed on a daily basis. There was particular hardship in Lwów and the surrounding area. Much of central and western Poland had escaped military threat and the presence of foreign armies, but Lwów was the arena of an extremely complicated conflict. During the partitions, the town was one of the most shining centers of Polish culture and also home to Pilsudski's strongest military centers. Lwów itself had a strong Polish majority; however, the villages of eastern Galicia remained Ukrainian. The only Polish element in the countryside was the intelligentsia and landowners. On November 1, 1918, when the Austro-Hungarian monarchy was in a complete state of impotence, the population of Lwów was surprised by a proclamation of the establishment of the Western Ukrainian People's Republic and by a Ukrainian military action which aimed to occupy the city. For the next three weeks there waged a severe and bloody battle. Not until November 21, 1918, did volunteer and regular Polish units come to the relief of the occupied city.[14]

2. Spiritus Movens 23

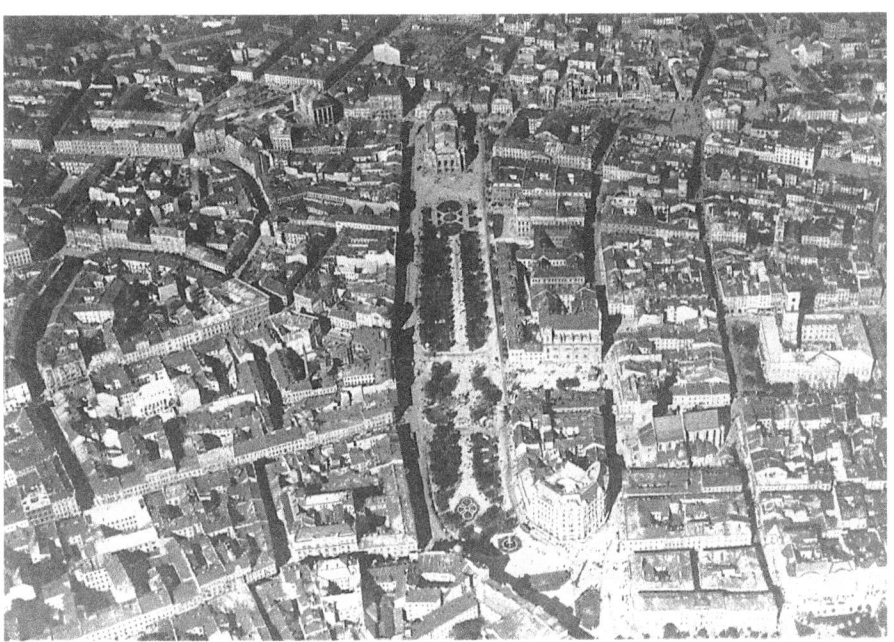

An aerial view of Lwów. (Courtesy of Dr. Tomasz Kopański, Warsaw.)

The defense of Lwów passed into history as an example of heroism, patriotism and the determination to unite this territory with Poland. Unfortunately, it was not a conclusive victory. Lwów and the immediate city outskirts continued to come under fire from Ukrainian artillery. The only railway line linking Lwów with Poland was sabotaged, and trains derailed several times. Practically every transport going to the city had to fight its way by force. There was no electricity, water or food supplies in the city. It is not surprising that the U.S. Food Administration considered food-aid for Lwów as one of its tasks. Merian Cooper was placed in charge of the mission there.

There is no conclusive documentary evidence on the basis of which one could reconstruct the genesis of the decision to send this particular officer there. On the basis of circumstantial evidence, and particularly the virtues of Cooper's character, one could imagine that news about the situation in Poland and the work of the Hoover mission evoked a noble impulse and persuaded him to go. Cooper's admission to the U.S. Food Administration is formally dated February 12, 1919. Merely two days later he was on his way through Italy and Austria to Poland. In Warsaw he boarded one of the first railway transports to Lwów. His experiences on the way left an extremely deep impression on him. The transport had to fight its way to Lwów, and immediately upon arrival, Cooper witnessed the death of a young woman by a Ukrainian grenade.[15]

Everything that had been said about Lwów and its battle turned out to be true. He threw himself into the midst of the relief action on the spot. The Headquarters of the American volunteers was the Potocki palace in the center of the city, but responsibilities rarely allowed one to enjoy life in a practically besieged town. Cooper became head of the U.S. Food Administration in Galicia and Lwów. He was immediately recognized as an individual who without regard for his own safety provided help and transports to the most dangerous areas and neighborhoods. He also distinguished himself as an excellent administrator and organizer. To relieve the position of the poorest, he waged a battle against profiteering and speculation. In April 1919, he appealed through the press to all ethnic groups to declare a battle against excessive increases in prices. His plan was straightforward and easy to reconstruct from his letter to the editor of *Chwila* ("The Moment"):

1. The daily announcements informing about the distribution of food should be prominently displayed. These announcements should not be hidden from the eyes of the public in some obscure part of the paper, and should not be restricted to a few words, which the public hardly understands.

2. The war against unscrupulous profiteers, selling food at exorbitant prices, should be constant and pitiless. Do not indulge in generalities. You should hire your own detectives. Use your reporters as investigators. Find out through them were that food at such high prices is being sold. Having established the facts, the names of the thieves who steal from the poor should be used as headlines, the names of the vile extortioneers, their addresses, what they sold, and at what prices, should be made public. They should be branded as thieves and murders of the children and the poor.[16]

Through this and many other similar campaigns, Cooper won immense popularity and earned gratitude from the inhabitants of the city. Colonel William Grove, Chief of Mission, wrote of him:

> Captain Cooper has handled a very difficult relief situation in the City of Lemberg (Lwów) during the siege and has the universal respect of all parties and factions in that town. He has devoted all possible energy

to the work and his administration has in every way been a credit to the American organization.[17]

No less enthusiastic was the attitude of the town authorities towards him:

> The representatives of the Polish Government, clergy, Community and of the Charitable societies whose signatures are put on the end of this letter, are sending to the Mission for Delivering of Food of the United States of North America, the most cordial and grateful thanks for the generous activity. Our mediator in this case will be the representative of this mission in Lwów, Sir Merian Cooper, Captain of the United States Army — who is known in our town as a true and frank friend of the suffering population of Lwów — and who worked, sacrificing himself and without taking care of his own life and health — visiting the environs of Lwów where maladies reigned — for bringing bread to the hungry inhabitants.[18]

Even far away in Warsaw, Cooper's efforts were appreciated. U.S. Attache Major Elbert Farman.[19]

Work conditions did not exhaust the Cooper energy. After over three months' work he clearly came to the conclusion that he could serve Poland much better with his aviation expertise than by working in food distribution. In Lwów he contacted General T. Rozwadowski, who had taken charge of the units in eastern Galicia from Piłsudski in November 1918. The offensive carried out by these units stopped the direct threat to Lwów. Taking advantage of this acquaintance, Cooper, clearly while still in Lwów, proposed to Rozwadowski that he serve in the ranks of the Polish Air Force and maybe even mentioned the establishment of an Air Force unit consisting of American volunteers. It is not known exactly when Cooper's conversation with Rozwadowski took place, nor even if it touched solely upon Cooper's enlistment, or whether the establishment of the volunteer air squadron had already been discussed. In any case, it must have occurred by March 1919 and definitely by April 29, 1919, the date when Cooper sent a letter to the Polish Head of State on this subject. Let us not forget that on March 21 Rozwadowski was appointed Head of the Polish Military Mission in Paris, and in the first days of May the General went to Paris. His role was doubly important. Not only was he personally convinced of the need to help Cooper, but only he could be a guide in the complexities of decision-making by the Polish Ministry of Military Affairs and the General Staff, and more importantly an efficient agent in securing direct contact with Piłsudski.

Visiting (business) card of Merian Cooper. It reads "Merian Coldwell Cooper, Captain of Aviation of the United States of North America," and in the lower left corner, "American Relief Administration. Mission to Poland." (Courtesy of Dr. Tomasz Kopański, Warsaw.)

It is interesting to note how Cooper and Rozwadowski's initiatives began to interact. After his arrival in Paris, Rozwadowski took on the organization of the volunteer legion. Though there is no hard proof, his initiative likely stemmed from Cooper's inspiration. Even if that wasn't the case, a squadron established at Cooper's initiative could be a substitute, or even a last resort, for the American legion. On the other hand, Cooper proved again how far ahead of his time he was. In 1915, he abandoned his studies at the Naval Academy in order to devote himself to service in the Air Force, which he felt had the greatest future. As soon as he achieved this, he suspended it on behalf of work in the Food Supply administration, which brought help to war victims. Again, once Lwów was liberated, he gave up his civil service for the Air Force in time for the defense of the Polish Republic against the Bolsheviks. He was there, where circumstances required, where there ought to be a man with the soul of a lion and the morals of a knight. Such an analogy can be extended in the sense that Cooper and his volunteers anticipated the danger of Bolshevism and necessity for U.S.–East-European cooperation to halt its expansion.

The next stage in Cooper's efforts was a letter to Piłsudski, sent on April 29, 1919. If one seeks a key document for the genesis of the squadron, this is it. After the introduction, in which Cooper explained the connections between his family and Casimir Pulaski, the young captain wrote:

UNITED STATES
FOOD ADMINISTRATION
MISSION FOR POLAND.

ADMINISTRACJA ŻYWNOŚCIOWA
STANÓW ZJEDNOCZONYCH.
MISYA DLA POLSKI.

Warsaw, Poland,
April 29, 1919.

General Pilsudske,
Chief of State of Poland,
WARSAW, Poland.

SIR:—

   General, the Count Casmir Pulaski was killed by the side of my great, great, grandfather, Col., John Cooper, at the siege of Savannah in our War of the Revolution, while he was serving with the regiment of which my direct ancestor was an officer. General Pulaski thus gave his life for my country while fighting with my own people. My family therefore consider it my duty, as is also my sincere wish, to offer my services to Poland during the period of its fight for its new freedom. For that reason I requested to be sent to work for Poland with the American Food Mission. As an officer of that mission, I have been in charge of the distribution of American food at Lwow during the past two months of siege and bombardment. However, I now feel that now my own country is not at war, that it is my duty to serve with the actual fighting forces. If the Polish Republic wishes to accept my services, I will immediately endeavor to try arrange my assignment or discharge to accept any commission to which the Polish Government may see fit to assign me, provided that I may be assigned for actual duty with fighting forces at the front.

   My previous military experience has been:—
   1. Four years training at the United States Naval Academy, school for active officers.
   2. One years service in Infantry on the Mexican Border, in the Mexican campaign.
   3. Instructor in Reserve Officers training camp and Cadet Captain of Aviation School.
   4. One years service as a pilot of aviation in France. I commanded the Army Command Flight during the St. Mihiel offensive, and served as pilot in the 20th Aero Squadron.

   If the Chief of State of Poland wishes to accept my services, I respectfully request that I be notified immediately, and I will take steps to try to arrange so that I may enter work with the fighting forces of Poland. I also would like to be informed at the same time, if possible, what rank I will hold, but I only ask to be assigned to forces in actual work at the front regardless of rank.

Very respectfully yours,

Merian C. Cooper,
Captain, Air Service, U. S. Army.

MCC:lr

Letter of Merian Cooper to Józef Piłsudski, Poland's Chief of State, April 29, 1919. (Courtesy of Central Military Archive, Warsaw.)

> My family considers it my duty, as is also my sincere wish, to offer my services to Poland during the period of her fight for freedom. For that reason I requested to be sent to work for Poland with the American Food Mission. As an officer of that mission, I have been in charge of the distribution of American food at Lwów during the past two months of siege and bombardment. However, I now feel, that now my own country is not at war, that it is my duty to serve with the actual fighting forces. If the Polish republic wishes to accept my services, I will immediately endeavor to try to arrange my assignment or discharge to accept any commission to which the Polish Government may see fit to assign me, provided that I may be assigned for actual duty with fighting forces at the front.... If the Chief of State of Poland wishes to accept my services, I respectfully request that I be notified immediately, and I will take steps to try to arrange so that I may enter work with the fighting forces of Poland. I also would like to be informed at the same time, if possible, what rank I will hold, but I only ask to be assigned to forces in actual work at the front regardless of rank.[20]

Above all the individual character of the letter is striking. Cooper does not mention the possibility of creating a squadron. Secondly, he most clearly foresaw that he would not be able to fight in American uniform and the questions about rank indicate this in the last part of the letter. It is crucial in as much as there is no earlier document in existence indicating that any of the later officers of the squadron considered service in this capacity, which indicates that the initiative was Cooper's. It is relatively important since with the passage of time and as the result of Cooper's incredible modesty, voices appeared which attempted to deprive him of his laurels in this matter. Regardless of the fact that a squadron was not mentioned, it is no reason to exclude at least two possibilities. Firstly, even if he had considered the establishment of a volunteer formation, perhaps he did not want to explain this to Piłsudski before he had gained official permission from him. Secondly, even if he did not yet have a crystallized intention, Piłsudski's positive attitude towards granting Cooper individual access opened the door to a wider plan succeeding in the future. Only via direct talks could both sides express their doubts. It is evident that neither the American legation nor Military Attache was involved or even informed about the meeting and the nature of Cooper's proposal. In order to get access to Piłsudski, it was necessary to have the protection of someone who was suitably close to him, such as Rozwadowski, and to keep the whole issue in secrecy.

The meeting with Piłsudski took place sometime in the beginning of May 1919, certainly before Rozwadowski left for France. The exact date is not known, it was not picked up by the press or in Cooper's own memoirs, not mentioned in publications linked to Piłsudski. The fact that the talks were held was confirmed not only by Cooper, but also by Fauntleroy in an interview in 1962. During this he said that in the course of his meeting with Piłsudski, Cooper obtained a commission as a cavalry officer, and that soon after he went to Paris to discharge himself from the AEF.[21]

Only part of Fauntleroy's account of Cooper's meeting with Piłsudski is credible. Fauntleroy's memory might have failed him 40 years after the event, and perhaps he wanted to emphasize his role in the establishment of the squadron. Piłsudski definitely did not give Cooper a commission in the cavalry. The Captain was not a cavalryman and Poland did not suffer from a lack of cavalry officers, rather the opposite. However, there was a lack of airmen. If Piłsudski were to agree or encourage anything, it would have been the establishment of an Air Force unit.

Unfortunately, there is no extant document giving the subject of the talks. The Head of State's meetings, especially those requiring secrecy, were generally not recorded. Poland was resurrected in the heat of war, and many official functions suffered on this account.[22]

Therefore we are forced to rely on Cooper's own memoirs and his later accounts. The Captain remembers that Rozwadowski arranged the meeting at his request. At the very beginning of the meeting Cooper offered the Commander-in-Chief his intention to discharge from the American Army and to join the Polish Air Force. It is clear that such a bold declaration surprised Piłsudski, who thought that Cooper's motive was to serve for fame and fortune. When Piłsudski expressed his objections, Cooper jumped to his feet to protest. He said that he would not take a cent more than a Polish officer's pay and that he wanted to obtain promotion by serving at the front. Piłsudski's objections vanished into thin air.[23] It must be remembered that Piłsudski was known for testing the perseverance of human character. In the same way, he tested the determination of the volunteer legionaries in 1914, and in the same way he tried to discourage young people who gave up their education to serve their country in November 1918. Secondly, he was certainly afraid that Cooper, who was used to American service standards, would be discouraged by the modest pay, the aviation equipment and the state of the Air Force. When, however, he turned out to be an officer of the highest and most noble motivation, Piłsudski gave the green light. There is still no concrete proof that only Cooper was involved, but Cooper himself in a later period appeared to say that he had received permission from Piłsudski to establish a unit. This is confirmed by a letter from 1942 in which Cooper unambiguously suggests that already by early spring 1919 he had thought about the establishment of the squadron and that he had received permission from Piłsudski himself. In a letter to Flight Lieutenant Witomir Bieńkowski of the Polish Squadron 303 of the Royal Air Force, he wrote:

> I will be delighted on my return to the United States to send you all the records I have concerning my services with the Polish Air Forces from 1919 to 1921 and to write you a description of the very founding of the Kościuszko Squadron, which actually was started by me in Lwów early in 1919 when I resigned from the American Army and went to Paris with the approval of Marshal Piłsudski to form it. Colonel Fauntleroy then took command as my superior officer and one of my closest friends. To him should go far more of the fame of those days than to myself, though I actually was the first pilot to join the Kościuszko Squadron.[24]

It must be added that in 1919 Piłsudski was not yet a Marshal and that the announced documents did not reach London. Cooper's inspiration and Piłsudski's agreement is indicated indirectly in an article in the *New York Times* from June 18, 1919. The newspaper correspondent reported:

> Several discharged American officers in Paris and many in the United States have offered their services to the Polish flying corps. Today I learned from the highest sources that these officers will be accepted. The Americans will be organized as quickly as possible into a foreign legion, which hopes to carry out the traditions of the Lafayette Escadrille. The movement is of greater magnitude than the American participation in French flying. One pilot, whose name cannot be divulged but who is an ace with an American Distinguished Service Cross has offered himself and 20 men as a fighting squadron.

As we know that Cooper was awarded, but declined to accept the Distinguished Service Cross, which further indicates him as the *spiritus movens* of the squadron. In another part of this article the *New York Times* correspondent discussed the possibilities of uniting the efforts of the squadron with the Haller Army, and there was a suggestion that they form the basis upon which to build a legion. However, there is no information about the motives of such a step, besides the need to take revenge on the Germans:

> They see in Poland a nation struggling to throw off the oppression of a century. They remember how Kościuszko came to the defense of

America during the Revolution and desire that these efforts for Polish nationalism be commemorated to this great hero of our struggle for independence.[25]

The information source for the *New York Times'* article was most certainly Colonel Howland, who could only have found out about the plan to establish a squadron from General Rozwadowski. He, in turn, must have had an outline of the plan by June 1919. Since Rozwadowski had been in Paris for a very short time when the article appeared, the source of inspiration for the squadron could only have been the plan put forward by Cooper. It is additionally confirmed by the 1920 article published in *Gazeta Lwowska* newspaper, which gives Cooper credit for originating and implementing the idea of a squadron.[26] There is yet another record to support this thesis. In his memo of May 9, 1921, Capt. Zbigniew Orzechowski, a member of the 7th Squadron, wrote that it was Cooper who initiated the volunteer squadron for Poland, and that Fauntleroy was just following him.[27]

There is hardly anything to suggest to the contrary. In the *Times* article even the squadron's patron and the motivation of the airmen are mentioned, in accordance with reports from other sources. Therefore, it is absolutely correct to state that Merian Cooper was the *spiritus movens* of the squadron and that his efforts in this direction dated back to spring 1919. On this subject nearly every author mentions Cooper as the initiator. Some bracket him with Fauntleroy, but they are in a minority. Yet others seek links between Cooper and the command of the Polish Air Force. Kenneth M. Murray writes about the decision to establish the squadron in agreement with the Chief of the Polish Air Force. According to him, Cooper was moved by the military situation around Lwów and presented the idea of the squadron to the Chief of Polish Aviation, Captain Jasiński, who in turn set the procedure in motion at the Polish High Command and encouraged Cooper to go to Paris.[28]

This sequence of events seems less likely. It is difficult to find a link between the American Relief Administration officer in Lwów, which was practically cut off from the rest of the country, and the CO of the Polish Air Force in Warsaw. In addition, a decision of that kind had to be made at a political level, and therefore most probably by Piłsudski. In this case, it would also have to have been suitably prepared and could only have been executed by Rozwadowski. Murray himself presents a somewhat different scenario in another part of his memoirs, which appeared in *Poland Magazine* few years before the publication of his book. According to this account,

Cooper conceived the idea of organizing the squadron during his rail trip through Germany, having left Warsaw for Paris after a visit to Piłsudski.[29] This report, nevertheless, has many weak points. First, if only Cooper's individual service in the Polish Armed Forces was the issue, there would be no need for him to see Piłsudski and go to Paris. He could just have waited for the official resolution of bureaucratic procedures in Lwów and then taken a Polish military uniform. His trip to Paris only makes sense if it was connected with an attempt to enlist a larger group of volunteers.

The next matter demanding clarification is the degree of inspiration for the squadron that came from General Rozwadowski. The General went to Paris after the airman's conversation with Piłsudski, probably with Cooper's verbal assurance regarding the possibilities of establishing a squadron. It was on Parisian soil that the idea of an American legion for Poland took root. It is difficult to imagine that while still in Lwów Rozwadowski could have foreseen the conditions prevalent among the discharged officers and soldiers of the AEF. He could not have thought of the legion without the cooperation of the higher-ranking AEF officers, and he could only have met them in Paris. It was only in Paris that the matter of the squadron could be linked to the would-be legion.

Even decades later, there are historians who still maintain that the squadron was established in Paris on the basis of General Rozwadowski's individual decision. "Unable to resist the requests of the American volunteers, he agreed to create a small American Air Force squadron for Poland under the command of Major Fauntleroy, who had hitherto been assigned to General Romer's mission."[30] That author, and thereafter a host of historians, claimed that the Polish Commander-in-Chief showed little interest in winning over Cooper. The source of this approach is to be found in a later political conflict between Piłsudski and Rozwadowski over the authorship of the plan for the Battle of the Vistula in 1920. Historians also have their own political sympathies, and some of them wish to disregard the facts. Rozwadowski undoubtedly played a key role in bringing the airmen to Poland, but he was not a decision-maker. It was Piłsudski who made decisions about the procedures and conditions of service, despite a mountain of other obligations.

Let us follow how he guided the matter. On May 14 the adjutant to the Commander-in-Chief of the Polish Army, Colonel Tadeusz Kasprzycki, wrote to Cooper:

> The Chief of State advised me to inform You that he will be really happy to see Your engagement in the Polish Army. He was really touched with the motives mentioned in Your letter.[31]

This document ought to be treated as a summary of the results of the Piłsudski-Cooper conversation, and more so because shortly after, a series of steps were taken which were to facilitate Cooper's enlistment in the Polish Army. Unfortunately, any other reply of Piłsudski's to Cooper's letter of April 29 is not known, neither is it known whether any other letter even left the offices of the General Staff at all. In any case, none have yet been found in Polish or American archives.

Piłsudski reserved for himself the right to evaluate a volunteer on the basis of a direct conversation. Kasprzycki's letter is Piłsudski's officially expressed agreement to Cooper's enlistment in the Polish Army. The subsequent documents from the General Staff established the procedures in this matter. All formalities from the Polish side were to be attended to by the Ministry of Military Affairs, whose officer Lt. Col. Jan Klim had already been informed and charged with responsibilities related to this matter. On May 20, 1919, Piłsudski issued an order to refer the matter of possible enlistment to the Chief of the Ministry of Military Affairs' Personnel Department. The Commander-in-Chief confirmed that since there were no objections from the Air Force Inspectorate to Cooper's admittance, it was necessary to facilitate the matter with his accord. The above consultations prove beyond any reasonable doubt that the decision on Cooper's admittance into the Polish Air Force was made in Warsaw on Piłsudski's orders.

At Piłsudski's recommendation, the next day (May 21) a representative of the Air Force Department of the Ministry of Military Affairs confirmed on behalf of Colonel Łossowski that there were no formal barriers to admitting Cooper to the Air Force. On this ground, the Personnel Department of the Ministry of Military Affairs submitted the following correspondence on June 10, 1919, to the Main Quartermaster of the U.S. Army: "The Personnel Department confirms that the General Staff of the Polish Army consents to the request of Captain Merian Cooper of the U.S. Army for his admittance to the Polish Army with the rank of Captain-Pilot."[32]

Although the Main Quartermaster of the American Army did not place any obstacles in his path, the Personnel Department of the Ministry of Public Affairs asked to be informed when Captain Cooper would be released from service in the American Army. This was because the decree nominating Captain Cooper for admittance to the Polish Army would be issued immediately after a decision in this matter had been received from the Main Quartermaster of the American Army.

The Polish military authorities even prepared an appropriate undated nomination document in July 1919. Cooper, on his part, started his own efforts from the middle of May. Firstly they were about his release from Colonel Grove's mission in Poland and then from the ranks of the AEF. On May 19, 1919, Cooper sent a report to the "Commanding General, AEF," in France stating that the American Food Administration was ready to release him and requesting reinstatement in military service. He stressed that he wanted to serve in the combat troops: "If impossible to station me with our own troops, I request to be assigned to duty with any Allied Units in Archangel or with the Russian or Polish Armies fighting against the Bolsheviks."[33]

It is this part of the report that is most exciting, but it nonetheless carries a certain distraction. Here he is ready to serve in Archangel or with Russian troops fighting the Bolsheviks. It could have meant that Poland was only one of the options. On the other hand, Colonel House's dispatch to the President, which has already been quoted, must be remembered. It was sent in February 1919 and contained a negative opinion about sending U.S. troops to Russia. That was the prevailing atmosphere of those days. Of course, House's dispatch was not a public announcement, but there were a few reasons for the Americans' reluctance to be further involved in Russia. If Cooper was aware that the chances of being assigned to service on the anti–Bolshevik front in Russia were extremely slight, then his "plan B" contained in the report was in reality his "plan A."

The recommendation of Colonel Grove, Head of the U.S. Food Administration in Poland, dated May 20, that Cooper return to military service was directed to Herbert Hoover in Paris, who authorized the decision to enable Cooper to leave the U.S. Food Administration.[34] This correspondence set in motion a positive chain reaction. On June 4, 1919, the Parisian U.S. Food Administration center issued its decision to the Warsaw branch, which ordered Cooper be sent to Paris. On June 22 the Chief of the ARA mission in Poland requested, however, to keep him in Poland until July 7. The motives of this decision are not clear, and it was probably the result of an administrative delay. It is important in that it indicates that the Captain remained in Poland at least until July 7, 1919, and that this was the reason for his delay.[35]

It was only after this date that Cooper could leave for the French capital. It turned out that he left immediately, and was present during the great parade on the anniversary of the storming of the Bastille on July 14, 1919. The matters formally connected with his return to the Army and discharge from the AEF were resolved by the end of July. On August 5, 1919, Captain Cooper was honorably discharged from the AEF at Gievres, France.[36]

2. Spiritus Movens

From the moment Cooper arrived in Paris, his basic task was to organize a team of airmen prepared for departure. The concern was not only that they be experienced but also that they be an ideal group of people, ready to serve under difficult conditions and even to sacrifice their lives for a foreign country. It must be stressed that Cooper presented every candidate with a true picture of the situation in Poland in every aspect of life and conditions of service.

First, he managed to interest Major Cedric Fauntleroy. Fauntleroy's deeds on the battlefield in France had gained him wide recognition. Fauntleroy's family came from France, which can be seen clearly in the way his surname was written in many documents *Faunt-le-Roy*, and in others in its modernized form as *Fauntleroy*. He was born November 22, 1891, in Churchill, Mississippi. He had already escaped from home by the age of 14 or 15, giving various reasons, and had always had an interest in mechanics, cars, and, in time, aviation. As Fauntleroy himself recollected, the great turning point in his life was the sinking of the *Lusitania*, which spurred him on to go to Europe. From February 1 until June 1916 he trained in a French pilot school at Issoudon, he spent the next 15 months in the field as a pilot, then he was C.O. of a squadron and Group Commander. He fought in the 94th *Hat-in-the-Ring* Persuit Squadron. In 1918,

Major Cedric Fauntleroy among Polish children. (Courtesy of Dr. Tomasz Kopański, Warsaw.)

he was sent to technical officer's training school, where he became an instructor. His next role was as Head of the Technical Commission for the collection of aviation apparatus for the U.S. Army. Apart from his exploits in the field, he also distinguished himself as a test pilot. He was undoubtedly a pilot of great experience, whose help in attracting the next volunteers was invaluable. A few months before his conversation with Cooper, Fauntleroy obtained a financially lucrative contract from the Polish Army as a technical advisor. They had been in contact with each other during a course at the training center in Issoudon, France, and this was another element cementing the relationship before a truly demanding test.[37]

Both of the airmen quickly agreed on their fundamental aim. Almost immediately they obtained a letter of recommendation from General Rozwadowski, which authorized them to enlist the next wave of volunteering airmen. *The New York Times* quoted that letter on August 28, 1919, along with news about the establishment of a squadron at the instigation of Fauntleroy and Cooper and about naming it after Kościuszko. Also in the article was the assertion that service in Poland would not last more than a year, and information about the unfavorable financial conditions.[38]

Many people were harnessed to the propaganda drive on behalf of the squadron, including acquaintances and mainly ex-pilots in various parts of Europe and in the U.S. The next pilot who managed to enlist was Lieutenant George Crawford. Crawford was born June 13, 1894, in Bristol, Pennsylvania, and graduated from Lehigh University as a professional mining engineer. He began his military training in May 1912 at Plattsburg Cadet School, although his military calling turned out to be the Air Force. In April 1917 Crawford began training at Mineola Field, Long Island, and was promoted to Lieutenant on October 1, 1917. From November 1 that year until the January 1, 1918, he was a pilot in the 1st Squadron in France, then for a month he served as an instructor at Issoudon. From February 1 to April 1, 1918, he was Commander of the 102nd Air Squadron, and then until September 12 he was a pilot in the 20th Bomber Squadron, where he probably came into contact with Cooper. That day, and thus more or less at the same time as Cooper, he fell into Germans hands. On December 1, 1918, he returned to France, where he was assigned to command the Aerial Navigators Experimental Squadron. From May 1 until September 1, 1919, he was a member of the American Relief Administration in the Baltic region. Fortunately for Cooper and Fauntleroy, in July 1919 Crawford was momentarily in Paris.[39] As a pilot he had over 50 operational sorties to his credit by the end of

July 1919, therefore his experience was a valuable asset for the squadron.

The next to volunteer was Lieutenant Kenneth Shrewsbury, who prior to his enlistment in the Air Force studied law at Harvard. After his training at Mineola Field and Issoudon, he was assigned as an Air Service supply officer to a unit at Tours. Before the German capitulation, he ferried planes by air from England to the continent.[40]

Edward C. Corsi of Brooklyn, New York, had an extremely interesting resume. He was one of the youngest pilots, born November 10, 1897, and by 1916 he had already enlisted in the Army as an ambulance driver. Then he served in the French Aviation Service, although documents give his official enlistment date as January 1, 1917. He completed Air Force training in September 1917 at the Bleriot School. He fought in the Escadrille Spad 77, and was wounded twice. He was promoted to the rank of Captain on July 1, 1919, shortly before talks about service for Poland.[41]

Edward C. Corsi. (Courtesy of Dr. Tomasz Kopański, Warsaw.)

The next candidate was a friend of Corsi, Lieutenant Carl C. Clark of the British Royal Air Service. Clark was born on June 19, 1896, graduated from Lawrencis College, Birmingham, and then from 1910 to 1914 trained as a Royal Naval Engineer. From the start of the war he served with the Royal Warwickshire Regiment and then in two other regiments, but in a similarity to Corsi, fate tossed him in the direction of the Air Force. On November 20, 1917, Clark graduated from the Central Flying School, Upavon, Wilts, where he "completed a course in the Military Wing and is qualified for service in the Royal Flying Corps." On April 1, 1918, he was promoted to the rank of Lieutenant in the Royal Air Service. During his Air Force combat career he was in the 1st Squadron, then the 50th Squadron, and the 61st Squadron. He trained in the Artillery and Infantry Cooperation School, Royal Air Force Pilots' School at Worthy Down, Winchester, at the "School of Aerial Navigation and Bomb

Dropping," and also trained in the art of night-bombing. In addition he was a test pilot. Discharged with the rank of Captain on May 11, 1919, he clearly sought a way to perfect his knowledge. Such an impressive resume allowed Clark to familiarize himself with a wide range of planes, from large bombers to small observer planes. Therefore there was no doubt that he could quickly adapt to planes that he was not familiar with, Austrian or Italian for example, which made up the majority of the 7th Squadron. Undoubtedly he could be counted on to help train other volunteers. This is why both Cooper and Fauntleroy accepted his application without a second thought.[42]

The next volunteer, Lieutenant Edwin L. Noble from Charlestown, Massachusetts, aroused certain doubts. Before his enlistment, he graduated in Electrical Engineering in 1915, from Sheffield Scientific School, Yale University. Similarly to the majority of U.S. airmen, he trained at Mineola Field and was then sent to France. Here he underwent further training (in August and September 1918) at Issoudon. After the cease-fire he was assigned to the Requisition and Claims Department of the AEF. It was his great determination that got him into the squadron and overcame any final doubts.[43]

The last to be won over at this stage of the recruitment drive was Captain Arthur H. Kelly, born in 1890 in Richmond, Virginia. He was a mining engineer by profession and ended up in the Air Force by choice, as did many of his colleagues. During his service in France as an observer and navigator of the 96th U.S. Bombardment Squadron he had two shot-down German planes to his credit. He was the only navigator, or observer as this function was called at the time, in the team of pilots who went to Poland.[44]

These eight candidates were the hardcore of the squadron, which grew in numbers even before it entered combat. All the officers mentioned above were extremely well qualified and determined to overcome any barriers that awaited them in an unknown theater of operation. An additional test was the terms of contract, signed individually with each pilot around August 26, 1919. The signature date was not the same on every contract. Some officers signed later and some contracts differed in the small print. One of the exceptions was Fauntleroy, who went into service with a previously signed contract as a Technical Advisor to the Polish Army. It ran until the beginning of February, 1920. The next exception was Cooper whose contract had been signed earlier than the rest, namely at the beginning of August 1919, and had a clause about non-remunerative service for that month. This was to cover the time it took to obtain

2. Spiritus Movens

LÉGATION DE POLOGNE
A PARIS
ATTACHÉ MILITAIRE

4, Rue de Chanaleilles (7°)

N° ??/

Paris, le 13 Septembre 1919.

ORDRE DE SERVICE.
-:-

    le Lieutenant M. CRAWFORD George, de l'Armée Améridaine, admis par le Général ROZWADOWSKI, Chef de la Mission Militaire Polonaise en France, à servir dans l'Aviation Polonaise, se rendra en Pologne le 15 Septembre.

    Dès son arrivée à VARSOVIE, cet officier se présentera d'abord au Général Commandant de la Place et ensuite au Général Inspecteur de L'Aviation Polonaise.

DESTINATAIRES:

Mr. le Lieutenant M. CRAWFORD.   Pour exécution.

Mr. le Général Inspecteur de l'Aviation   A titre de renseignement.
    Polonaise

General Rozwadowski's letter of recommendation for every pilot issued before their departure for Poland. Paris, September 13, 1919. (Courtesy of Central Military Archive, Warsaw.)

Rozwadowski's recommendation letter, which was intended for carrying out recruitment.

    A common feature of their contracts was the basic financial conditions, rights and obligations and also the fact that all of the contracts of the first eight airmen were actually signed in Paris, before their departure for Poland. However, it was characteristic that the place of signing the contracts was given as Warsaw. The change in the place was, firstly, probably to enable the dismissal of accusations of recruitment on foreign territory and in the ranks of AEF. Secondly, it meant that the party making the contract was the Polish Ministry of Military Affairs and not the Head of Mission in Paris, whose authority in these matters could not reach that far. The text of one of the contracts explains the rights and obligations.

> Contract.
> August 3rd 1919 in Warsaw. The following subscribers, Major Sigsmund Platowski, Assistant Chief of the Department IV, Ministry of Military Affairs. In the name of the Ministry of the Military Affairs of the Polish Republic and the officer of the United States of America Army, Mr. Merian Cooper having his steady residence in Jacksonville, Florida, USA on the other, have on the base of order No.1739 IV, Secret, of the Ministry of Military Affairs, signed a contract on the following conditions.
>
> 1. The Ministry of Military Affairs of the Polish Republic accepts on military active service in the Polish Army Mr. Merian Cooper in the rank of Captain, pilot, which is given him after examination of his military papers for a term of six months from the day of the signature of this contract.
> 2. From the moment of the signature of this contract, Mr. Merian Cooper engages himself to obey to all the rules existing for the Polish Officers in the way of military discipline, responsibilities and service in general.
> 3. From the moment of the beginning of the active service in the Polish Army, Mr. Merian Cooper will obtain from the Polish Finances:
>   a) The pay received by the Polish Officers of the rank of Captain.
>   b) The supplementary indemnities given to the Officers of the same rank.
> 4. Mr. Merian Cooper will also obtain all the rights and privileges given to the Polish Officers.
> 5. In case of illness or accident medical assistance will be assured in the same way as for the Polish Officers to Mr. Merian Cooper.
> 6. Mr. Merian Cooper has the right every year to one month of leave to his original country, the time of traveling not being included.
> 7. Mr. Merian Cooper can obtain the first leave only after 6 month of service in the Polish Army.
> 8. Being on leave the travel will be gratuitous on the Polish Railways.
> 9. All the cost of travel to Poland and back Mr. Merian Cooper will have to pay himself, as for the time of traveling the Ministry of

Military Affairs does not pay any indemnity.

10. If one month before the expiration of this contract either side does not mean to retire, the following contract is valuable automatically for three more months and so on.

11. The Ministry of Military Affairs does not want no longer the services of Mr. Merian Cooper after the end of the termin, there will be no forfeit pay by the Ministry of Military Affairs.

12. The non-observation of anyone of the conditions of this contract by Mr. Merian Cooper and especially the faults condemned by the Military Tribunals to the loss of commission for the Polish Officers will effect an immediate rupture of the contract without any consideration of the termin referred to in 11 and no forfeit paid by the Ministry of Military Affairs.[45]

Edwin Noble. (Courtesy of Paul Konys, Rocky River, OH.)

The conditions of the contract were the results of experience in work on the establishment of the squadron, on the modest financial resources of the Polish State, and the conditions that had already developed to win over reinforcements. The memo entitled *Conditions of Acceptance into the Polish Army of Foreign Officers*, as well as other documents, confirms this. It was sent by the Deputy Minister of Military Affairs, General Kazimierz Sosnkowski to, among others, the U.S. Military Attache, Lieutenant Colonel Farman. It was assumed that the contracts would be signed individually for a period of six months with the possibility of their extension. It was stipulated that the remuneration would match that of Polish Army officers, and that they would maintain the rank held in their own army. This is so important because it shows a uniform attitude to the issue of possible reinforcements from other sources in the future. Nevertheless, there was an exception. It concerned Harmon Rorison, who joined the Polish Army as a lieutenant, although in the U.S. Army he had held the rank of captain. This error was caused when his rank was incorrectly written in the correspondence dealing with his enlistment.[46]

After the contracts had been signed, the Polish General Staff and Ministry of Military Affairs granted permission, respectively, on September 3 and 10, 1919, for the unit's establishment.[47] At this stage, there were still no details available about how it was to be implemented. In fact, soon after the arrival of the airmen in Warsaw, the plan to form a separate unit was abandoned and what was already in existence was handed over by the Polish personnel to the Americans. On September 13, General Rozwadowski issued a letter of recommendation for each officer directing each one of them to the Chief of the Polish Air Force, General Staff in Warsaw.[48]

The very content of the contract, leaving aside the rest of the accompanying elements, excluded the separation of the squadron as a foreign unit. The squadron consisting of American volunteers was to fight under Polish supervision, in Polish uniforms, on the payroll of and using the equipment of the Polish Army. The airmen knew that the conditions of the contracts were dictated by the objective limitations and because the American military and political authorities refused to allow the creation of larger autonomous units.

The establishment of the squadron did not preclude the possibility of expanding into a larger formation. This is confirmed, perhaps, by the fact that Paderewski consented to the efforts of Paul Baer, a reserve officer of the U.S. Army, to organize another squadron, and to a return to the idea of a volunteer legion in the summer of 1920, during the greatest crisis of the Polish-Bolshevik war. There will be more about both of these episodes later.

3 | Motives

During the war of 1919–1920, Poland's war effort was supplemented by individual officers and units of several nations. As a matter of fact, there were more French than American officers in Poland, but they never formed a regular fighting unit of their own to fight the Bolsheviks. The French served for the most part in an advisory role to the Polish General Staff and military commanders on the ground. Ukrainians and White Russians fought for their own state, and only Americans had no clear state or national interest at stake. This is why the airmen of the 7th Squadron occupy a particular place in the history of this conflict and in the memory of the Polish people. What is equally interesting is that after the end of the war, Americans became the uncompromising enemies of communism. In many instances the airmen informed the American public about dimensions of the Bolshevik threat to peace and stability. Their relationship to Poland remained consistently friendly during the following years when Poland experienced subsequent catastrophes. Col. Cedric Fauntleroy, in the late autumn of 1920, appealed for military help for Poland, and warned that the Bolsheviks' plans also encompassed America. On the eve of Nazi aggression in 1939, he proposed to come to fight for Poland again, this time against the Germans. During the Second World War, he and Merian Cooper kept in contact with the Polish 303rd Squadron of the Royal Air Force, which inherited the mantle of the 7th Kościuszko Squadron. The officers of the squadron remained in contact with the diplomatic-consular representatives of the Republic of Poland, and with Polish organizations even after the end of World War II, when Stalin's dream of occupying Warsaw came true.[1] One can say, without exaggeration, that they fully repaid the debt to the homeland of Kościuszko and Pulaski.

One of the most intriguing and frequently asked questions is about the individual justification of the decisions which led the airmen to Poland. None of them had any family ties to Poland, and apart from Cooper there was little sign of any emotional ties to Poland. Financial considerations did not enter in to the picture at all. A Polish officer's pay was barely a small percentage of his American counterpart. In addition, the Polish State was suffering from a scarcity of hard currency, and under war conditions inflation was a natural danger. Therefore, there was no doubt that service in Poland would not be lucrative.[2] It was also difficult to ascribe pure military fame as a motive. The conflict was taking place on the periphery of Europe, where it was difficult to find even half the correspondents who were present in any West European capital. In addition, the danger was greater than on the western front for the simple fact that the enemy was less predictable. Falling into the hands of the enemy meant that one would almost certainly be shot or would suffer heavy imprisonment, forced labor and starvation. Communication with one's family was more difficult and the possibility of contact with one's own diplomatic representative was limited. The US had no official relations with Bolshevik Russia, and there were no channels of assistance through which they could look for prisoners of war or intervene on their behalf. Cooper, the *spiritus moves* of the Squadron, knew this and did not hide this state of affairs from the enlisted pilots, so the individual motives must have been more than intriguing.

An analysis of the airmen diaries and opinions reveals a surprising element. The fundamental driving force was to repay the debt owed by America to Poland, whose sons Gen. Thaddeus Kościuszko and Gen. Casimir Pulaski fought for American independence. In his letter of April 29, 1919, to Jozef Piłsudski, Merian Cooper wrote:

> General, the Count Pulaski was killed by the side of my great, great, grandfather, Col. John Cooper, at the siege of Savannah in our War of the Revolution, while he was serving with the regiment of which my direct ancestor was an officer. General Pulaski thus gave his life for my country while fighting with my own people. My family therefore consider it my duty, as is also my sincere wish, to offer my services to Poland during the period of its fight for freedom.[3]

This element is present in the correspondence of other squadron officers. Kenneth Malcolm Murray, who joined the squadron in the last phase of the Polish-Bolshevik war, wrote in the introduction to his memoirs:

The work of this little known legion, the pilots of the Kościuszko Squadron thus repaid, in part, America's debt to Poland for the gallant service rendered in 1776 by those two great Polish patriots, Casimir Pulaski and Thaddeus Kościuszko, who gloriously bared their swords in the cause of our American independence.[4]

Apparently, the same motives directed Edmund Graves to Poland, who was the first to pay with his life for his adherence to his ideals. In a posthumous article, one of the Lwów newspapers quoted Graves, who was thought to have said: "I wanted to repay Poland for the deeds of Pulaski and Kościuszko."[5]

Edward C. Corsi, who was in Poland from the beginning of the squadron's activity, confessed that his presence in Poland was a repayment of duty for the devotion of Kościuszko and Pulaski, and also the defense of an American ally — the democratic *Rzeczpospolita* (Polish Republic). That was not all, after his return to the US, he wrote a book on the subject of Poland and her democratic traditions.[6] The significance of Kościuszko and Pulaski as positive symbols of Polish-American relations was so obvious that it influenced the name of the squadron. This was not only Cooper's opinion. In the weeks after his arrival in Poland Major Fauntleroy developed a project named the *Polish-American Air Group*. In a letter to the Deputy Minister of Military Affairs in Warsaw of November 1, 1919, he writes that the names of Kościuszko and Pulaski were resonant throughout the U.S., and this ought to be taken advantage of.[7] A *New York Times* article of 1919 confirms the magnetism of Kościuszko's name and its motivational power. No less surprising was the maturity of this conviction — and on this level in particular — that it was absolutely essential to combat Bolshevism. Merian Cooper wrote in the spring of 1920 to US Senator Duncan U. Fletcher:

> I became interested in the Bolshevik question when I was a prisoner in Germany. I was sent to a hospital way over in Silesia in a little town near Breslau. In Silesia I came to know a number of Russians, prisoners like myself, many of whom spoke English or French. From them I began to learn what Bolshevism really was, and the ambition of the Bolsheviks to bring all the world under their sway. I thought that America would one day have to fight them, and I still think so unless the Germans and Japanese swallow up Soviet Russia and thus form a great German-Russian-Japanese Alliance. In that case I know we will have to defend ourselves. We will be the only people in the world really worth plundering, and that combination would make a coalition of world adventures who would like nothing better than to make us pay

to the utmost limit.... Because I realized that the Bolsheviks would surely try to work against America by propaganda and because I thought it very likely that we might have to take the field in Russia, I wrote to our General Staff in France offering to go into Russia, either as an American officer or to resign from the American Army and join one of the White Russian armies fighting the Bolsheviks.... When this was pigeon-holed, I asked to be sent to Poland with the Food Mission on the Bolshevik front. Here I learned more about Bolshevism, and finally determined to get in the fight against it. I therefore resigned from the American army and offered my services to Poland.... Right at present the Bolsheviks are preparing to commence a drive on this front. Denikin and Kolchak are beaten, so the offensive will be very strong. If Poland falls or is forced to make peace due to lack of military supplies and finances to carry on the campaign, it means quite surely one of two things — either the Bolsheviks will sweep across Europe, or the Germans and Japanese will be able to establish their alliance with Russia, and Poland will once more discontinue to exist as a nation. If Poland falls and Bolshevism sweeps Europe, or if the triple alliance is brought about by the crushing of Poland, I believe with all my heart and soul we will be plunged in war again within ten years.... I know that the Bolsheviks consider America as an enemy, and they will surely try, if not by force of arms then by propaganda, to overturn our government. I know that to be impossible. The American people are not of the stuff of which Bolsheviks are made. But if the Russian soviet government continues to exist, or if it forces a peace with Poland, powers will be turned loose which can cause much bloodshed in America, trouble in every direction, and most surely will harm our nation.[8]

The maturity of Cooper's conviction is to some extent surprising in the sense that he foresaw a direct threat to America. Thus, he thought that by fighting on the Polish front he was also protecting the interests of the U.S. Cedric Fauntleroy, Commander of the 7th Squadron, reasoned in a similar way. In a speech shortly after the signing of the ceasefire in the Polish-Bolshevik war, he said, "Personally, I feel that Poland has put up a battle against Bolshevism for the last two years not only for Poland, but for civilization and for the world. I am not saying this is what I think; I have proven what I believe; I have been there, Gentlemen, for 16 months fighting these same red hordes."[9]

Elsewhere, on the same subject he said: "Among many people, and more especially in America, Poland is heralded as being the aggressor in this war against Bolshevism. Imperialistic Poland is a byword for the presses of America — Poland out for territorial rights.... The world does not know what Bolshevism means; otherwise, they would not herald

Poland as imperialistic Poland. Bolshevism stands for and sanctions everything that I am opposed to; that is the reason why I am fighting."[10]

Reflecting on his motives, he wrote in 1933 that after the 1918 Armistice between Germany and France was signed, the Polish Government requested the American Air Service to recommend a Technical Advisor to help develop a Polish Air Service. General Mason M. Patrick, Chief of the American Air Service, selected Fauntleroy to fill this position. Fauntleroy, however, resigned after the seriousness of the Bolshevik invasion became obvious to him. He felt that he could be more useful by organizing a squadron of American Pilots to help repel this threat to the existing social order.[11]

Fauntleroy gives also a more comprehensive argument, which was precisely corresponding to the political philosophy of Józef Piłsudski. The Polish leader was the author of a plan for a federation with the nations that lay between ethnic Poland and Russia. A political entity established from such a base could resist Russian and German imperialism and fill the vacuum in that part of Europe after the destruction of the Austro-Hungarian monarchy. Fauntleroy explains Piłsudski's objectives in his offensive on Kiev:

> It had three purposes: First, because we had allies with Ukraine, [it] would give the allies of Poland and Ukraine one hundred and ten million population. The second purpose was to create a strong Ukraine and take the capital of Ukraine, Kiev, and [the third was] to get enough Ukrainian territory to enable us to turn over to the Ukrainian Army the southern front, allowing us to withdraw our troops and concentrate them on the northern front.[12]

The squadron pilots' anti–Communist attitudes can be regarded as surprising, especially considering the lack of direct contact and negative experience. Fauntleroy's holiday itinerary in autumn 1920 confirms the fact that they were consistent. In October of that year, he returned to the US for four months, to organize support for Poland and to warn Americans against the Bolshevik threat. He repeated that Communism would not restrict itself to the borders of Europe, that it threatened America and Western civilization. Very few really wanted to believe him at that time.[13] Another squadron pilot said that he took part in the war for "the preservation of Christian civilization against the all-encompassing threat of Bolshevism."[14]

Obviously there were also other motives. One of the strongest was a need to help those in the city of Lwów, who were threatened by famine and aggression. The Galician capital found itself in the midst of international public attention in November 1918, when a battle broke out between the forces of the Western-Ukrainian People's Republic and the Polish population. From November 1 to 22, 1918, women and schoolchildren fought on the barricades. At this point in time Polish regular forces did not yet exist. The defenders were aware of the historical importance of the city and the significance of their own attitude, more so because it could decide whether it would in future belong to the resurrected Polish state. The people's stance made a deep impression on Cooper, who got to Lwów three months later. As he wrote in his memoir, it was one of the main motives for creating the air squadron to fight for the Polish side:

> Lwów stands, as I would say, on the border of Western Europe and has always been a bastion of western civilization against barbarous invasions from the east.... I am reminded of numerous episodes of battle, famine, and monstrosity which I saw in this country, which has been completely destroyed by a terrible five-year war. There, brother had to fight against brother, because the Polish lands were partitioned by three strong powers and the Polish nation was enslaved for one and a half centuries.[15]

Even time could not dim the memory of the defenders of Lwów in Cooper's mind; it remained with him until the end of his days. In his memoirs Cooper clearly mentions the stance of women in the defense of the city, and in the 1973 publication issued by the veterans of the Polish 303rd Squadron, he wrote:

> As I think back over the rough, harsh, tempestuous, glorious years 1919–1920 in Poland, my crude pen falters at the task. What memories for me — the first U.S. Air Force officer, 1919, in Herbert Hoover's A.R.A. Lwów, Poland, during the siege of Lwów!— yes, it is true, I saw them — those children and women fighting in the trenches and so that summer 1919 I resigned the American Service and then fought for Poland. Col. Fauntleroy and I formed the Seventh Fighter Squadron, Polish Air Force — and first he, then I, then Crawford, led it in battle![16]

Other Americans also recognized the importance of the city and the need to send aid. It was thanks to them that information about the city's situation was able to reach other volunteers. The U.S. Military Attache in Switzerland, Major Earnest H. Schelling, visited Poland between

January 13 and February 1, 1919. In his report to the Military Intelligence Division in Washington, he stated:

> In Lemberg (Lwów) city surrounded on three sides by Ukrainians, water supply out, electric plant shut down. Railroad line to Przemyśl open but cut practically every day as Ukrainians hold villages on both sideline, Poles only railroad.[17]

Few weeks later he again returned to the importance of Lwów for Poland:

> The Poles are putting up a most gallant fight to save Lemberg (Lwów). Lemberg represents to them their political capital, the only place where they could develop their nationality unhindered. It is a city with an overwhelming majority of Polish population, and their fighting for it against such odds is largely a question of sentiment.[18]

Elbert Farman, the USA Military Attache in Warsaw, also reported similar observations. In a report from October 16, 1919, he wrote, "The statement of the [Polish] authorities has been confirmed by a visit to the front. It was shown that the army is reduced practically to rags. They have no underwear and as cold weather approaches the shortage in clothing becomes more critical."[19]

A report by the U.S. Military Attache in Bucharest, Colonel Yates (who had the chance directly to observe the situation of Lwów and its inhabitants), confirmed that other officers who had visited the city also regarded Lwów as significant.[20] Thus there is no doubt that regardless of Cooper's personal experience, the opinions of officers stationed in Poland, or those who visited it from time to time, could influence the decision about the expedition to Poland. It is also certain that individual considerations also influenced these decisions. For some of the officers, the experience gained on the battlefield in France demanded verification in battle conditions at the outskirts of Europe. For others, it was a form of escape from the unknown conditions of a return to the U.S. and the search for another avenue of earning a living. This last reason was perhaps not the most important, since all the officers had decided on the same pay as officers of the Polish Army, which at that time that did not rise above a dozen or so dollars a month.

It is hard to overlook the idealism evident in the officers' decision to come to Poland's rescue. The presence of this idealism is proved not only on the battlefields but also in the officers' acceptance of low pay and their general attitude toward Poland after the end of wartime demands. Finally, the last motive, which was of a political and military nature, was Polish appeals for aid. From the very moment of Poland's rebirth in November 1918, until the third Silesian Uprising in May 1921, Poland was engaged in military struggle or was threatened by invasion on several fronts at the same time. The Russians and Ukrainians pressed from the east, the Germans threatened from the west, and by January 1919 the Czechs occupied several Polish counties in the south. It is possible that a desire to aid the underdog played a role here.

It is worth noting the warm attitude towards America evident in Poland. In the space of merely a few months after regaining independence, the US enjoyed an unrivaled position in unofficial popularity ratings. Elbert Farman reported on January 10, 1920:

> There is no doubt that American influence is greater in Poland than any other foreign influence. All but the extreme Left are very friendly towards America. This influence is due to the feeling that we are disinterested, to the American aid given to Poland, food, children relief, Red Cross, etc., and to a very considerable degree to the personality of the American Minister. The present American Minister is the most influential foreign representative in Poland.[21]

It is necessary to add that besides the ARA and the work of Hugh Gibson (the first U.S. envoy to Warsaw), the American airmen contributed to the image of the U.S. in Poland by providing tangible help without expecting any reward.

4 | Paris — Warsaw — Lwów

After the contracts had been signed, preparations were made for departure to Warsaw. It was predicted that the American pilots would depart in the middle of September 1919. The matter of choosing a route was simplified somewhat by the fact that there was to some extent a rail route already in existence, which went through Germany. From April to July 1919 several tens of thousands of soldiers of Haller's Army had been transported by this route. However, there was always the possibility of obstruction by the defeated Germans, and transports of special significance became the subject of negotiations and petty decisions. The first period after the cease-fire in November 1918 was the most difficult. As the result of strong German opposition, many transports from Central Europe to France had to pass through Austria, Switzerland and Italy. But this route was too lengthy and went through too many borders, and the Allies stressed the opening of a shorter route.

The airmen were not traveling with any military equipment, and they were traveling incognito. This was important since at that time Poland and Germany were in a state of undeclared conflict. The most inflammatory issues in this situation were the anti–German uprising in Silesia, the problem of Gdańsk's (Danzig's) future, and the remaining disputed territories where the plebiscites were to be held. Therefore, the Germans could not look favorably on any strengthening of the Polish Army, especially by highly qualified airmen of the American and British Armed Forces. It must be remembered that a substantial group of Allied officers served in the Allied Commission for Upper Silesia, established in August 1919 by the Supreme Command of the Allied Forces. The U.S. army delegate there was Colonel Goodyear. The Commission's task was to observe the situation in Silesia and prepare conditions for the transfer and assign-

On their way to Poland, September, 1919. (Courtesy of Paul Konys, Rocky River, OH.)

ment of these territories by the Allied Forces. In the first version of the plan to use the America airmen, as we remember, the military authorities in Warsaw had planned to direct them to Silesia, just as Paderewski had.

Taking into consideration all the events mentioned above, the airmen's trip was carefully camouflaged. Firstly, they were equipped with uniforms of General Haller's Army, but en route between Paris and Warsaw they could not even wear those uniforms. To avoid unnecessary publicity, Col. Howland recommended that they wear substitute uniforms. Since one of the conditions of the contract stipulated that the volunteers cover the cost of their journey to Poland, they joined up with a Red Cross transport and in Coblenz they joined an "American Typhus Relief" train going to Poland.[1]

Just before their departure, there was a parting of both the Polish military authorities in Paris and of Paderewski. It was a rather warm occasion, which lasted two hours in the Hotel Ritz, where Ignacy Paderewski had his headquarters. Apart from being Prime Minister, Paderewski was also a delegate at the Peace Conference in Paris. After Fauntleroy presented the squadron, Paderewski was supposed to have said, "Nothing has ever touched me so much as the offer of you young men to fight and,

4. Paris — Warsaw — Lwów

if necessary to die for my country." The next ceremony in honor of the airmen was organized by one of the most fervent promoters of the whole venture, Gen. Tadeusz Rozwadowski, and attended by the newly appointed Polish Minister to the United States, Prince Casimir Lubomirski, Col. Howland, and Gen. Ewing. D. Booth, AEF Chief of Staff. The presence of the latter needs a little explanation. It seems to confirm that, independently of Gen. Howland's role, the higher AEF authorities also recognized the nature of the expedition and were not opposed to it. The Ukrainian historian R.G. Simonenko said that the presence of Gen. Booth confirmed that the volunteers were an element of international intervention against Russian Bolshevism. The aims of the airmen reached far further than the occupation of Kiev. According to Simonenko, they aimed to march on Moscow.[2]

The seven volunteers left Paris September 16, 1919. Only Fauntleroy traveled by train in luxurious conditions under the terms of his previous contract. The rest, after changing at Coblenz, arrived in Warsaw on September 24. The volunteers went straight from the railway station to *Pole Mokotowskie*, where the airfield and the headquarters of the Chief of the Polish Air Force were located. Their arrival caused a certain amount of surprise, since not all the preparations have been made. After formalities had been disposed with, they were lodged in a hotel.

Deployment was a wearisome matter, more so because at the beginning the Polish authorities were not sure where the volunteers would serve. Whether to create a completely new unit or hand the airmen over to one that already existed — with unknown officers — was difficult to decide. There were many inherent problems; for example, what language were orders, correspondence, communications, and battle documentation to be in, and in what way should the volunteers behave if they fell into enemy hands. Their contracts obliged them to serve in the Polish Army, but they were still citizens of the United States. In the Polish Armed Forces' experience, the treatment of prisoners in the Russian Bolshevik war was way below universally accepted international norms. Great thought was given to how to combat the propaganda possibilities of the Bolsheviks against the Americans' presence in the Polish ranks. As is well known, the Bolsheviks saw in every guest of the Polish Government an emissary of the imperialists and bankers who threatened the peace and well-being of the homeland of the world proletariat. Every form of aid was synonymous with an international plot to harm Soviet Russia. The matter of the deployment of the volunteers oscillated from using them to train cadres at the rear to using them in direct service on the front.

The only person who could fundamentally deal with all these issues was Józef Piłsudski, who met with the American pilots in Belvedere after a visit to the Polish-Bolshevik front in the vicinity of Mińsk. The exact date of the meeting is unknown. From indirect sources it can be dated to between the end of September and the beginning of October, 1919. Piłsudski tried to test the determination of the Americans who had come to Belvedere. He painted a discouraging picture of the conditions under which they were to serve. He spoke of the lack of equipment and the difference in training. "You will not be satisfied by teaching our young airmen." This was picked up by Fauntleroy, who categorically declared that he, as the other airmen, had come to fight at the front and not to serve at the rear. This certainly convinced Piłsudski, who encouraged them to "show what they could do."

The Chief of the Air Force, Jasiński, was present during the conversation. Fauntleroy, with Jasiński acting as an interpreter, led the conversation on behalf of the Air Force. The rest merely listened. The atmosphere of the meeting was not idyllic. Piłsudski showed his colder side and did not reveal his own preferences and attitudes, although he forced the pilots to declare theirs. Finally, he agreed to send them to the front, which Fauntleroy had determinedly requested, and promised to attend to all the details. Ultimately it was a significant strengthening of the Polish Air Force, which was then still in its infancy.[3]

Some ascribe Piłsudski's harshness during the meeting to a lack of trust in the Air Force itself. During the Great War the Air Force had performed poorly. The extremely harsh weather, the swiftly changing frontline, the lack of permanent landing strips, the weakness of the industrial infrastructure, the lack of and fragility of the equipment, the airmen's weak observational results, and the inefficient bombing discouraged any thoughts of costly innovations. For Piłsudski an additional disappointment was the first public air show at the Mokotów Aerodome (*Pola Mokotowskie*) in Warsaw on August 23, 1919, a few weeks before the Americans' visit to Belvedere. Piłsudski, surrounded by numerous guests, observed the flight of a Roland CL II piloted by Captain Kazimierz Jesionowski and Lieutenant Karol Słowik. It was a modified German plane, which for ceremonial purposes was decorated with characteristic red and white checkers and numbers alluding to the year 1918, when Poland regained independence. This air show was intended to prove the readiness of the Polish military, but the Roland's acrobatics ended tragically. Due to a technical failure, the plane plummeted to the ground, burying the pilots. Considering the symbolism of the show, it must have been an exceptionally depressing experience for Piłsudski, who a few days later took part in the funeral of the pilots.[4]

In reality, the Americans arrived in a country which not only lacked a developed Air Force, but whose independence was still in its infancy. The genesis of the Polish Air Force dates back to 1915–1916. While still in the Pilsudski Legion, Janusz Beaurain proposed the organization of an air squadron. His initiative, announced in a volunteer unit completely dependent on Austrian supplies and possessing no technical backup, was unusually courageous. To Piłsudski's credit, it must be noted that the staff of the 1st Brigade of the Polish Legion applied to the Austro-Hungarian military authorities to organize an Air Force squadron. At this stage the quest did not meet with a positive reply. Nevertheless, Beaurain and three other candidates were directed to the 34th Austro-Hungarian Squadron on the Italian front. Characteristically, Beaurain together with Stefan Stec and Leopold Toruń became the core of the regular Polish Air Force, which first engaged the enemy in the defense of Lwów in November 1918. What is more, Lt. Stec was responsible for the design of the combat Air Force logo, red and white checkers, which he had already painted on his own plane while serving in the Austro-Hungarian armed forces.[5] This was a major insubordination and quite a challenge on his part. This logo was used in independent Poland, survived WWII, and has served excellently to this day.

In November 1918 the Polish Air Force consisted of a small group of Polish officers trained in the armies of Poland's occupiers and a cluster of the most varied and often most obsolete types of planes, or just their parts, which the Poles had managed to save from evacuation or destruction. In the four days before Piłsudski's return from a German prison (November 14, 1918), the Aerial Navigation Section of the Ministry of Military Affairs was established. In the first weeks of independence, it was difficult to speak of any coordination of activities or logistical support. The main airfields in Cracow, Lwów, Poznań, Warsaw and Przemyśl had independent groups of airmen, who responded to apparent threats, organized equipment repair and training, and activated courier links. They led the first reconnaissance and combat sorties. Since some cities were cut off, the courier links between Cracow and Lwów or Lwów and Warsaw were particularly important. It is assumed that from November to December 1918 there were approximately 217 aircraft, but in March 1919 the Air Force had closer to 350. However, these figures do not indicate the number of aircraft that were essentially combat ready. These made up a small percent of the whole. The return to Poland of the Haller Army certainly strengthened it in April and May 1919.[6]

The situation of the Air Force at that time was evaluated, perhaps a little harshly, by American Military Attache Elbert Farman, who wrote in one of his reports:

> The Poles have very little, if any, aviation corps, as these matters go nowadays. In fact I believe that aside from such as many as may have been brought up with General Haller's troops, their entire machines numbered 14, of which only 2 or 3 were in good conditions and 50% usable if one wanted to take a chance. These are mostly of the German Fokker type, but, I understand, it is their intention to increase the amount considerably, but to the best of my knowledge no steps have been taken to this end other than the endeavor to recruit officers from the Allied armies for service with the Polish in the aviation corps.[7]

It is difficult to investigate whether Farman, writing about foreign officers, had the Americans in mind. There are no direct indications. One can allege that he had several Italian and French officers in mind, who had higher functions in the Polish Air Force. One of them, Capt. Camillo Perini, was at the head of the Polish Air Force for a while. Cooper and his companions came to Warsaw after these reinforcements to the Air Force had already been made, moreover in a situation when there was relative calm on the frontline. The reorganization of the military structure had been completed in preparation for the unification of the whole army. Until that time it consisted of several elements of separate origins. An important part came from the Piłsudski Legion, but no less numerous was the cadre of the previous Polish Corps in Russia, which had been organized there since 1917. The Greater Poland (or "Wielkopolska") Army of Gen. Dowbor-Muśnicki that fought against the Germans to unite Greater Poland to the Republic had yet other origins. And one cannot pass over General Haller's Army. Its core was made up of emigrants from the United States. Similarly divided was the officers' corps, fostering different schools of thought and training, and advocating different tactics and strategy. The ceremonial unification of the Polish Army took place on October 19, 1919, with the participation of Piłsudski, Józef Haller and General Dowbor-Muśnicki. That ceremony was held in Cracow, the ancient capital of Poland.

The Americans' departure for Lwów preceded an unexpected but appreciated reinforcement of their personnel. On October 12, 1919, that is, after the Belvedere meeting with Piłsudski, two additional airmen arrived from England, Lt. Edmund Pike Graves and Lt. Elliott William Chess. Graves was born in Newburyport, Massachusetts, in 1891 and in

1913 graduated from Harvard Law School. During the First World War he served in the British Royal Flying Corps, and after he obtained his pilot's license in Canada, he was directed to the School of Aerial Gunnery at Fort Worth, Texas. At the beginning of 1918, he became an instructor of aerobatics at the School of Special Flying in Toronto. His passion for dangerous aerobatics dates from that time, a passion for which eventually he paid with his life. Since he was assigned to the school, Graves did not see combat action, and probably because of this he volunteered for service in Poland.[8]

Lt. Chess, nicknamed *Chesski,* came from El Paso, Texas. He trained in aviation in 1917 in a few Canadian training centers. In February and March 1918, he underwent additional training in the British Isles, after which he served as Aerial Messenger to the King. After his move from Britain to France, he flew 60 combat sorties, gaining the recognition of his superiors. Cooper and Fauntleroy didn't get to know these two candidates previously, which was a certain departure from the recruitment in Paris, but both were ready to prove their qualifications under Polish skies. The contract signed by Chess is dated September 1, 1919, the same as the original volunteers. Unfortunately, Graves' contract has not been found, but one can guess nonetheless that it was signed under similar circumstances and backdated, as in the case of Chess. This was probably so that all the pilots terminated their six-month contract simultaneously, and the renewal of all the contracts could occur on the same day.[9]

Prior to departure for Lwów, the tactical allocation was decided upon. At first the 4th or 6th fighter squadrons were considered, but quickly enough the concept of creating a new squadron or of the Americans completely taking over an existing unit was rejected. It was decided that it would be most advantageous to co-opt the volunteers to a unit that was already in existence, leaving the remainder of the Polish Flying Personnel to be supplemented by Americans. The ultimate choice fell upon the 7th Fighter Squadron, which at that time was stationed in Lwów. It was one of the best units and in November 1918 was still called the 3rd Air Combat Squadron. It was established at Rakowice, the airfield at the outskirts of Cracow, in the first half of November of that year, on the Austrian Pilot School's base. Its equipment, for the most part obsolete Brandenburgs with Austro-Deimler 160 KM engines, and one Offag 51, were the only combat aircraft to fall into the hands of the Poles. Already by the end of November the Squadron had been directed to Lwów, where it was installed at Lewandówka airport, and on December

Lewandówka airfield in Autumn 1919. (Courtesy of Dr. Tomasz Kopański, Warsaw.)

21 it was turned into the 7th Air Squadron and assigned to the 2nd Air Group, commanded by Capt. Stefan Bastyr.[10]

The air base at which the Squadron was stationed also possessed a colorful history. The Austrians constructed it on the northern periphery of Lwów in 1915. Lewandówka's position was very advantageous, since it was near a railway line, which facilitated delivery and possible evacuation. In comparison with airport standards of the time, it was large — two miles long and one mile wide, with many permanent hangars and well-equipped workshops. Therefore, it was a valuable attribute for the Austrians, who feared handing it over to the Poles. At the end of October 1918, shortly before the collapse of the Austro-Hungarian monarchy, three airmen of Polish origin came to Lwów on holiday and managed to capture Lewandówka. They were Lt. Stefan Bastyr, Lt. Stefan Stec, and Eugeniusz Roland. This achievement enabled communications to be established between Lwów and the outside world. More than that, Lewandówka was a staging point on the courier route between Kiev and Vienna. On November 5, 1918, one of the Austrian planes, unaware of the political development that had occurred in Lwów, landed at Lewandówka on the way to Vienna and fell right into Polish hands. In this way, the Poles gained another functioning aircraft and news of the situation in Kiev. On the same day, Lt. Bastyr and Lt. Beaurain took off on their first combat sortie, during which they bombed Ukrainian positions at Peresenkówka railway station. In fact, it was the first bombing raid carried out by the Polish Air Force.[11]

The Americans reached Lwów nearly one year later. Their train reached the city on October 17 at eight o'clock in the morning. They were sent to Lewandówka the next day, where Polish pilots were waiting for them. At that time the 7th Squadron was commanded by Ludomił Rayski, an officer of great experience who knew foreign languages, which was immeasurably useful since the Americans naturally did not know Polish. When the Americans arrived, the 7th Squadron already had a lot of combat experience. There was also a reorganization, which was accompanied by rearmament with modernized equipment.[12] The Americans were welcomed not only by Rayski, but also by other officers who were not chosen solely for their combat ability but also for their knowledge of foreign languages.

All the pilots and the adjutant (non-flying) of the squadron managed to understand English and also German or French. They were, First Lt. Jerzy Weber (who served officially as the Squadron translator), First Lt. Władysław Konopka, Sec. Lt. Aleksander Senkowski and Sec. Lt. Ludwik Idzikowski. They had all served during the First World War, though in different armies. For example, Weber served in the Imperial Russian Air Service, as did Idzikowski. Senkowski, however, came from the Austrian Air Service. Rayski, who undoubtedly stood out from the group, formerly served as an officer in the Turkish Air Force.[13]

Before October 24 Rayski handed over command of the Squadron to Fauntleroy, though he did not officially leave the Squadron until January 1919. This was probably in order to ensure a smooth transition. Nevertheless, Fauntleroy was already making decisions that were far beyond normal functions of a commander. Almost from the day following their arrival, he also took steps to reorganize the squadron. This concerned the development of the squadron into the "Polish-American Air Group." The pretext was the announcement of reinforcements expected from the United States and Western Europe, but the decision may have been spurred on by political developments. A report of the III Department of the High Command of the Republic of Poland from October 31 stated that in France a new squadron was being formed from American airmen, "who requested to be named after Pulaski. They are requesting permission to be enlisted into the Polish Army."[14]

It turned out that these reports were exaggerated. Events of later weeks proved that no group of volunteers arrived in Warsaw from Paris, but because the announcement came from Polish sources it was able to

Top: American pilots immediately after arrival to Poland. *Bottom:* Lt. Rayski and C. Fauntleroy, Lewandówska, Autumn 1919. (Courtesy of Dr. Tomasz Kopański, Warsaw.)

stimulate the imagination. As a matter of fact, there is no proof that Fauntleroy even knew about this. At any rate, on November 1, 1919, without any visible connection to the previous day's report, he submitted correspondence to the Head of the Air Force in Warsaw informing him of Gen. Rozwadowski's recruitment of Capt. Paul Brewster in Paris. Fauntleroy also requested a consultation with him about the evaluation of any newly enlisted officers and a verification of their military ranks.[15] Still more significant was Fauntleroy's action on the same day, namely a memo to the 1st Deputy Minister for Military Affairs General Sosnkowski. In this he wrote:

> With the aim of propaganda and interest in the whole of the United States, I request in the strongest terms that the organization of the American Air Force officers in Poland be named the "Polish-American Air Group" and that it be divided into two units, one named the "Kościuszko Squadron" and the other, the "Pulaski Squadron." These two names incite extraordinary interest and sympathy in the United States, where the former name is well known in the North because he served in Washington's Army. Whereas Pulaski is highly regarded in the southern states where Gen. Pulaski gave his life in defense of the besieged Savannah for the freedom of the United States. The naming of one of the squadrons after Pulaski will be an interesting historical memento. Gen. Pulaski, during the cavalry charge on the front of the regiment commanded by Col. John Cooper, a direct ancestor of Capt. Merian C. Cooper, an exceptional man of the first wing of our present squadron and whom I would like to appoint as commander of the Pulaski Squadron.

In a later part of the letter, Fauntleroy requested that the Polish military authorities draw up a document about this matter, with the aim of publishing it in the United States. He was even prepared to take command, if only the "Polish-American Air Group" was established and consisted of two squadrons with historical names.[16] Fauntleroy's project met with interest. His correspondence was dispatched for evaluation by the appropriate Departments and Sections of the Polish High Command, who only a few days later prepared a preliminary opinion. Section 3b of the High Command, or the Chief of the Air Force, replied on November 6, 1919, that: "...it takes the position, that Maj. Pilot Fauntleroy's project with appropriate support from national factors, would bring great advantages, with consideration given to the fact that in the U.S. general public opinion evokes greater influence on all diplomatic action than any where else."[17]

Army's Intelligence had an equally favorable attitude about the idea, although they did not send the appropriate correspondence to the V Department of the High Command until December 9, 1919. It was the general military and political considerations that decided the matter, and also the fact that Fauntleroy's project did not include new financial obligations. Fauntleroy's idea also reverberated in America. *The New York Times* in its November 9 edition most clearly endorsed the plan. Quoting Major Baer, the editor of the *Times* wrote:

> Poland has 800,000 men in uniform who have sworn to regain their lost provinces and to maintain their new national independence against all foes.... On their battlefront they are fighting not only Bolshevist but Germans in Russian uniforms. You must know that Germany has refused to give up certain territory she now holds until the United States ratifies the Peace Treaty. Maj. Baer is making his Headquarters at the American Flying Club.[18]

The anti–German conclusion was most clearly supposed to encourage the journey to Poland. Baer's efforts to establish another squadron unfortunately did not yield any measurable results. There were no further announcements, and he himself fell into financial difficulties which prevented him from continuing his work. In a letter to Paderewski from January 2, 1920, Baer recalled that he had already, while in Paris, committed himself to Paderewski and to organizing another American Air Squadron. He thought, however, that it was essential to run a huge propaganda campaign on behalf of Poland in America. He planned a trip to Poland with a movie crew, so as to organize a series of film shows, presentations, and public lectures to facilitate recruitment: "As Poland was concerned she was shrouded in mystery to the Americans, and before more funds could be hoped for, Poland must have publicity in this U.S.A."

In another part of the letter, he emphasized, however, that he had already exhausted his own time and resources, and without further support he would not be able to achieve his aim. He promised that he would repay Paderewski the 25,000 francs he had borrowed from him.[19]

From the fragment of the letter quoted, one can see that Baer tried not only to continue with the recruitment of volunteers but also to raise funds to this end. Unfortunately, there are no details as to how much money he raised and what ultimately happened with respect to his overall plan. There are no traces of any information on that subject from available sources.

The efforts described were not the only letters of undertaking connected with Polish-American air force cooperation. One can even suspect that it was not the sole form of support for the "Polish-American Air Group." On December 28, 1919, Col. Howland prepared a memo on the subject of the need to establish a permanent air route between Warsaw and Paris. The route was to be maintained by three planes, one stationed in Paris, one in Warsaw and one running between the two. They were to serve not only the diplomatic staff, but also the organizational needs of charities present in Poland. Howland also permitted the use of two free seats for passengers. Since the planes were supposed to land in Berlin, it was also possible to serve the recipients of correspondence there. Howland, moreover, made it known that he had secured the support of the Knights of Columbus and the American Red Cross to the tune of 200,000 francs, and of the Polish authorities, who were obliged to ensure the delivery of fuel and spare parts, and to maintain servicing in Poland. For 200,000 francs it was possible to buy planes, but financial assistance was also needed from the State Department to cover day-to-day expenses. Thus, there were many arguments for opening such a line of communication. Howland considered that air transport would not only be more efficient, but also safer and cheaper.

> The foregoing facts are being covered in a cablegram to be sent by Ambassador Wallace to Mr. Polk at Washington, asking simply for the necessary authority from the State Department to utilize as much of the funds now being used for courier and telegraph service as may be necessary to maintain the aeroplane service.[20]

One can, of course, argue about the connection of this project to the presence of the airmen of the 7th Squadron in Poland. However, if one considers that its author, Col. Howland, was known for his previous cooperation with Rozwadowski, and if one adds the timing of his action, it is possible to intertwine this project with a wider intention of enlisting additional airmen and guaranteeing better communication for transferring them to Poland. Unfortunately, the intention of activating air channel between Paris and Warsaw did not take off.

Col. Benjamin F. Castle's arrival in Poland has a certain connection with Fauntleroy's, Baer's, and maybe even the Howland initiative. He was a banker and, as the man in charge of the American Flying Club in New York City, the most vocal patron of the squadron in America. His arrival is dated December 19, 1919. The sources and memoirs are silent, however, on the subject of the visit, although one concluded unambiguously that "although he did not do actual flying with [the squadron], he helped a great deal with the 'behind the scenes' organization work."[21]

If Col. Castle was only concerned with securing funds from American creditors, which was his official reason for visiting Europe, he would not have visited Lewandówka. It seems that he was in some way involved with the plan to create the Polish-American Air Group, possibly by generating support on behalf of the squadron at the American Flying Club. It is difficult to speculate further, as other researchers into the squadron do. For example, the Ukrainian historian P. Simonenko suggests that Col. Castle's visit was connected to the plans, as he writes, of American imperialism. According to him the 7th Squadron was intertwined with anti–Bolshevik intrigue, and it was no accident that it was to be stationed in the vicinity of Lwów. In Simonenko's opinion, the point was to link the Polish offensive of 1920 with the activities of Gen. Peter Wrangel — leader of the White Russian counterrevolutionaries in the Crimea, and with the landing operations of the Allies on the Black Sea coast.[22]

Views of this nature, which persist even decades after the events described, indicate how the Bolshevik authorities saw the presence of the Americans, with what unease their involvement in defending Poland has been viewed. It is not necessary to explain here that neither the squadron nor Poland was carrying out any operations to facilitate any landing on the Black Sea. It is easy to imagine what a propaganda counteraction would have been sparked off in Russia if Fauntleroy had succeeded in organizing the Polish-American Air Group. In a certain sense Fauntleroy left possibilities open for the future. In the period prior to the Col. Castle's visit, he divided the squadron into two formations. The first, named *Kościuszko,* was led by Corsi, and the second named *Pulaski,* by Cooper. Lt. E. Chess, Lt. C. Clark, Sec. Lt. E. Noble, Sec. Lt. Idzikowski, Lt. A. Senkowski, and Lt. J. Weber were placed in the first formation. In the second, apart from Cooper, were Lt. H. Rorison, Capt. A. Kelly, Lt. G. Crawford, and Lt. W. Konopka. Fauntleroy was still in command of the whole squadron.[23] The Polish Minister of Military Affairs, Gen. Józef Leśniewski, and Gen. Gustaw Macewicz of the Inspectorate of the Air Forces sanctioned Fauntleroy's decision on December 16, 1919.[24]

From the moment that it arrived in Lwów, the squadron began to familiarize itself with new equipment, conditions, and regulations. The weather conditions diminished the number of training flights, and this was important since the Americans had no prior experience with the squadron planes. By summer 1919, the 7th Squadron got 12 fighter planes,

Spad S.VII CI's and Offag-Albatros D. III's. Until the end of October the squadron carried out over 130 training flights, taking advantage of hints from Rayski and the remaining Polish pilots. One of them was about extinguishing the engine at the touch down in order to avoid somersaults. Training work was not disturbed. The Bolshevik Air Force at that time was engaged in action against Denikin. The Ukrainians, in turn, aspired to an alliance with Poland. Only reports of the heavy German Gotha transport planes flying between the Bolsheviks and the Germans alarmed the Squadron from time to time. However, they never managed to make contact with these planes.

More or less at the same time, the squadron obtained its insignia. Its designer was Elliot Chess, who, according to one source, designed it on a menu of the Hotel George in Lwów. He presented crossed blackbirds on the background of Cracow folk hats, which symbolized the Kościuszko Uprising of 1794. This was placed on a background of the 13 red stars and 13 red and white stripes. The numbers matched the 13 original colonies of the United States, which fought for independence. It is difficult to imagine a more suitable set of symbols close to both nations and so ideally connected to the patron of the squadron. It is not surprising that the insignia served excellently throughout the inter-war period, the 1939 September Campaign, and WWII.

From the beginning the Americans demanded direct participation in operations on the Polish-Bolshevik front, where at this time an autumnal silence had fallen. Weather conditions prevented active reconnaissance and training flights, but there were no orders to move the unit closer to the frontline. They took advantage of the time to familiarize themselves further with their surroundings and the town, and to carry out a range of charitable acts. The Americans decided to get involved with the protection of the youngest defenders of Lwów, who after the bloody battles of 1918 had become orphans, bereft of any means of self-support. The airmen, as one journalist wrote: "decided to adopt a certain number of these boys and take care of their upbringing. To this end, they have assigned 8,000 crowns for the moment. The first boy whom they adopted is 15 year-old Jan Wronowski, an ex–Corporal of the 5th Infantry Regiment of the Polish Army."[25]

This was not the only act of its kind. The Americans distributed food supplies, helped in the work of the representatives of American charities in Lwów, and visited both the well known and less well known families of Lwów. They were often to be seen at the Red Cross Headquarters, which had been set up in the Potocki Palace. Close relations with the

Albatros Oefag D III aircraft of the 7th Squadron. (Courtesy of Dr. Tomasz Kopański, Warsaw.)

maintenance crew were also on the agenda. Cooper's memoirs from Christmas 1919, throw an interesting light on the relations between the Americans and Poles. After a dinner in their own group, a deputation of Polish non-commissioned officers came to the American quarters with an invitation to a Christmas Eve dinner. The oldest of the non-commissioned officers presented Fauntleroy with a certificate with a likeness of the Major and the caption, "to the Commander of the *Kościuszko*

Aviation Squadron, the representative in Poland of the democratic spirit of freedom of the United States of America, from his Polish soldiers." The most amusing part of the picture was the background, which showed planes and the many spires and buildings of Lwów, and on the other side a village and rustic scenery with the caption "New York." Clearly, images of the wild West overwhelmed the realities of the metropolis in the imagination of the amateur artist.[26]

The celebrations of the first anniversary of the liberation of Lwów, on November 22, 1919, marked a certain interlude. Piłsudski's attendance was announced so the preparations gathered even greater momentum. Despite the fact that ultimately the Head of State did not come to Lwów, the celebrations went ahead as planned. The airmen's were asked to stage an air show over the city center, near the Potocki Palace. Corsi, Graves, Chess, Idzikowski, Konopka, and Orzechowski were delegated this task under the general command of Fauntleroy. The crew performed over *Mariacki* Square in a V formation and flew over the applauding crowd many times. The aerobatics show was going exactly to time, when Graves flew off from the group to show a few "double barrels." Suddenly, around 200 meters from the ground, the left wing of his plane fell off and the plane crashed full speed into the Potocki Palace, igniting a huge fire. Graves tried to save himself by jumping from the plane, according to one of the sources, but he was already too low to save his life. Another witness described his death thus: "seeing the plane crashing, I stood on the pavement, following the picture of the catastrophe with fear. Then the plane crashed into a turret on the left wing of the palace. The noise of a terrible explosion reverberated in the air and at that moment the pilot was thrown out of the plane and plummeted head-first to the ground. I ran together with a few witnesses in the direction of the palace and threw myself into helping the pilot. He lay in a puddle of blood with a smashed skull, and blood spurted out of his ears and lips, and it seemed to me that I could feel the weak beating of his heart, but as one of the doctors who arrived later said it was only an illusion, because his death was instantaneous."[27]

In must be added that knowing the technical condition of the aircraft of the Squadron, the C.O. of the III Air Group issued a strict order forbidding any aerial acrobatics below the 500-meter ceiling.[28]

Crowds of Lwów's residents attended Graves' funeral, which took place on November 26. Official delegates included Dr. Gałecki, the government delegate, Polish generals, French officers who were in the city, representatives of religious affiliations and the city authorities. Dispatches

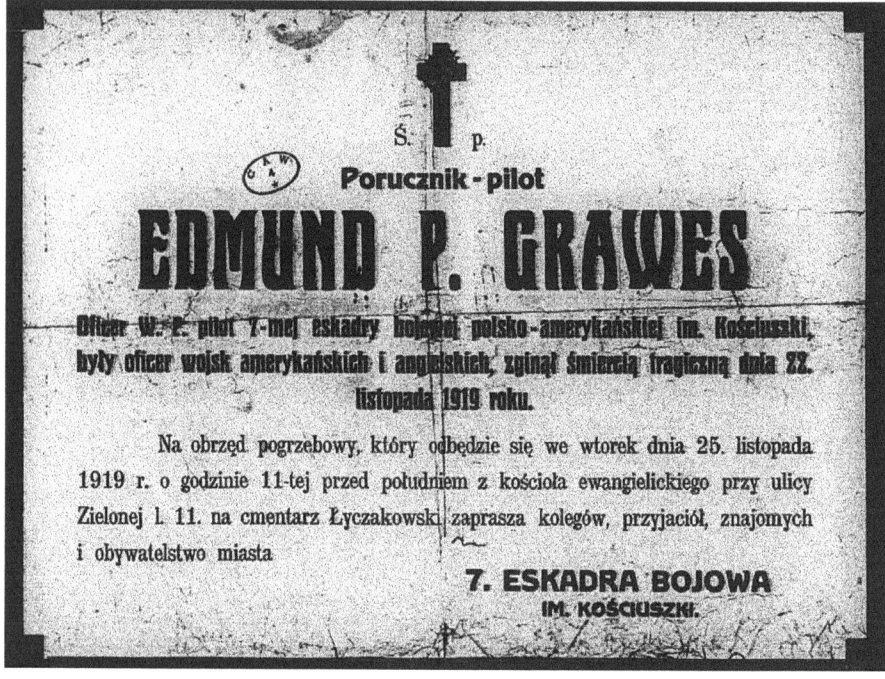

Obituary of Lt. Graves. (Courtesy of the Central Military Archive, Warsaw.)

arrived from all over the country. Pastor Doctor Kesserling delivered the homily in an Evangelical church in both Polish and English. The funeral procession consisted of a chariot made from the remains of the plane, with a propeller at the front. At the moment when the body was lowered into the grave one of the squadron planes flew low over the cemetery, paying their last homage the airmen's way.[29] The squadron historian wrote:

> It was an unhappy event in every way, but it served to bring about an interesting psychological change: the slight sense of being foreigners in a strange country was swept away from the fellows, and they became a part of the land. The blood of their comrade was sown in the soil, and the men were thus welded the stronger to the land of their service.[30]

For the people of Lwów, Graves' death served as a catalyst, on the basis of which an even stronger affection and gratitude emerged for the airmen from over the ocean.

The loss of an experienced pilot such as Graves forced the group to seek a swift replacement. Fauntleroy announced the upcoming arrival of Paul Brewster, a very well trained and experienced pilot who ultimately did not arrive. However, the volunteer who did arrive was Capt. Harmon Chadbourn Rorison. Rorison graduated from the School of Military Aeronautics, Ohio State University (July 6, 1917–September 6, 1917). From there he went to the U.S. Aviation School at Mineola Field, Long Island, which he graduated from on the first of November that year. Commissioned as a 1st Lieutenant, Aviation Section, Sig. R.C. on November 3, he was sent to France and reported on the continent on January 24, 1918. In the famous center at Issoudon, he completed training as a "Chasse Pilot," and learned how to perform a nighttime sortie. He also took an Aerial Gunnery Course at Cazaux, France, and on May 23 was assigned to Air Service Production Center No. 2 at Romorantin, France. After September 26, 1918, Rorison served in the 22nd Aero Squadron, 2nd Pursuit Group, First Army.

Shortly before the armistice he had the distinction of shooting down Rorison's decision to come to Poland was assisted not only in France but also in the United States. After his discharge from the Army on October 8, 1919, the Adjutant General advised to him that the Department of War had no objections to his departure for eight months, after which he was to report on his return to the United States. The favorable attitude of the Military authorities is notable. It is possible that at this stage they permitted individual service in Poland because it would provide data on a totally unknown theater of war and on the Bolshevik military machine. Rorison was preceded by a letter of recommendation from a relative, the Vice-President of the J.G. White Engineering Corporation of New York, addressed to the U.S. envoy Hugh Gibson. There is no evidence to confirm that Gibson made use of it; most probably it was not needed. The contract with Rorison was signed on November 27 with conditions identical to those of the other volunteers. By the 30th of that month, "Little Rory" had already reported to Lewandówka and was immediately pressed into service.

Weather conditions prevented systematic training or the carrying out of courier-communication assignments. The register of sorties carried out in the autumn and winter months indicates that the squadron was condemned to a frustrating wait for the weather to change or for political-military decisions. It was difficult to expect the latter before the arrival of spring. The airmen were forced to develop resistance against swinging moods, changeable weather, and lack of knowledge as to what form their activities would take and when the offensive would begin.

Cooper and Fauntleroy in front of the Squadrons Albatros, winter 1919/20. (Courtesy of Dr. Tomasz Kopański, Warsaw.)

However, they did carry out sorties when it was at all possible. During October, the squadron succeeded in carrying out an impressive number of 131 sorties. The average length of the flights did not exceed 30 minutes, which indicates training exercises, limited to the area immediately surrounding Lewandówka. In the same month, all of the Polish Air Squadrons, including the 7th Squadron, counted 185 training flights and barely over 146 hours in the air. In November the squadrons carried out only 81 sorties, in December only 38. In November the bombing activities used 2,500 kilograms of explosives, then a month later barely ten bombs were dropped of an unknown weight. 1920 began with equally adverse weather conditions. Altogether the squadrons of the Polish Armed Forces recorded only 49 flights totaling 57 hours in January; in February, however, they carried out 145 flights totaling 158 hours. The sorties clearly became longer during these months, calculated on gathering information about the strength of the Bolsheviks on the vicinity of the front. In this last month 1,316.5 kilograms of bombs were dropped. March 1920 brought another halt. The total number of sorties carried out by all the squadrons was 69, dropping only 234 kg of bombs. That month was particularly difficult, not only because of the low temperature but also because of the low cloud level, which obscured visibility. April, which brought the beginning of Piłsudski's Kiev offensive, bore fruit, since 150 sorties were carried out in over 231 hours. The bombardment was heavy, for that time, 2,400 kg of bombs. Apart from that, the squadrons took hundreds of photographs of enemy positions and strategic installations. Documents do not record the precise number of flights carried out in this month by the 7th Squadron. It is only known that in January 1920 the Kościuszko Squadron carried out 19 sorties, and that was more than any other unit. For example, in the same month the 3rd "Wielkopolski" Squadron took off on 14 sorties. In February, the proportions were overturned. The Kościuszko airmen carried out 20 sorties, but the 5th Squadron carried out as many as 47, and the 6th Squadron, where some of the airmen's friends served, 43 sorties. All the squadrons mentioned reported after two dogfights in the air.[31]

The difference in the number of flights is not surprising given the weather conditions and difficulties with the equipment. Not only because in the winter it was especially difficult to move and navigate but also because there was a constant lack of spare parts, reinforcements and fuel. The airmen's flying tasks were alternated with attempts to replenish supplies, and to this end Fauntleroy and Cooper went to Warsaw and Cracow several times.

Those who remained took tasks of supporting the maintenance of courier links. The contact maintained with the military outposts nearest the front was most often supported by air links. The pilots also carried communications officers and provided orders. On their return, they took back mail and reports. Sometimes they landed at the planned point, and at other times, when conditions did not permit landing, they dropped the orders at designated drop points. At the beginning the procedure of identifying designated drop points for orders was not formalized. It was not until the effectiveness of this type of service had been confirmed that precise instructions from the heads of the Air Force appeared, regulating the methods of indicating the positions of their own units and the command posts of larger units. For example, infantry units in the vicinity of the front had to mark their positions with white sheets about 1×1 meter facing the enemy line. In other words they had to mark the extent of the area under control of their own forces. The Brigade Command indicated this by using two parallel sheets which measured 1×3 meters. They were to light a bonfire next to the sheets and send patrols to the drop area to collect the reports. In order to recognize friendly forces flares had to be fired.[32]

The reports were put in special tubes that protected the contents and were easy to spot at a distance. It is necessary to bear in mind that

Fauntleroy in front of his Albatros, winter 1919/1920. (Courtesy of Dr. Tomasz Kopański, Warsaw.)

not all the outposts had suitable landing strips. Some of them were frequently covered by snow, preventing planes from landing. This was another reason why working on procedures for the dispatch of reports and their collection was so important. The attitude of the population could also be a particular problem for the courier service. The further east, the less support there was for Poland and the Americans, and the stronger was the Bolshevik influence. The Bolshevik influence even reached Lwów. On February 14, 1920, there was a fire in a hangar at the 4th Lwów Air Park caused by a communist saboteur. A fire that broke out the day after Graves' funeral, at Lewandówka, was attributed to a similar cause, at least in the opinion of a Ukrainian historian of the 7th Squadron.[33]

Problems and the harsh conditions of service resounded in the Americans' correspondence with the outside world. On February 28, 1920, Fauntleroy wrote a letter to the Secretary of War, Newton D. Baker. He explained that the conditions under which they served in Poland were difficult for the average American to imagine, and he appealed for 20–30 planes to be sent with spare parts. He emphasized that it was in the U.S. government's interest to comply with the request since the Bolsheviks were determined to overcome every government, including the American. Unfortunately, Baker was evasive in his reply.[34] Col. Castle's appeal to the President in support of Fauntleroy was to no avail.

Frustrations with equipment were a part of life for the airmen. On November 30, 1919, Cooper received an order to transport Maj. Holms of the British Military Mission in a two-seater Brandenburg to Kamieniec Podolski some 100 miles south of Lwów. However, shortly after the plane took off, Cooper was forced to land because of technical difficulties, and the pilot and the British Major had to stay in Dziryn a few days before Cooper could deliver Holmes to Kamieniec Podolski.

The English were engaged in sorting out complicated issues of East Galicia nationalities and the future of the entire region. Despite the negative opinion of Petlura, they pressed hard for a settlement between the Ukrainian Peoples Republic and Anton Denikin's "White" Russia, which was an exceptionally difficult task. Around Christmas time an additional crew comprising Crawford and Shrewsbury went to Kamieniec Podolski in order to check whether a stock of military supplies left behind by the Austrians and seized by the Poles was of any value whatsoever for the squadron, and also to observe possible enemy movement and activity near the frontline. After these officers, Noble and Rorison went on January 7, 1920. Kamieniec Podolski was of great strategic importance since it lay on the point of three borders, the Russian-Ukrainian, Polish and Romanian. From there ran the shortest route to the main concentration of "White" Russian armies, which had been gradually pushed back towards the Crimean peninsula. It is not surprising then that the squadron airmen received orders to prepare a landing strip in a neighboring city.

At the end of January 1920, rumors spread about a concentration of Bolsheviks on the Podolski Front who were ready to attack. To find out the truth of the situation, an order was issued to deliver orders from Lwów to Tarnopol. Lt. Elliot Chess was the first to make an attempt. Shortly after take-off, however, he was forced to return to Lewandówka because of engine problems. When he landed he was slightly injured. Taking no account of this, he boarded Cooper's Albatros and took off again, and this time he delivered the tube with the orders to its destination. However, there were further problems on landing. The airfield at Tarnopol was covered by a thick layer of snow, and Chess's plane nosed over. Suspecting that Chess would have problems, Cooper took off in his wake, but soon after take-off the engine lid of his plane opened and blocked his view. Cooper was forced to return to Lewandówka, and during the landing his own plane flipped over. Such a situation is indicative of the flaws in the equipment, which was difficult to get going in winter weather conditions. The next day Corsi took off for Tarnopol with the next report, and Cooper again the following day. A strong wind blew Corsi far off course, forcing him to land in the village of Kopczynka, around 50 miles from Tarnopol. On a wide field he met with an unpleasant adventure — he was shot at by a Polish soldier who noticed that the nose of his plane was painted red. However, everything ended well: The

Winter 1919/1920. From left to right: Corsi, Kelly, Fauntleroy and Rorison. (Courtesy of Dr. Tomasz Kopański, Warsaw.)

soldier recognized the pilot just in time, and there were no injuries to report.

Cooper immediately went in search of Corsi, but his plane was forced to land three kilometers from Tarnopol because of lack of fuel. Finally he got there on peasant sleighs a few hours later. Fortunately, his was the last courier run to the front of that kind. On the last day of January, Noble, who had taken care of that particular landing strip, returned from Kamieniec Podolski.[35]

The long period of combat inactivity induced Fauntleroy to write a letter directly to Piłsudski, without regard to chain of command. It was an expression of his frustration, but also of his good will, with a tinge of romantic rowdiness close to that of medieval Crusaders.

> The Kościuszko Air Squadron, made up of American Airmen, has been serving in the Polish Armed Forces for the last three months. When we arrived in Poland, we had only one request, that we would be sent to the most active part of the front — to battle. Despite that request, up to now we have been kept far away from the frontline. Once more, we obediently ask the Head of State to hear our only request and to send us to the most active part of the front — to fight.[36]

There is no way of judging whether the letter provoked any positive result, since it was difficult to compromise strategic plans to the temperament of particular units. However, the fact is that the next assignments were in direct preparations for an offensive. On February 17, 1920, the 7th Squadron received an order to send aircraft to Tarnopol, which was the subject of more rumors of the possibility of a Bolshevik attack. Fauntleroy, Cooper, and Senkowski left for Tarnopol, but the departure of Clark, Chess, and Rorison ended in accidents. Some of these types of accidents were caused by the weather conditions, others by faults of equipment that lacked appropriate hangars for protection against moisture and frost. Tarnopol had none up until that time, and Fauntleroy appealed for hangars to be sent from Warsaw.

The issue of the hangars and of fuel was one of the problems of airmen all over the eastern front. The most widely available hangar was the French type called the *Bessoneau,* which in the conditions of mobile war when the hangars were frequently dismantled seemed impractical. The 7th Squadron used these hangars. Austrian hangars were also used, but in fewer numbers. These were basically designed for one plane, but when the occasion demanded were able to fit two. The hangars' main problems were their susceptibility to being surrounded by the enemy and their transport mobility between one landing strip and another. Some of the squadrons tried to keep their hangars and landing strips as close as possible to the battle zone; others acted with more prudence, which lengthened the air operation time. According to one of the instructions from the Chief Command of the Air Force, there were to be two hangar companies for each Air Division to attend to the transport of hangars. In practice, however, there was barely one hangar company with the 2nd Army, and everything fell on the shoulders of the officers and the ground crews of each squadron. Since the landing strips were often changed and the meteorological conditions were severe, the few hangars that existed were quickly worn out. As usual in such cases they were saved by the technical ingenuity of the support services, which were of the highest quality.[37]

At the beginning of the year, the first in a series of organizational shuffles preceded the Kiev Expedition. On January 2, 1920, Maj. Sergiusz Abżółtowski became head of the Air Force, replaced as of February 25 by Lt. Col. Aleksander Serednicki. He served in this capacity until September 17, 1920, when he was replaced by Capt. Stanisław Jasiński, already known from his contacts with the Americans. At the same time as the formal liquidation of the previous division into the Operation Groups

Crash of Lt. Clark's aircraft, February 17, 1920. (Courtesy of Dr. Tomasz Kopański, Warsaw.)

and fronts, the High Command also reformed the organization of the Air Force. An order from March 10, 1920, placed it under the command of the Head of the Air Force of the High Command of the Polish Army, which as of that day consisted of four sections. Lt. Włodzimierz Baczyński, the Head of Section I (Tactical), had the most contact with the American airmen.[38]

The *Ordre de Bataille* of the Air Force of March 1, 1920, directed the 7th Squadron to the area of the Podolski Front. It was subordinated to the III Air Group in Tarnopol commanded by Capt. Stefan Bastyr. However, the squadron's airport remained Lwów. At that time the squadron consisted of 11 planes, 12 pilots, 2 navigators (observers), 31 mechanics and 3 cars. It was already known that the 7th Squadron had better equipment and more of it than any other Polish unit. Some historians even write that it was favored.[39]

In March, all the squadrons were assigned to specific Infantry Divisions and Operation Groups. The squadrons on the Podolski Front were assigned as follows: the 5th Squadron to the 12th Infantry Division, the 6th Squadron to the 5th Infantry Division, and the 7th Kościuszko Squadron to General Wacław Iwaszkiewicz, the C.O. of the Front.

Foreseeing that combat would commence in late winter or early spring of 1920, 387 fighter planes were purchased mostly in France, England, and Italy. The greatest number, 137, were to come from France, 115 from Italy, and a lesser number from England. The possibility of buying equipment from the U.S. was lost due to earlier purchases by other states and the low quality of what remained after that. These ambitious plans testified to the importance of the Air Force's role.[40]

The popular view in historical literature that the Air Force was underestimated in the war is contradicted by an anonymous officer-airman, the author of a memo entitled *Several Words About the Air Force in Poland*, addressed to the Chief of General Staff in March 1920.

> All efforts ought to be concentrated on the Air Force corps, on bombardment, and as far as possible on one type of aircraft. Avoid buying abroad, get permission for the transport (of technology) and build methodically.... Let us not forget that at the current moment in world war, the Air Force is a vastly important weapon for who knows how to use it. Its mobility during battle, speed of attack, precise information that is given, the demoralizing influence that it has on the masses, greatly impresses the enemy, who isn't used to it. It is necessary to act, and counteract mainly, to hit shortly, swiftly, and accurately. Get rid of the incompetent officers and take the advice of those who are capable. Give command to those who can take over the responsibility.[41]

Also in early 1920 work began on the organizational structure, equipment needs, and the combat possibilities of the Air Force. Due to material shortages, attention was concentrated on the need to ensure effective aircraft repair. It was stressed that with the exception of the 7th Squadron, the quality of the machines in the majority of air squadrons was bad. It was recommended that the Air Force Department take on the issue of repairs. The airmen's training was also criticized.[42] A report from March 6, 1920, states that of the 19 squadrons supposed to take part in the Kiev Expedition, only 12 could be counted on to be in combat readiness by April 15. In any case, of the total number only 11 squadrons were assigned to the eastern front. It was assumed that due to the alleviation of the German threat, some of the units facing the Germans would reinforce the eastern front. The High Command placed five squadrons in reserve, and as war was approaching, there were further shifts towards strengthening the eastern front.

The problems of the air force were also of interest to the American Attache in Warsaw and his superiors in Washington. Farman's report of January 8, 1920, was devoted to the general structure and situation of

Flying equipment of the Kościuszko Squadron at the Lewandówka airfield, December, 1919. Aircraft #5 belonged to Cooper. (Courtesy of Dr. Tomasz Kopański, Warsaw.)

the Polish Air Force. According to Farman, any fighter squadron was supposed to consist of 10 planes, as many pilots, and 30 mechanics, and the Kościuszko Squadron was in a good shape because they had 13 pilot-officers. As regards salaries, captains earned 600 marks, plus 250 marks for officer airmen and an additional 50 marks for every 6 flying hours per month. The flying equipment, Farman wrote, belonged to the older type:

> Squadron No.7 (Kościuszko Squadron) is equipped with ten Albatros III one-seater planes, 220 H.P. Daimler motors. The motors are very reliable and good, except the rubber connections, which are bad. Some of the metal stampings are not good. The plane itself is structurally weak. It has monocoque (three plywood fuselages). This is good but warps very easily. There are two machine guns firing forward through the propeller. These guns are Austrian 30.30 (model not known) self-oiling system.[43]

Farman at that point did not know that the Schwartzlose machine guns were being used by the Squadron. They were located on the rather uncomfortable gun stand, without any swivel action, making it extremely difficult to aim efficiently. There was additional difficulty because the ammunition belts were still made of canvas and were folded up in rolls of their own making, which often caused the weapons to seize up. As for bombardment, the maximum bomb capacity of a single plane was 100 kg. There were no view-finders. Lighter bombs were thrown overboard, and heavier bombs through the doors in the observer's cabin in other makes of planes. The most popular were light bombs, weighing barely 2.5 kgs, called "little mice," were manually thrown onto targets of attack. According to the memoirs of the pilots, this brought extraordinary results.[44]

In a report soon after, Farman estimated the size of the Polish Air Force at 19 squadrons, in which there were 200 trained airmen. The organization was based on the French system, but there was no appropriate training system. Some air force units trained new pilots themselves. Farman considered the best air school to be at Ławica, near Poznań, where there were the best planes and ten French instructors. As for equipment, he stressed that a contract between Polish firms and the Italian Rosaldo company, which had opened an assembly line in Lublin, had antagonized the French, who considered Poland to be their sphere of influence.[45]

These remarks reflected progress compared to the picture he had painted of the beginnings of the Polish Air Force. Progress was also illustrated by the request from the Chief of the Air Force for an alliance between Poland and the Ukrainian Armed Forces Mission in Warsaw. Col. Pavlenko appealed for an Air Force squadron to provide the Ukrainian Army with ten planes so that they could carry out propaganda assignments, and to train ten Ukrainian pilots in Polish schools.[46]

On March 5, 1920, the 7th Squadron experienced its first combat

Personnel and flying equipment of the Kościuszko Squadron awaiting inspection. (Courtesy of Dr. Tomasz Kopański, Warsaw.)

contact with the Bolsheviks. Rorison, on that day, during a patrol flight in the direction of Wolpyniec, unexpectedly came across a large Bolshevik unit concentrated around the railway station. He was not entirely sure that it was really the enemy until he was fired at. Fortunately, he had a few 12-kilogram bombs on board, which he began to drop on the Bolsheviks. The losses he caused turned out to be extremely serious. Rorison practically disabled a whole Bolshevik regiment, inflicting heavy losses on their artillery, cavalry, and infantry. Details on that subject were confirmed by information gained by the Polish Intelligence.[47]

On the next day, the squadron received orders to relocate to the airfield at Mikulińce. Corsi went ahead of the squadron to prepare work on the erection of the hangars and to familiarize himself with the conditions on the spot. The choice of a landing strip, made from the air, turned out to be a deeply plowed field, on which landing was limited and even posed a danger to pilots' lives. Snow covered the unevenness of the terrain, which only became apparent when it partially melted. Corsi tried to inform the remaining airmen of the situation, to prevent them from embarking on a transport, but unfortunately to no avail. His telegram did not arrive in time and on March 13 the squadron stores set off in railway cars in the direction of Mikulińce. The inadequacy of the airfield was confirmed on the spot and Fauntleroy arranged for a change in orders. On March 18, new orders directed the squadron to Bereświca, but this airfield also appeared to be merely a mirage. Two days later the next orders arrived, directing the squadron to Rovne, but they were not carried out. Before the railway cars with hangars and equipment even arrived in Rovne, there was another change in orders. The 7th Squadron was to report to the town of Płoskirov. The exchange of dispatches with command lasted a few days before the final order of March 27 was issued, directing the squadron to Połonne, around 45 kilometers from Starokonstantynów. Połonne was chosen by the Supreme Command of the Polish Armed Forces as one of the main landing strips for the Kiev Expedition. It was planned to collect fuel supplies there for a month, and to leave two spare hangars, which after the start of the march on Kiev were to be transported to Żytomierz, Berdyczew and Koziatyń. Replenishment of emergency fuel supplies were also expected there. They finally arrived but with great delay. Thus, it fell on the 7th Squadron to carry out the operational missions of the airfield, which was of strategic importance.

It was not necessary to be an officer of the General Staff to guess that there was a limited number of days to the beginning of the offensive. On April 8 all work on the airfield at Polonne was finished and on the same day the first reconnaissance sorties took off from the new landing strip. On the following day, Fauntleroy, Crawford, and Rorison went as far as Żytomierz, where at last they came across a concentration of Bolshevik units. Since they were not carrying bombs, the three airmen were forced to attack solely with machine gun fire. They forced the Bolsheviks to disperse. The losses inflicted during this attack stopped the advance of an enemy column for the next few days. On April 10, an order arrived to attack full force the river station at Czudnów, where according to intelligence reports, the Bolshevik Headquarters was located. Fauntleroy, Cooper, Rorison, Crawford, and Senkowski took off, reaching the target site without further problems. The first object of attack was the bridge at Teterew, which was destroyed by Rorison's accurate bombardment. In turn, a building suspected of being the headquarters was attacked using machine guns. The mission was successful. The squadron succeeded in destroying an important crossing over the Teterew and throwing the enemy brigade headquarters into disarray, although it turned out that the Russian staff officers had been absent from the building during the raid.

Since no one had been present, another raid was carried out immediately. Flying a plane that had been damaged by a machine gun, Rorison led Fauntleroy, Cooper, and Senkowski in an early-morning raid. This time at Czudnów they were met by organized machine gun fire and artillery. To limit the effectiveness of the enemy fire, the pilots attacked from the front, dropping to very low flying levels. The speed and low altitude prevented the enemy from opening effective fire.[48] It was the first attack of this kind in the war. In short, this technique became part not only of the 7th Squadron's repertoire but also of the remaining Polish squadrons during this war. They attacked in short, individual charges, one after the other. It not only inflicted serious losses, but also had a demoralizing effect on an enemy unaccustomed to dealing with the air force. Apart from that, it maintained constant pressure on the enemy. The pilots started attacks by dropping bombs, and after running out of bombs, they hit the enemy with machine gun fire. This sequence was particularly devastating in attacks on the cavalry. The explosion of bombs and the noise of the planes' engines frightened the horses, and the machine gun fire dispersed the marching columns. Pilots returning from the previously mentioned action at Czudnów performed an exemplary attack of this sort. Approximately ten kilometers west of the city, Rorison came across a cavalry column, which he immediately attacked with a nosediving charge:

> Up hill and down dale, the cavalry tore across the face of the country while the four planes whirled and dove again until, actually weary of the sport, they drew off and headed for home, leaving but a sweating, cursing remnant of the Bolos to crawl into a nearby wood and rest from their strenuous ride.[49]

Of course, this technique was perfected as the campaign developed, and the new equipment was beneficial to this end. On April 10, information arrived about the delivery of Italian Ansaldo A1 Balilla planes in Warsaw. The Group Command of the Air Force announced that the 7th Squadron could take five of these aircrafts. Five airmen headed by Fauntleroy took the next train to collect the planes, and Cooper took command in his absence. Thanks to his resilience, in the last ten days before the beginning of the offensive on Kiev the squadron managed to replenish their technical shortages and fuel supplies. During Fauntleroy's absence, on April 12, there was an inspection of the 7th Squadron carried out by the C.O. of the 2nd Army, Gen. Antoni Listowski, and the Commander of the 13th Infantry Division, Gen. Jan Romer, who was accompanied by Gen. Vial from the French Military Mission. At around five in the afternoon, cars with the officers arrived at the spacious airfield located southwest of Połonne. There was a hangar erected at the airfield, which housed the 13 Albatros planes, eight of which were combat ready. Listowski was impressed by the overall discipline and readiness of the unit.

He also complemented the design of the Squadron's insignia, which he saw for the first time.[50]

The inspection was brief and probably was more concerned with checking the mood and readiness for battle, and for the airmen to familiarize themselves with the generals and the assignments they were to carry out. There were soon particular links forged between the 7th Squadron and the 13th Infantry Division, with whom they not only fought on the front but also shared their views on the role of the air force in the future war. The visiting generals announced that they would return to the squadron when the remaining pilots returned. In fact, this did not happen. Prior to the start of the offensive, only Capt. Camillo Perini, Chief of the Air Force in the Headquarters of the High Command, carried out an inspection. In any case, it was the next sign of the approaching offensive.

In order to carry out necessary repairs and above all to calm the Bolsheviks, for a few days after April 13 there were fewer sorties. They only dropped propaganda leaflets, patrolled the immediate vicinity of the front line and responded to a few alarms. The most important flight was the attack on a rail station at Czudnów, where they dropped two bombs.[51]

On the 15th, the 7th Squadron was alerted to the appearance of a Bolshevik plane near Derewiczki. Cooper, Corsi, and Noble took off in search of the enemy, but to no avail. After almost an hour they returned to the airport. On the afternoon of the same day, Clark and Corsi took off in search of a Bolshevik dirigible, which had been spotted east of Kamienny Bród. The dirigible exploded before the airmen got there. On April 16, Gen Romer issued an order to attack the Bolshevik positions in Żytomierz and Berdyczew. Corsi, Clark, and Noble took off in the direction of the first of these cities. Berdyczew was not attacked effectively until the next day.

Cooper and Konopka noticed a concentration of Bolshevik forces in Berdyczew and attacked them without suffering even the slightest graze. On the same day, Corsi observed a Bolshevik regiment on the road from Szalejki to Sulejów. Through airborne fire they succeeded in inflicting losses upon the column and effectively dispersed them. The same airman, still on the same day, went to Żytomierz together with Noble, where they observed 6 locomotives and a concentration of up to 200 enemy railway cars, full of military material. They attacked the concentration and inflicted significant losses. On April 18 and for the next few days, the squadron continued sorties with propaganda materials, combined with observation of the front line. The intensity of flights was also

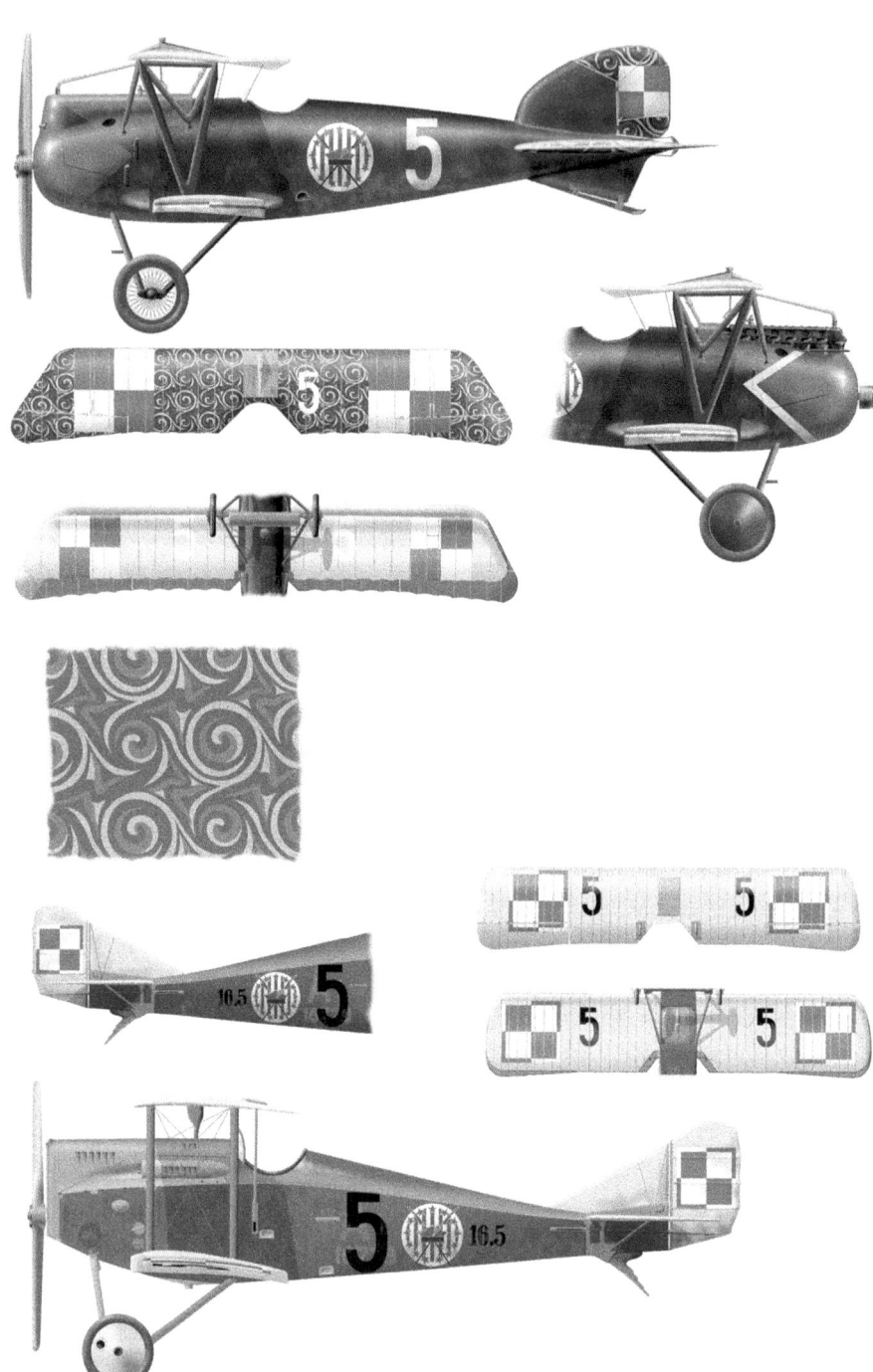

far less. The fact was that they wanted to make the Bolsheviks less vigilant before they began their own offensive.[52]

Meanwhile Cooper sent Lt. Weber by car to Nowogród Wołyński, approximately 30 miles north of Połonne, in search of fuel. To the same end, he sent some people in the direction of Starokonstantynów by horse cart. Both expeditions were successful. In addition, on April 23 a message from Lwów arrived about the delivery of petrol and emergency supplies, which they had appealed for by telegraph. Thus the airmen were already fully prepared for the offensive, even more so because on April 22 the French Capt. C. Roussin mentioned it during his visit to the airfield at Połonne.

For the 7th Squadron, the offensive began with their assignment to the 2nd Air *Dyon** operating on behalf of the 2nd Polish Army under the

*("Dywizjon" consisted of from two to five Air Squadrons. This term was used from April 13, 1920, and replaced the "Air Group" used from the inception of the Polish Air Force in 1918)

Opposite, top: The Albatros (Oef) D. III (no. 253.222) with 225 horse power Austro-Daimler engine (no. 23443), was the first aircraft used by Merian Cooper in Poland. Purchased in Austria was delivered to the Central Airforce Depot in Warsaw on July 31, 1919. It was marked by the Squadron's logo and designated number 5 after being delivered to Lwów. The plane crashed on November 22, 1919 with Lt. Graves on board during an air show to commemorate the second anniversary of Lwów's liberation from the Ukrainians. Albatros (Oef) D. III, no. 253.218, was equipped with 225 Horse Power Austro-Daimler engine (no. 23514) and two 8mm "Schwarzlose M7/12" machine guns (no. 45048 and 45027). It was delivered to the 7th Squadron on August 21, 1919. This aircraft was marked identically to his first plane; additionally the nose of the aircraft was painted red to indicate the "Pulaski Wing," which was to be commanded by Cooper. Captain Cooper used this aircraft in April and May 1920 during the Kiev Expedition, including combat flights over the city of Kiev. By May 29, 1920, Cooper logged 33 hours and 20 minutes on board this aircraft. During the retreat of the 7th Squadron from Berdyczew, the Albatros was set afire by Capt. Cooper due to an engine failure, which did not allow it to be flown out. ***Bottom:*** Ansaldo "Balilla" (no. 16726, Poland serial number 16.5) was equipped with SPA 6A, 220 horse power engine (no. 3231) and two "Vickers," 7.62 mm machine guns (no. 1366 and 1625). This plane was purchased in Italy, delivered to Poland on January 9, 1920, and was transferred to the 7th Squadron on May 25, 1920, together with four other "Balillas." This transport reached Berdyczew on May 31, 1920; however, due to the lack of mechanics the plane never took flight and was transported to Lwów on June 19, 1920, as part of the transfer of the 7th Squadron equipment. At the beginning of July 1920, it was finally assembled and flown. It was designated number 5, much as Cooper's earlier planes, and shot down by the Bolsheviks on July 13, 1920, after only two hours in the air.

command of Gen. Antoni Listowski. The army consisted of, among others, the 13th Infantry Division led by Gen. Romer, the 15th Infantry Division and the Ukrainian Division. Besides the 7th Squadron, the 2nd *Dyon* consisted of the 2nd and 9th Squadrons initially. The 2nd Army also included the 5th *Dyon*, consisting of the 3rd and 16th Squadrons. The 2nd Army carried out their attack from the region of Szepietówka, Połonne, and Starokonstantynów, south of the 3rd Army's flank and Gen. Edward Śmigły-Rydz's Group. The 2nd Army's order was to attack in the direction of Berdyczew and Koziatyn. Even further south there was the 6th Army under the command of Gen. Wacław Iwaszkiewicz, whose task was to provide auxiliary strikes from the direction of Płoskirów, Winnica, Bar, and Mohylów — along the River Dniestr. The 6th Army was supported by the 3rd *Dyon* which was made up of the 5th, 6th, 15th, 17th, and 21st Squadrons. The 3rd Army, under Piłsudski's direct command, took the main burden of attack in the direction of Kiev. It attacked from the vicinity of Rovne, where the HQ of the High Command were located. The 3rd Army was supported by the 5th *Dyon,* made up of the 16th and then the 3rd Squadrons. On April 17, Capt. Perini took on the responsibility of the Chief of the Air Force of the High Command. The final formations of the individual armies underwent a certain reorganization during the activities. At any rate, the entire Polish Air Force at the very opening of the campaign on April 25, 1920, stood at over 200 aircraft. The decisive majority of these were located in the east. Bolshevik Russia possessed a similar number of aircraft, although the estimates of various researchers vary.[53]

The airmen of the 7th Squadron, the whole army, even the whole of Europe wondered what Piłsudski's aims were, and what results the conflict would bring.

5 | Objectives of Piłsudski

To understand better the genesis of the war and Piłsudski's aims, it is essential to present a general background of this conflict. Between ethnic Poland and ethnic Russia stretches a belt of land several hundred kilometers wide, inhabited by a population that is neither Russian nor Polish. After a few centuries of political union with Poland, Ukrainians, Lithuanians, Baltic nations, and even to some extent Belorussians succeeded in creating their own national movements at the turn of the twentieth century. Poland was the dominant political power until the end of the eighteenth century, but by the time of the second and third partitions of Poland (1793, 1795) Russia had taken over control of those areas. In spite of this, the Poles were a dominant element of both the economy and culture of those territories. For many of local leaders the tradition of a multinational Polish Kingdom, or *Rzeczpospolita,* with its privileges and freedom, was still an attractive example. All these matters were incomprehensible in the West, where all Polish claims to territories east of the Bug River were treated as imperialistic, even after two important declarations of the Bolshevik regime. In the Peace Decree of November 8, 1917, they announced:

> The Government regards as an honest or democratic peace ... an immediate peace without annexations (i.e., without the seizure of foreign land, without the forcible taking over of foreign nationalities) and without contribution.[1]

The decree was issued at the Second All-Russian Congress of Workers' and Soldiers' Deputies in Piotrogrod (St. Petersburg). Subsequent documents included the Declaration of the Rights of the Nations of Russia from November 15, 1917, guaranteeing the rights of self-determination to break away and to create independent states. Even more important was the decree of the Council of the Peoples Commissars from the August 29, 1918, about the annulment of the partition treaties in relation to Poland.[2] According to many lawyers, these proclamations restored the *status quo ante* and legitimated Poland's claims to lands within her 1772 borders. Of course, politicians in Warsaw realized the impossibility of openly claiming the return of those territories, mainly because of the awakening national consciences of the nations inhabiting these lands. Anyway, this option remained more or less in the propaganda arsenal.

Fundamentally, there were two approaches to the territorial shape of the state. The National Democrats headed by Roman Dmowski pursued the incorporation of the borderland areas into the Polish state and the gradual *polonization* of those people. Piłsudski countered Dmowski with his federation program, or the construction of national states friendly to Poland, which would fulfill the national aspirations of the Ukrainians and the Lithuanians and would separate Poland from Russian threat. In February 1919, following the German armies' retreat from the "Ober-Ost," the Bolshevik armies moved west. When they met Polish military outposts in the vicinity of Bereza Kartuska, armed conflict ensued. At the same time there were battles and skirmishes between Poles and Ukrainians in East Galicia. The conflict on this part of the frontline was complicated because there were at least three political entities that claimed principal state authority in Ukraine. It is common knowledge that until 1914 the Ukrainians, who did not have their own state, were divided by the Austro-Hungarian and Russian border. The eastern part of their national territory belonged to Russia and created a group of politicians opposing Russian domination. From this base came the later ally of Piłsudski and Ataman of the Ukrainian People's Republic, Semen Petlura. Part of western Galicia under Austro-Hungarian control, and the capital Lwów, was turned into the Western Ukrainian People's Republic with Evhen Petrushewich at its head. Its policy was decidedly anti–Polish. In addition there was the Ukrainian communist movement controlled from Moscow and led by the Bulgarian born Christian Rakovski. This triangle remained unchanged, with the exception of attempts at cooperation by both of the national wings of the Ukrainian movement against Poland. There was also a small but relatively influential group around the "Hetmanate" government of Pavlo Skoropadski appointed at the end of World War I, when the Germans occupied Ukrainian territory.

The situation underwent some changes from the conclusion of the

5. Objectives of Piłsudski

May–June offensive of 1919, in which the Polish Army forced the Ukrainians back beyond the Zbruch River. Shortly after, namely in August 1919, under the pressure of anti–Bolshevik armies, the so-called White Russians, Kiev fell. The Tsarist generals did not even want to hear of independence for Ukraine. They fought all factions of Ukrainian political life opting for the breakaway of Ukraine from Russia. The occupation of Kiev signified the extinguishing of all hope of an independent state. Quite simply the Ukrainians did not have the resources to fight both Poland and Russia. Petlura was first to grasp the political situation. Since it was impossible to fight all the real and alleged enemies of Ukraine, it was necessary to ally, even at the cost of territorial concessions, with a partner who guaranteed political independence. It was Piłsudski's idea of a federation that seemed to offer the most promise of an independent Ukrainian state. After a few weeks of hesitation, Petlura, in November 1919, sent Andrij Livickij to Warsaw with the aim of preparing for talks about a military-political alliance. This was the origin of the Polish-Ukrainian alliance, which was finalized in April 1920 by a political pact on April 21 and a military convention on April 24.[3] With this ally Piłsudski moved on Kiev. However, as time showed, the mirage of an independent Ukraine disintegrated. This happened as a result of the relative apathy of the population, which had suffered six years of war. It was also due to the impossibility of ensuring a longer period for the organization of a state apparatus and administration after the Polish armed forces had taken Kiev on May 7, 1920.

The Americans also made their own observations on the subject of Ukraine. Their interest was of an indirect nature and to a certain extent was economic. In the period of 1918–1920, Ukraine was no less seen as an important element since she occupied a lot of space in the military-political reports of the American Military Attache in Warsaw. In the middle of 1919, Elbert Farman evaluated Ukrainian matters in the following way:

> Colonel [Stanisław] Haller had conferences with ... Piłsudski on the subject. The former felt that from a military point of view, there was much in favor of an armistice. First, as long as the Allies desired no operations be undertaken against the Ukrainians, it was best to use the troops elsewhere; second, a combined action of the Poles and the Ukrainians against the Bolshevists would be very desirable. From the political side there was a well-known desire of the Allies for an adjustment of the Polish-Ukrainian question. The Poles, therefore, accepted the principle of an armistice and proposed that they should occupy the

line of the Zbrucz [River] and guarantee the Ukrainians from any danger from their side.... In Galicia, I talked with many Ukrainians and Jews without the presence of an interpreter (many of them speak German). They all stated they did not want to fight that those who forced them to were a few of the leaders and that they were tired of the war and wanted only to live in peace. They said that during the Polish occupation, they had been allowed to live in peace and that they could and did live in peace with the Poles.... The idea that the Poles in Galicia were trying to conquer and subject the people who were defending themselves and their nationality seems to be prevalent in some quarters. Without reading any Polish propaganda, without listening to any explanations from their side, but merely by going over the ground, I am convinced that such is not the case. The majority of the population in this country districts is said to be Ruthenian, but the civilization of the land is Polish, the towns are Polish and practically all the educated people are Polish. The Ruthenian element is not enough educated ... to run a government. This is proven by the testimony of many including the Ruthenian priest above-mentioned and by notes of an Austrian officer serving with the Ukrainians, which are transmitted under separate cover. Regardless of the final ruler of the country, I am convinced that neither peace nor order can exist until all the Ukrainian forces have been withdrawn from Galicia. Their savage methods, complete lack of control on the part of the officers, if there are any who desire to control them, will only continue to increase the feeling against the Ukrainians and make final settlement more difficult.[4]

Even if we dismiss Farman's harsh opinions about Ukrainians, the document testifies to the aspirations of the Polish party to settle for a compromise. This report preceded the arrival of the American airmen, who came at a time of relative peace at the front after the end of the June offensive by the Polish armed forces. They had reached the Zbruch River, which became the border of Polish territorial aspirations. From August 1919, when the Polish armed forces occupied Minsk, there was something resembling an interval of semi-peace, in which Moscow and Warsaw were preparing for a general settlement. Piłsudski entertained no doubts whatsoever that Lenin and Trotsky intended to overcome Poland and bring the revolution to the West. On the other hand, the old Russian regime represented by Denikin, and from April 1920 by Gen. Peter Wrangel, refrained from recognizing of Poland's independence and her territorial claims, postponing everything until the post-war Constitutional Assembly ruling. The clearest expression of relations between White Russia and Poland was Denikin's letter to Piłsudski of November 29, 1919, which was full of threats and expected Piłsudski to allow a

Russian administration on the territory occupied by Poland.[5] Knowing what he could expect from the White Russians, Piłsudski decided to sound out the position of the Bolsheviks. Talks between the Polish and the Russian delegations of the Red Cross served this purpose. These were held in 1919 in Białowieża and Mikaszewicze. Although the official pretext was the exchange of prisoners, in reality it was a means of sounding out Lenin's stance. While Piłsudski's delegates clearly let them understand that Poland was not supporting the Whites, they also demanded that the Bolsheviks stop picking on the Ukrainians. These talks did not bring the desired results — rather the opposite. Reports from Polish intelligence from the turn of 1919 and 1920 indicate that there was a progressive concentration of Red forces on the border with Poland. For Piłsudski it was clear that since Poland's power did not match that of Russia, it was necessary to carry out a preemptive strike, for which the ideal strategic point would be Ukraine. Deprived of Ukraine's resources and food supplies, Russia would be too weak to threaten her neighbors. This was the basis for the decision to attack Kiev. The American airmen participated in this attack.

Piłsudski's motives were not entirely clear to western observers, and Poland was suspected of militaristic and imperialistic designs. Did some people think that Piłsudski was an irresponsible trouble-maker? The reports of Hugh Gibson, the first American envoy in Warsaw, reveal interesting details on this very subject. Shortly after his arrival in Warsaw, he had talks with Piłsudski, after which he reported to Washington:

> I asked the General what were his objectives in the eastern campaign, whether he expected to push on to the eastern boundaries of Lithuania or had some military line in view. He replied with a twinkle in his eye that he was pushing forward to a psychological line and went on to explain there was a clearly defined frontier between the ideas of East and West, that he proposed to push forwards as far as people held to individual ownership as a temporary protective measure. On the other side of this line he said the people held to communal ownership.... Piłsudski went on to say that he felt Poland should be moderate in her claims and that she had suffered in the eyes of her friends from exaggerated ideas of enthusiastic Poles who want to take in broad territories. He believes it would be a misfortune if the demands of these people were granted since Poland could not assimilate so much.[6]

Gibson's subsequent reports reflected the issue of Polish territorial claims. One of these matters arose after the Bolshevik proposals for peace were sent to Warsaw at the end of 1919 and in January 1920. In his reply, Piłsudski presented a range of conditions and Gibson wrote about these in the report as follows:

> He dwelt on the fact that the provisions concerning the frontiers of 1772 were inserted at his own desire. By these provisions he did not wish to take over these territories for Poland. He explained that an immediate entente cordiale with Russia was out of the question in view of the resentment remaining in the minds of the people but that it was the duty of farsighted patriots to prepare the way for an eventual understanding with the Russian people, that so long as the partitions were unacknowledged resentment would persist, but that as soon as Russia abandoned her claims to these ill-gotten territories public animosity would soon die down, thus leaving the way open to better understanding. Once this was done he did not pretend to say what should be done with the territories in question. They should, he felt, be given a chance to set up orderly government under the League of Nations or in any other way that satisfied the Powers. For Poland he desired ownership only in the territory that was undeniably Polish, feeling that if the Poles were successful in establishing effective government there the neighboring peoples would eventually come asking some form of affiliation with Poland. His tone was entirely reasonable but he made a strong plea for moral support and advice from the Great Powers, particularly from America, the latter being according to him the only country which had no selfish interest to serve in her dealings with Poland.[7]

The envoy did not mention here the famous manifesto *To the Inhabitants of the Lands of the Former Grand Duchy of Lithuania*, of April 1919, issued shortly after the Bolsheviks had been thrown out of Vilnius. This became a dominant element in the shaping of Polish policy in the east at that point. It proclaimed freedom and equal rights for all nationalities living in the extensive lands of the already non-existent Grand Duchy of Lithuania, which was linked to Poland from the fourteenth century by a personal union.

Even if, as later events showed, the attempt to construct a chain of states between Poland and Russia failed, was it possible from the Polish point of view to allow a strict ethnic border with Russia to be marked out, passing barely 100 kilometers from Warsaw, just as Lord Nathaniel Curzon wanted, in his note of December 2, 1919, better known under the date of December 8 of that year. It turned out that the Curzon line was not compatible with the views of many military experts, including Col. Harry Howland. In a report of February 18, 1920, he wrote:

5. Objectives of Piłsudski

> While it may be possible for Poland to consider the present eastern front as a basis for the future frontier, it cannot be considered or accepted as an armistice line pending peace negotiations with the Bolsheviks. From the military viewpoint, therefore, especially in view of the present military situation, only a line naturally strong, susceptible of defense and resistance, and one constituting a certain barrier between Europe and Bolshevism, can be considered.
> <u>Strong Barrier Against Bolshevism necessary</u>. [underlined by Col. Howland]
> In a conference between Marshal Foch, Allied Commander in Chief, and General Rozwadowski, Chief of the Polish Military Mission, it has therefore been decided that an acceptable armistice line will be one taking in the Dvina River, from the dividing line between Poland and Lithuania on the north to Vitebsk on the south; thence the line of the Dniepr River from Orza to Kiev....
> While the Soviet authorities may be sincere in their desire for peace, Poland, from past experience, frankly distrusts the Bolsheviks and feels that as long as they remain in power she must maintain a military barrier against them.[8]

It is also worth quoting parts of the report of the same officer, who visited Poland in the first few weeks of 1920 to investigate the situation on the spot. In a report from January 27, 1920, he wrote:

> While the situation in the west, as result of constant German intrigue and active propaganda, is one that requires constant watchful alertness, and will soon demand serious consideration and action, it is the situation confronting Poland on her eastern borders that particularly is full of menace to the Polish State and presents the possibility of dire consequences not only to Central Europe but to the world as well unless aid be speedily extended to the Polish Government. Poland is not only maintaining a military barrier against Bolshevism on the eastern front, but is also desperately endeavoring to maintain a sanitary barrier against an ever spreading epidemic of disease as well.[9]

Therefore there was no doubt that the conclusions and recommendations of direct observers, both political and military, indicated a good measure of understanding for Poland's situation vis-a-vis a powerful and unpredictable neighbor. It turned out, however, that it did not entirely suit the intentions of the decision-makers in Washington. One of the cornerstones of American policy towards Russia became the preservation of her territorial integrity, which contradicted the postulate of self-determination of nations, announced forcefully by Wilson. Some politicians attempted to compare the 1776 revolution with the Red Revolution in Russia.[10]

Shortly after these Bolshevik peace propositions from the beginning of 1920, the Polish envoy in Washington reported that the position of the State Department towards Poland was characterized by indifference. In February 1920, Lansing, in a note to Gibson, stressed that the United States could not "take responsibility for advising Poland on policy toward Russia."[11] Lansing's successor, Bainbridge Colby, maintained that line precisely. Boris Bakhmietieff, Russian ambassador of the Kierenskij government in Washington, had a significant influence on this politician's views. He was a supporter of Russia's territorial integrity within the 1914 borders. An echo of his attitude was found in the so-called Colby Note of August 10, 1920, which was shown to and in a way consulted by the Russian representative.[12]

The Secretary of State wrote that with the exception of Poland, Finland, and Armenia, the Russian borders ought to be defined by the Russians. He announced that the United States would not participate in the possible peace negotiations; however, at the same time he stressed that America was supporting the preservation of Poland's independence and territorial integrity. He obviously referred to the line marked out by Curzon. As Gibson noted, Colby "read the statement about what America thought about Bolshevism, bowed to the audience, and made an unapplauded exit."[13]

It is obvious that American airmen were not aware of the differences of opinion between the State Department and the United States' representatives in Warsaw. They fought in an atmosphere defined by elements beyond their control and were at risk from the multiplicity of consequences. The lack of official support from the Department of State made many questions difficult to settle. One example was the impossibility of helping Merian Cooper, who had been taken prisoner on July 13, 1920.

The main burden of the Polish offensive was to be born by the land forces. In January and February 1920 two new classes of recruits were admitted to the Polish armed forces, which supplemented the rank and file to such an extent that in the spring of that year the Ukrainian part of the eastern front was reinforced by 55,000 men. On March 8, 1920, the High Command divided the whole eastern front between four armies. The 6th Polish Army was stationed at Podole and the 2nd Army at Wolynia. The 3rd Army, which was to mount the main attack on Kiev, found itself in the middle of reorganization. The choice of direction and the time of attack were determined by forthcoming signals about the concentration of the Red Army to the north of *Błota Poleskie* (Pripet Marshes). In order to prevent communications between the Bolshevik north and south theaters of operation, Piłsudski recommended taking control of an important rail junction. The Polish attack of March 5, 1920, led to the occupation of two key strategic points at Mozyrz and Kalenkowicze, which cut the Red Army into two separate groups unable to cooperate with each other. The main attack of the forces, consisting of eight infantry divisions, five cavalry brigades and an operational armed group of Ukrainians, took placed on April 25, 1920, in the direction of Kiev. The first objective of the operation was the control of Koziatyń, a vital center, which became the meeting point of the 14th and 12th Red Armies. Koziatyń had already been occupied by a Polish cavalry group on April 27. A day earlier, the important center of Żytomierz had been taken. In the space of a dozen or so hours the Bolshevik 12th Army was smashed to such an extent that they did not manage to regain their fighting ability before the end of the war. On April 29, Poles took Winnica, and thus opened up the road to Kiev. An Operational Group under the command of Gen. Śmigły-Rydz attacked Kiev. It was their task to occupy the city, make safe the crossing and open the bridgehead on the eastern bank of the Dniepr River. The action in this direction moved so quickly that the American Military Attache expected the city to be entered by the first days of May. Significantly, it happened on May 7. Leaving the destruction of the 12th Army and the significant weakening of the Bolshevik 14th Army aside, a lot of war material and transport equipment fell into the hands of the Poles. Apart from that, the Ukrainians gained time to achieve their plan of establishing an independent state. Unfortunately, it was not successful. As a result of the break in the frontline at Samhorodek by Budenny's cavalry on June 5, 1920, the front started to shift to the west. Budenny not only buried the hope of an independent Ukraine, but seriously threatened the independence of Poland herself.

6 | IN THE KIEV OFFENSIVE

On the day before the offensive on Kiev, the 7th Squadron, with Cooper as a temporary CO, had only four pilots ready to take off. The rest, headed by Fauntleroy, went to Warsaw, where they collected new planes. They did not manage to return before the start of the offensive.

On April 24, with orders from Gen. Romer to go on reconnaissance, the 7th Squadron sent one plane after another in the direction of Berdyczew. All enemy movements were followed, and reports were filed on the condition of the roads, railway lines and bridges. Directly after his take off at 6:00 A.M., Shrewsbury flew in the direction of the Teterew River, which divided the Polish and Russian fronts. He saw that in Czudnów there were 70 abandoned box cars, without any sign of the enemy personnel. There was a similar situation in Michajlenki, which was halfway along the road to Berdyczew and situated closer to Korownica, where Shrewsbury noted five abandoned railway cars. He also noted that the bridge over the Piątek River along the village of Raczki was in good condition, as was the bridge at Gołodka, which spanned both banks of the Gnilopiatki River. No less interesting, even the strong bridge to the north of Berdyczew had not been destroyed by the Bolsheviks. It looked as though they had left their positions in haste, and this was also confirmed by the fact that another 300 railway cars had been abandoned at Berdyczew. Shrewsbury landed at 7:35 A.M. Rorison carried out a reconnaissance sortie in a parallel direction.[1]

On the day of the start of the offensive, the squadron's duties included reconnaissance on behalf of the HQ of the 2nd Polish Army in Szepietówka. This action was also on behalf of the Headquarters of the Commander-in-Chief Józef Piłsudski in Nowogród Wołyński, which was 55 miles north of Połonne. On April 25 at 5:30 A.M. Cooper led Konopka,

6. In the Kiev Offensive

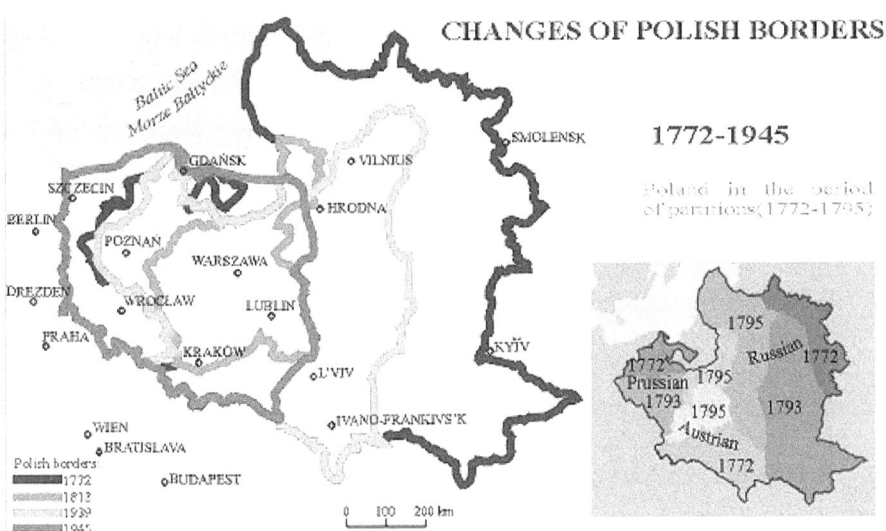

Map of Poland. Changes of borders from the first partition (1772). (Courtesy of the Head Office of the State Archives, Warsaw, Poland.)

Clark, and Shrewsbury on reconnaissance in the direction of Berdyczew. Beyond Miropol, about 20 kilometers from Połonne, the pilots saw the Polish Infantry moving forward; at the next point, near Noworunia, they came across Polish cavalry patrols. They encountered abandoned railway equipment everywhere and abandoned Bolshevik positions. Thus it was in Pulin, Adamowka, and Kurne. Clearly the Bolshevik advance guard had abandoned the occupied parts merely on hearing that the offensive had started. After a two-hour flight, the crew landed at Połonne, where, after they had reported and eaten, Cooper received an order to support the cavalry battle, which according to the report was to take place in the vicinity of Miropol. At 9:40 A.M. Cooper took off with Lt. Noble. Flying in the direction of Miropol, they did not come across any battles, but in Raczki, around 25 kilometers west of Berdyczew, Cooper located a small train escorted by a cavalry unit made up of Cossacks. Both airmen attacked the train with machine guns. They did not succeed in destroying the locomotive engine however. After the end of the attack they both proceeded in the direction of Berdyczew, where they saw a long train ready to retreat from the city. Without much thought they attacked, using about 350 rounds of ammunition. Unfortunately, they had no bombs since Cooper's plane accidentally had lost its only bomb shortly after take-off. The attack was not conducted from a high altitude. Thanks to a swift maneuvering above the train, they took advantage of the element of surprise. The Bolsheviks (simply called the "Bolos" by the Americans) opened fire with machine guns and even artillery. The Americans managed to silence at least three of the five artillery pieces. On their return they saw a huge Bolshevik cavalry camp north of Rajki and a small railway train with escort on the road to Piątek. However, 15 kilometers from Czudnów they saw Polish patrols occupying the small towns of Serbinówka and Stołpów. Directly after landing, an order was waiting for Cooper from the headquarters at Nowogród Wołyński, requesting that two planes be sent in the direction of Żytomierz. Konopka and Clark were assigned to that mission; however, not long after they had taken off they were both forced to return to Czudnów. The next order to fly in the same direction came from Nowogród Wołyński at 2:50 P.M. This time Noble and Shrewsbury took off. They reached the large city without any mishaps. They found it without any military personnel, the last Bolshevik troops having been loaded onto their own railway cars. Both airmen attacked them with machine guns, using about 300 rounds of ammunition. Continuing the flight, they noticed three Bolshevik artillery batteries north of the city, which they attacked with one bomb. They returned to the airfield at Połonne at 5:00 P.M. During the whole day, the 7th Squadron was in the air for 19 hours.[2]

On April 26 the whole headquarters train of the 2nd Polish Army arrived in the vicinity of Połonne. Its proximity saved time in the delivery of reports, but also put the squadron under constant pressure due to the presence of Gen. Listowski. Perhaps it is because of this that the squadron received the honor of delegating one crew to guard Piłsudski's train on that day. The train stood out from the others by its cleanliness, indicating that it carried important cargo, which would make it a target for enemy air force attack. Because the Bolshevik formation and strength of their air force was unknown, the escort was required, and the honor fell to Shrewsbury, who treated his assignment with imagination. On the road between Nowogród Wołyński and Szepietówka, not only did he safeguard the train against possible attack, but he also entertained the Marshall. During the hour-long escort, he alternately flew up and then low, simulating an air attack. Another time he carried out dangerous

Opposite: **Polish military I.D. card of Lt. Edwin Noble. It reads as follows: "Height: 162 cm, brown eyes, blond hair, oblong face. American (pilot) in the service of the Polish Army. Doesn't speak Polish." (Courtesy of Mr. Paul Konys, Rocky River, OH.)**

OPIS.

Wzrost: 1 m. 62 ct.
Oczy: piwne
Włosy: blond
Owal twarzy: podłużny
Szczególne znamiona: Amerykanin ur. w Sisbee w W. T. ma szram po postrzale

pieczątka

podpis wystawiającego (dowódcy)

, dnia 19

Edwin L. Noble
podpis właściciela legitymacyi.

L. p. 47.

KARTA IDENTYCZNOŚCI.

Imię i nazwisko: Edwin L. Noble
stopień: podporucznik
przydział służbowy: 7 Eskadra Lotnicza (obserwator)
rok urodzenia: 1891
religia: protestant

pieczątka

podpis wystawiającego (dowódcy)

Ważność legitymacyi na rok 1919

..., dnia 17. XI 19 19

pieczątka

podpis wystawiającego (dowódcy)

Bezpośrednio przełożone dowództwo:

Drukarnia D. O. G. Lwów

aerobatics for Piłsudski's amusement. The atmosphere accompanying this assignment departed from that of all other duties that had to be carried out during the war.³

Shrewsbury's duties ended at the junction of the railroad in the vicinity of Szepietowka. It was not the first flight of the 7th Squadron of that day. The remaining crew, Cooper, Noble, Clark, and Konopka, had earlier gone on reconnaissance in the direction of Berdyczew on behalf of the 2nd Army. Cooper took off at 5:00 A.M. His report after a two-hour flight confirmed the advance of the Polish armed forces in the direction of Czudnów, and what was most important, the reoccupation of Berdyczew by the Bolsheviks, valuable information for Gen. Listowski's Headquarters. That day Clark distinguished himself in particular. He took off three times and was in the air for about six hours, and all this despite a severe headache. During his second flight he attacked machine gun positions and a group of 150 railway cars, attacking them from the altitude of 30 meters. After this attack, he shelled one more train near Piątek, where he succeeded in damaging a locomotive engine. After its return to the airfield, Clark's plane had nine bullets in one of the wings. The wing had to be changed, and Clark boarded another plane and carried out his third combat sortie of the day.⁴

On April 26 Lt. Noble had an exceptionally active day around the Bolsheviks. He took off for the first time at 5:45 A.M. with the task of defining the situation of Polish cavalry units near Biełopol, 18 kilometers from Berdyczew. During this flight Noble attacked the Bolshevik artillery position near Berdyczew. He decided to confuse the vigilance of the artillery and he shut off his engine high enough, as though he had been shot. At this moment the artillery ceased their fire and started — literally — a victory dance. Then about 300 meters above the ground, Noble turned on the engine again and opened machine gun fire violently, inflicting serious losses on the Bolsheviks. During the next sortie of that day, Noble, escaping in the direction of Berdyczew, attacked a column of a few hundred horse carts, disrupting their march for a long time. The culmination of the day was the expedition by four squadron planes under Cooper's command, between 5:00 and 5:30 P.M. The target was also Berdyczew and the Bolshevik forces withdrawing from the city. Again, Cooper, Noble, Clark, and Konopka took part in the expedition.

Among the four pilots, Noble distinguished himself by attacking an armored train standing still at Berdyczew railway station. During the attack, he was seriously wounded by a "dum-dum" bullet in the right elbow. Despite intense pain and a significant loss of blood, he managed

Edwin Noble in front of a railway first-aid station. (Courtesy of Dr. Tomasz Kopański, Warsaw.)

to maintain control over his plane and return about 80 kilometers to the airfield at Połonne. Shortly after landing, he slumped forward, unconscious onto the controls. He was immediately administrated first aid and taken to the American Red Cross hospital, where he was tended to by Major Charles Phillips. After a week Noble went to the army hospital at Kovel, and then to a hospital in Warsaw. Unfortunately his wound was further complicated by infection, and he was even threatened with the loss of his arm. Feverish efforts were initiated to transfer the pilot to the Red Cross hospital in Paris. It was not easy, considering the state of the war and the difficulty of traveling across Germany. They succeeded, but only after a few weeks. There was no question of further flying. The squadron had lost its first pilot in combat. What is more, his elbow remained immobile for the rest of his life.[5]

On the next day the 7th Squadron was surprised by an order to stop its flights. It was caused in part by the Poles' occupation of Berdyczew and the subsequent retreat of the frontline from the airfield that had been used until that time. It was also due to the need to preserve the equipment. Gen. Listowski himself visited the squadron's wagon-mess canteen and congratulated them on their results from the previous day. He also expressed his regret at Lt. Noble's injury and the hope that the squadron would be able to immediately accompany the Headquarters to Berdyczew. To the surprise of the General, Shrewsbury took off the very same day to find a new landing strip for the 2nd Air Group. The frontline had shifted by dozens of kilometers to the east, beyond the range of effective reconnaissance of the Albatroses. The 7th Squadron had to relocate as near as possible to the frontline to carry out its next assignments. That is also why Cooper and Weber drove by car at 4:00 A.M. in search of another landing strip, on Shrewsbury's trail. A suitable field was located in the vicinity of Berdyczew, in a place that had been used previously by the Bolshevik air force. According to the local people, the Bolshevik planes had escaped towards Kiev without the slightest intention of facing the Polish Air Force.

On the next day Cooper returned to Połonne to direct the remaining equipment to the new field. On Friday, April 30, Cooper, Konopka, and Shrewsbury relocated the aircraft to the new landing strip, from which that same day they took off on a few reconnaissance sorties in the direction of Markowa, Lipki and Sobolewka. Shrewsbury reported that at 3:00 P.M. that the Polish 3rd Army had not yet reached the Markowa-Sobolewka line; however Cooper, who took off at 4:30 P.M. noted that the Polish cavalry was barely six kilometers from Fastov.

Albatros (Oeffag) D III aircraft of the 7th Kościuszko Squadron. (Courtesy of Dr. Tomasz Kopański, Warsaw.)

The next day brought more orders. On May 1, Gen. Listowski wrote in his diary: "We are preparing for new action, which as usual the 'Commandant' [Piłsudski] has kept secret. Meanwhile he demands intensive work from the airmen, intelligence about Bolshevik intentions ... in the south and on the left bank of the Dniepr River. Our objective and the work of our airmen is — the rail junction of Cwietkowo and Chrystianowka."[6]

Around 10:00 A.M. the same day Clark carried out a reconnaissance sortie along the railway line between Berdyczew and Winnica, reporting that Polish tanks were already in Winnica. It was then that Fauntleroy returned, which was a much-awaited event. That day he flew into the airfield at Połonne, at the head of a group of 7th Squadron pilots equipped with new aircraft. In Warsaw the 7th Squadron had been allocated the Ansaldo A-1 Balilla, a single-seater Italian biplane. On April 23, shortly before the beginning of the offensive, Fauntleroy had tried to take off for the first time in the direction of Łuck, but the weather forced him to return. It was not until the April 30 that Rorison succeeded in reaching Lublin in the new Balilla. However, the next day a regrettable accident

Lt. Senkowski in front of his Balilla aircraft. (Courtesy of Dr. Tomasz Kopański, Warsaw.)

occurred, shortly after Fauntleroy had landed in Łuck in order to refuel. Immediately after landing, "Faunt" left his plane on the runway; meanwhile Chess, who was obviously suffering from poor visibility, landed exactly on top of his machine. The accident caused irreparable damage to both aircraft. Fortunately nobody was injured. Fauntleroy, together with Crawford, Chess, Senkowski, and Rorison arrived at Polonne on May 1, but there was a move to Berdyczew, in general direction of Kiev. On the next day, the 7th Squadron was complete, and Fauntleroy took back the command.

Clark inflicted the most serious losses on the enemy in an attack on a railway station near Berdyczew, where he killed at least six Bolsheviks. Senkowski, who took off after him, noted 1,000 Polish cavalrymen 50 km east of Berdyczew. He did not see any Bolshevik presence as far as Skwira. At 2:40 P.M. Clark took off again to check whether the rumors of a Bolshevik division in Lipowiec were true. In the evening Clark, Konopka, and Senkowski took off again in the direction of the old airfield at Polonne. However, Shrewsbury during earlier flights had already noticed an extremely good landing strip in the vicinity of Biała Cerkiew, approximately 30 miles southwest of Kiev. The relocation had become necessary because the frontline had shifted forward again to limit the

Lt. Chess' Ballilla after accidental touchdown on top of Fauntleroy's aircraft, Łuck airfield, May 1, 1920. (Courtesy of Dr. Tomasz Kopański, Warsaw.)

range of the planes taking off from Berdyczew. On the evening of May 2, Shrewsbury traveled by car to Biała Cerkiew to secure the landing strip for the 7th Squadron. The lightning swift movement of the Poles also surprised the American Attache, who reported to Washington:

> Winnica, Żmerynka junction taken by Poles, who reached left bank of Teterew April 29. 15,000 prisoners, one aviation squadron, 100 locomotives, 3,000 railroad cars, several armored trains and numerous tanks and armored cars were captured by them.... It is probable that within a few days, Kiev will fall.[7]

On May 3 Corsi, Clark, and Senkowski flew from Połonne to Berdyczew. That afternoon an order arrived to carry out reconnaissance in the area around Skwira. Clark carried out this task and noticed a huge Polish column on the march from Skwira all the way to Biała Cerkiew. Clark did not manage to spot the presence of the Bolsheviks at Biała Cerkiew. Fauntleroy's flight had similar results. He flew on the same day to Lipowiec and reported after his return to HQ that the Polish Armed Forces had already occupied that city.

Gen. Listowski noted in his diary: "The American pilots of the 7th Squadron are performing miracles. They have already reported the cavalry's approach towards Biała Cerkiew. They flew over the city during the units' entry into the city." Listowski also noted the arrival of the American Attache, Lt. Col. Farman, at the 2nd Army HQ.[8] On the next day, Rorison was assigned the task of reconnaissance of the situation around Biała Cerkiew. It turned out that the Polish forces had not yet left the city, as HQ had expected. Visibility was hampered by fog and rain to such an extent that on his return, Rorison was forced to land in Powołocz. He managed to conceal the plane in a barn and found himself spending a night as the guest of the local priest.[9]

Over the next few days, rain prevented any air action whatsoever, but this did not hamper land maneuvers. On May 7 the Polish forces occupied Kiev. That day, the squadron met with their next, and fortunately temporary, loss when Lt. Weber was attacked from a machine gun position near the village of Ostryjka and a bullet damaged his plane. Forced to land in enemy territory, Weber suffered serious injuries to his face. He managed to get to his own armed forces, where a doctor of the 26th Infantry Regiment tended his wounds and recommended hospitalization. Weber refused, made his report on the situation and remained at the airfield. His presence, even on the ground, turned out to be valuable for the squadron over the following few days.[10] On May 8, Fauntleroy flew to Biała Cerkiew, took over the new airfield, and then recommended the transport of the remaining planes there. This occurred at the end of the offensive. Evaluating the first stage of the campaign, Farman reported:

> Poles reached all final objectives on May 10. Also advanced line to Berezina along the Dniepr. Part of two Bolshevik divisions and five armored trains which were surrounded at Korosteń forced their way out, but with this exception the operations were a complete success. In 48 hours cavalry reached strategic points in Bolshevik rear causing retirement and reorganization of Bolshevik lines. Success of operations and light losses of main forces were due to this well executed and rapid advance. Cavalry could have entered Kiev May 4, the initial success was so complete, but the High Command, fearing reverses, forbade this. Bolshevik 12th Army was completely destroyed.... Practically entire combatant strength either killed, wounded or captured.[11]

The American Military Attache entered Kiev right behind the Polish spear units, thus he had the chance to make a range of first-hand observations. What is interesting is that he stressed how favorably the Ukrainian population accepted the Poles, and the relief that was evident from the liberation of the country from the Bolsheviks.[12] This atmosphere

Polish military I.D. card of Lt. K. Shrewsbury. It reads as follows: Height: 172 cm, blue eyes, dark hair, oblong face. American [pilot] in the service of the Polisy Army. Doesn't speak Polish. (Courtesy of Dr. T. Kopański.)

was strengthened by a swift cleansing of the city and repairs to the waterworks. While Poles were undertaking these tasks they solved a range of problems concerning the management and functioning of the city services. In the next report, written after Kiev had been taken, Farman stressed that the Poles had no intention of moving past the line of the Dniepr River, and that they were not going to support a further march by the Ukrainians. However, as he presumed, they could look favorably on Ukrainian cooperation with Gen. Wrangel. Farman presented also his own general hypothesis, according to which the dispersal of the Bolsheviks would have been possible in 1919 if Gen. Denikin had recognized Polish territorial aspirations.[13]

With the occupation of Kiev, a basic political aim of the campaign seemed to have been achieved. Ataman Petlura was able to enter the city, and from there he could build the administration and launch a propaganda campaign. However, from a military point of view, the situation did not look rosy. The Bolshevik armed forces suffered huge losses, but because they declined to engage in a decisive battle, they maintained the possibility of carrying out a counter-offensive, especially after the arrival of reinforcements by uncommitted forces such as the 1st Horse Army (called "*Konarmia*") under the command of Semion Budenny. The key to Polish success was to maintain their strategic initiative, but controlling the line and stopping their advance at the Dniepr River meant squandering the initiative into the hands of the enemy. The Polish Army limited itself to building a bridgehead on the eastern bank of the Dniepr River to protect the city from artillery fire. They expected the swift rebuilding of the Ukrainian national forces, who, in Piłsudski's plan, ought to have taken on the burden of defense. This, however, didn't happen.

On May 9 Rorison carried out a combat sortie, during which Bolshevik bullets hit the sleeve of his jacket. Senkowski flew from Polonne to Biała Cerkiew. On the following day, Crawford and Senkowski carried out reconnaissance in the direction of Kaniów, Czerkassy and Śmielna. A rail bridge over Dniepr at Kaniow was destroyed, however the bridges at Czerkassy seemed to be in good condition. Corsi and Clark carried out the next flight of that day. In Medwin they saw a 50-man strong infantry unit, which they shelled. In Majdenowka and Zwienogudka they shelled a small cavalry unit, causing significant losses. On the town square in Zwienogudka, they noticed a larger unit of Bolshevik recruits on exercise, which turned out to be easy prey. The recruits were not used to air attacks, and besides that they were abandoned by their NCO. After his return, Corsi reported personally to Gen. Listowski's HQ in Berdyczew, as he was consistently obliged to do: "A report had to be made every day, someone had to do it, and Corsi never failed, rain or shine, cloudy or clear, he flew back and forth with the regularity of a railroad schedule."[14]

On the basis of these and other reports, Gen. Listowski was able to confirm the enemy concentration in the region of Korsuń and Sotnik.[15] On May 11, after his return, Crawford lodged his report in Biała Cerkiew. Rorison and Senkowski flew in the direction of Piatagory and Włodarpa, but they did not see any further enemy activity. However, on the next day the 7th Squadron received orders not to carry out any flights. One way or another the period of at least ten days following the capture of Kiev was a time of slowing down the pace. The squadron pilots forged closer contacts with the local people, including the prettier part of the population of Biała Cerkiew. That time was used to repair equipment, and the 3rd Technical Park played an efficient role in this. Its service was

Takeoff of the Squadron's Balilla. (Courtesy of Dr. Tomasz Kopański, Warsaw.)

highly rated and was confirmed by Fauntleroy's letter to Lt. Leopold Toruń, written in the deepest heat of battle:

> Please accept my most sincere thanks for the splendid work that the 3rd [Technical] Park has been doing for the Kościuszko Squadron. It is much to little to say that in my opinion the 3rd Park surpasses in every way the 2nd Park. Without the fine aid that your Park has been doing for us we should certainly have been in great difficulty. Please give Lt. Peter my very best regards, and thank him also for the work he has done for us.[16]

Franciszek Peter was an officer of the 6th Squadron. After some of the 7th Squadron pilots had been transferred to Kiev, the Americans were able to fully evaluate the devastation caused by the war that had lasted for 6 years and the degradation suffered during the period of Bolshevik occupation. Pauperization touched all, including the highest social echelons. Ladies of upper class extraction worked as waitresses in cafes, and valuable pictures, works of art, table services, unique pieces of furniture, and books were sold for pennies at bazaars. Cooper, in his memoirs, described the amazing works of art he found at such low prices that he bought a few old prints. It was a clear sign of desperation and the only way to get the resources needed to leave Kiev. Cooper described the sad pages of the city's history with an immense outpour of sympathy for its inhabitants.[17]

Maj. Jerzy Kossowski was in command of the air units in Kiev. He was not merely the leader of the Air Group, but also Chief of the Air Force of the 3rd Army led by Gen. Śmigły-Rydz as of May 3. Kossowski led the air operations on the bridgehead on the Dniepr River, and the airmen of his *Breguet Squadron* carried out bombardments in the vicinity of Dymirki, Browar, and Boryspol on the eastern bank of the Dniepr River. The HQ of the 3rd Polish Army was concerned with possible enemy concentration.

The 3rd Air Squadron was the first air unit to enter the city. This was on May 8 at 4:00 P.M., when the airmen occupied the broad Post Wołyński airfield, which was excellently situated on the railway line from Kiev to Fastow. The pilot's quarters were on the periphery of Sołomianki. Since the hangars at Post Wołyński had been burnt, it was necessary to erect new ones, and a general reparation was needed to revive the airfield's functions. There was danger of new destruction to the landing strip on the very same day. Before evening a Bolshevik plane (Farman) from the 21st Air Regiment tried to bomb the airport, but the bombs fell far wide of the their target. Despite this, the pilot reported the destruction of a few planes, for which he received the Order of the Red Banner.[18]

The basic route of reconnaissance for planes taking off from Kiev was the line of the Dniepr River to the north and mainly to the south of the city. The city was prepared to receive a detachment of the 7th Squadron from May 14. Fauntleroy flew first that day, and after having researched the conditions, recommended transfer of several crews to Kiev. It was the result of Fauntleroy's arrangement with Gen. Listowski's HQ and the HQ of Gen. Edward Śmigły-Rydz, the commander of the Polish forces in Kiev. For almost three weeks Cooper, Clark, Corsi, and temporarily Weber, settled there, the rest took off from the airfield at Biała Cerkiew. The U.S. Military Attache reported to Washington:

> The Kościuszko Squadron arrived at Kiev on the 17th. Although another squadron had been in the vicinity for several days, no flying had been done since the capture of the city.[19]

Farman was not precise about the date, nor about the complete abandonment of flights. There was a lot of information contradicting this, including this entry in Gen. Listowski's diary. That day he noted that "the 7th Squadron is working effectively."[20]

6. In the Kiev Offensive

Balilla of the 7th Kościusko Squadron. (Courtesy of Dr. Tomasz Kopański, Warsaw.)

Despite lesser enemy activity, they stepped up their observation of the targets, particularly after the Polish units captured the railway station at Darnica on May 9 and reinforced the bridgehead on the eastern bank of the Dniepr. One of the greatest successes of that period was Crawford's action on May 10. He took off together with Senkowski to patrol the Dniepr. Shortly after take-off Senkowski was forced to return to the airport, and Crawford decided to continue his flight alone. Finding himself over Czerkassy, he noticed seven ships, three of which were steamboats full of soldiers. Crawford had no bombs, but fortunately he was equipped with explosive ammunition. Without hesitation he attacked the largest ship and managed to hit the ammunition supplies, and it went up in flames. The Bolshevik soldiers jumped into the river in panic. Crawford spent a little too much time on his prey. On the way back to the base he ran out of fuel and was forced to land around 15 km from the airfield.[21]

On May 15 two events were noted; the first was connected with Senkowski, the second with Rorison. Senkowski took off that day in search of a target and found an artillery battery, which he shelled with his machine guns. Unfortunately, his machine gun malfunctioned and he shot the propeller of his own plane twice. He was lucky enough that his machine gun then shut out completely, saving his own life. Further shots to the propeller would have undoubtedly led to a catastrophe. Rorison had better luck, and during his flight he attacked a nest of machine guns. A Bolshevik bullet damaged his main fuel tank, and he was forced to return and land 2 km from Korsuń. Even the CO of the 2nd Army noted that a pilot of the 7th Squadron had been lost, following his fate over the next few days.[22]

Crawford went in search of Rorison on May 16, but the news of the pilot's loss spread to other units. Meanwhile "Little Rory," without any knowledge of the terrain or the local languages, walked for 45 km before he was found by a Polish cavalry unit. His plane was recovered by the Polish Infantry. A few parts had been stolen in the pilot's absence, but the aircraft was swiftly repaired and pressed into action again.[23]

On May 17 Corsi also experienced a similar adventure, namely a forced landing beyond his own airfield. Freshly rescued from his own forced landing, Rorison went with Cooper by car in search of the lost man. The very same day, he managed to chance upon a trace of Corsi. By the next day the plane and the pilot were already in Biała Cerkiew. Apart from that, the other event of the day was Crawford's reconnaissance sortie in the direction of Świella. On May 19, Crawford repeated his flight in the same direction. This time he happened upon a 200-strong Bolshevik cavalry at Korsuń, which he immediately attacked. After he had dispersed them, he turned his efforts against a machine gun nest that was shelling a Polish Infantry rail transport. Crawford immediately attacked the Bolshevik position and silenced it. On the same day, Senkowski flew in the direction of Humań.

On May 20th Clark, Weber, and Senkowski took off at 7:30 A.M., and Clark and Weber made another flight in the later hours. On that day Crawford flew towards Czerkassy and attacked a Bolshevik infantry unit west of Korsuń on his way. Fauntleroy discovered the presence of an infantry division with cavalry and artillery near the town of Medwin. He strafed them with 250 rounds of ammunition, after which he returned to Biała Cerkiew. After landing he discovered that a Bolshevik bullet had hit the oil tank. Fortunately, the pilot reached the airfield before the damage affected the performance of the steering of the plane.

The next day passed largely without incident due to bad weather and the fact that the fuel supply had been exhausted. Only Weber and Clark flew from Kiev to file their reports. By the next day, the weather

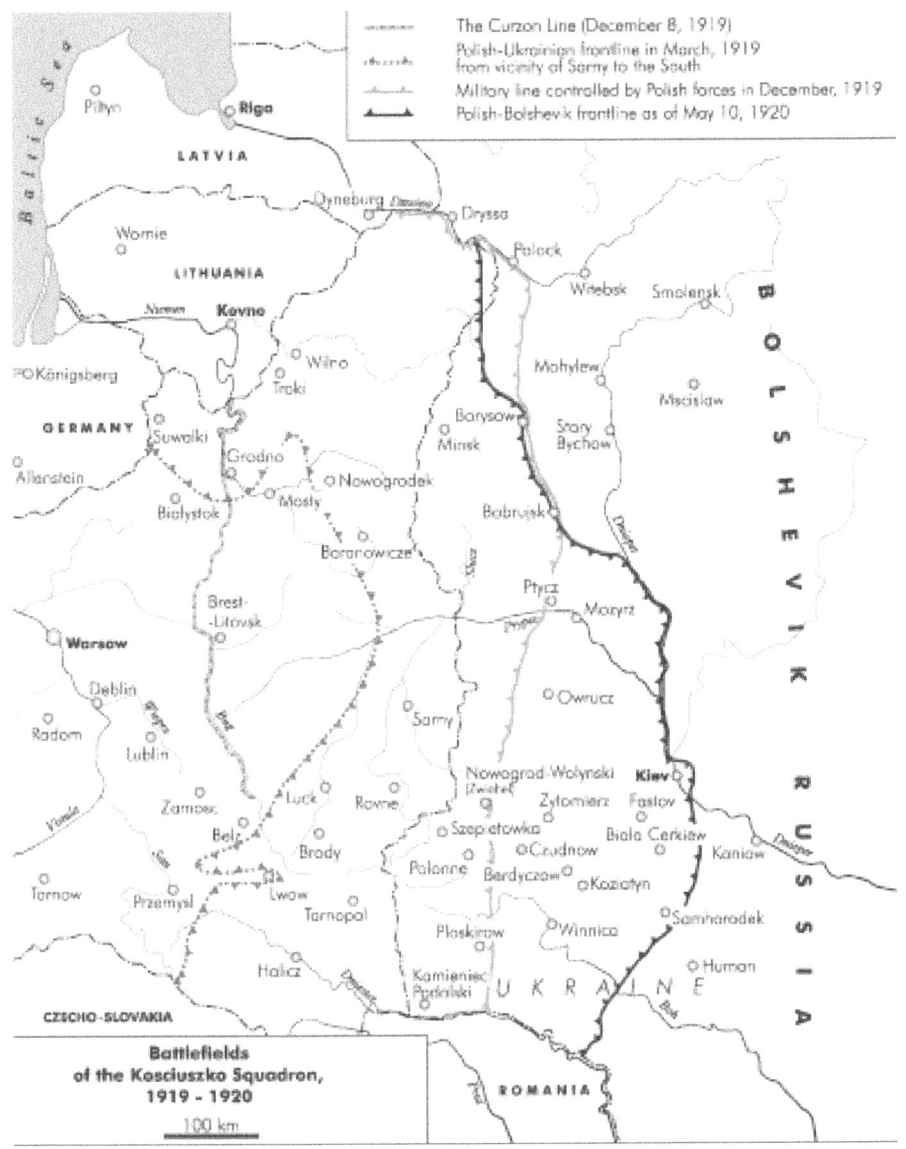

Map showing the 1919–1920 theatre of operations between Lwów and Kiev. (Courtesy of Mariusz Kędzieuski, Cracow.

was better, but the continuing lack of fuel prevented any airborne action. On May 23, Weber carried out a 100-minute sortie, taking off from Kiev. On the 24, Senkowski took off for Kaniów, and Crawford for Talnoje and Stawiszcze, but besides Weber only Shrewsbury and Clark took off from Kiev.[24]

These were the last days of relative stability on the frontline. On May 23, the airmen of the 3rd Squadron carried out productive sorties the length of the Dniepr River in a southerly direction. They discovered that the Bolsheviks were using the river landing facility at Rżyszczew and the bridges on the Dniepr at Czerkassy, 160 km south of Kiev. They succeeded in damaging a vehicle bridge and a rail bridge and even a train which was within firing range at that time.[25]

On the 25, Weber was in the air despite his previous injuries and carried out a 45-minute flight. Crawford took off in the air at 7:15 A.M. His flight was extremely long (2 hours and 55 minutes) and was exceedingly productive. Near Humań, he noticed a huge cavalry unit which he estimated at 6,000 horses. Only the *Konarmia* possessed so many cavalrymen, and its presence in this part of the frontline was a complete surprise. The HQ was convinced that the unit was still engaged in battle with Wrangel, 200 miles east of the Polish theater of operation. When Fauntleroy reported to the HQ, he was treated with disbelief; however, a similar report was on the desk of the Chief of Staff the 13th Infantry Division.

Crawford was one of the first airmen, but probably not *the* first, to discover the presence of the *Konarmia*. Debate surrounding this subject continues to this very day. Some historians credit this to the 7th Squadron, but there are differing opinions. An article describing the activities of the air force in battle with Budenny, written by Lt. Col. Edward Lewandowski, related that the 21st Squadron had located Budenny near Humań by May 24. This fact is confirmed by a commendation order for the 3rd *Dyon*, issued by the 6th Army HQ on September 11, 1920.[26]

In turn, the "farewell order" of Gen. Józef Haller of May 9, 1921, summarizing the actions of the 7th Squadron, does not mention that the squadron had discovered Budenny's presence, but stressed that it had fought with him efficiently.[27] And in a report summarizing the air force's actions in the war in 1920, the American Attache wrote: "The arrival of Budenny's cavalry at Humań was witnessed by American Aviators of Kościuszko Squadron."[28]

To witness does not necessarily mean to discover. Of course, it did not change the value of services rendered by the squadron. The effectiveness with which they fought was most important, not who was first to detect the enemy presence. Anyway, the result of Crawford's flight confirmed that a formidable enemy had made an appearance. This information had colossal significance, considering the lack of information

6. In the Kiev Offensive

from Polish Intelligence, which up to that time was working extremely effectively.

Meanwhile, to the huge surprise of Polish HQ, Budenny did not try to cross the frontline. He moved back and began to march parallel to the line of Polish outposts, causing even greater confusion. It was not known where and when he would decide to attack, and the extension of the frontline made all preparations from the Polish side extremely burdensome. Budenny's movement prevented the Polish troops from engaging him in battle. On May 27, a few columns of the *Konarmia* marched in the direction of Koziatyń. The Polish 13th and 7th Infantry divisions were waiting for the Bolshevik horsemen. Wishing to effectively oppose the cavalry, Gen. Listowski requested to place at his disposition two units that were expected to march to the northern front. On May 28, the 13th Infantry Division under the command of Gen. Jan Romer was placed under command of the 6th Army. Due to this, the meeting point for the frontline of two divisions became from that moment the contact point for two Polish armies. It had vital consequences for the further course of battle. On the same day, the 13th Infantry Division was additionally reinforced by the 7th Kościuszko Squadron. On the next day, Budenny stopped by the banks of the two small rivers called Sob and Roś, around 25 km from the defensive position of the 13th Division. On May 29, a fierce battle began between the 13th Polish Division and the *Konarmia*. The 50th Infantry Regiment under the French Colonel Paqualen moved ahead despite of the HQ orders. This resulted in a gap in the Polish line of defense and caused unusually bloody clashes with the 6th Division of the *Konarmia*. Finally the Polish forces managed to stop the march of the Bolshevik forces on Koziatyń on June 2 and forced them to retreat. Budenny was by no means discouraged, only looking for another point of attack elsewhere. There was such a point near Samhorodek where the forces of the two Polish Armies met. Due to heavy rainfall in the first days of June, the concentration of Polish forces arrived late at this contact point, so that the attack by the *Konarmia* on June 5 chanced upon an unusually weak resistance. Budenny attacked with two cavalry divisions against only six companies of Polish infantry, two heavy machine gun companies, a few cavalry squadrons, and three artillery batteries. On June 5, 1920, there was a definite breakthrough of the frontline, and the Bolsheviks took full advantage of it.[29]

From the beginning of the battle with Budenny, the Air Force carried exceptional responsibility. The HQ wanted swift intelligence data so that they could prepare orders to fight effectively. Since the frontline was unusually thin, the planes' machine gun action and bombardment was more than once the only form of balancing the enemy's fire potential. Starting May 26 the number and intensity of flights increased dramatically. On May 27, Lt. Chess carried out an hour and a half flight in the direction of Taraszcze-Olszanica, during which he attacked the Bolshevik cavalry from the altitude of 100 m. During this charge one of his wings was shot by 14 bullets. Fortunately, he managed to return to Biała Cerkiew. On the same day, Lt. Senkowski located the movement of two Bolshevik cavalry divisions near Chrystianówka. Not taking account of heavy enemy fire, Senkowski attacked the column with machine gun fire. During combat a Bolshevik bullet hit him in the leg. Despite his wound, Senkowski managed to maintain control of the plane and return to the airfield 80 km away. He refused medical treatment until he had lodged a written report and even after that he refused recommended hospitalization.[30]

Shrewsbury attacked Budenny's forces with one bomb and 250 rounds of ammunition. On this exceptionally active day, Chess took off once more, this time with Weber, who due to a defect in his aircraft was forced to land prematurely. Fauntleroy sent out a rescue team in search of him. The bruised Weber was transported to a first aid station, where his wounds, which turned out not to be threatening, were treated. He also refused to be sent to the hospital. Weber and Senkowski were unable to carry out flights, but they helped in carrying out the order to evacuate the airfield at Biała Cerkiew.

The change was the necessary result of the retreat of parts of the Polish units. Budenny unexpectedly demolished the weaker cavalry units blocking his advance on the road to Biała Cerkiew. In the morning hours of May 28 Fauntleroy flew on an intelligence sortie and found spearheads of the enemy cavalry only a few kilometers from the city. An immediate evacuation was carried out, which Lt. Weber conducted indefatigably. If he had decided to go to the hospital, as advised, the squadron's equipment would have most certainly fallen into Bolshevik hands. At the same time Fauntleroy and the rest of the pilots who were capable of flying began to fight the advancing Bolsheviks. Their attacks were so effective that they temporarily stopped the enemy march. The next task was to find a new airfield. Fauntleroy and Crawford took off with this aim. They sought a suitable part of the terrain in Fastov, where Crawford had gone by car. Finally, however, an order arrived to lead the squadron to Koziatyń.[31]

On Friday the 28th, the equipment was relocated and on May 29

6. In the Kiev Offensive

Relocation of Squadron's equipment, June 1920. (Courtesy of Dr. Tomasz Kopański, Warsaw.)

the 7th Squadron's equipment arrived at Koziatyń, escorted by Lt. Weber. In Koziatyń, the Kościuszko boys shared an airfield with the 9th Squadron, whose commander allowed them to replenish their fuel, ammunition, and bomb supplies. He also permitted them to share his mechanics. At the same time, the part of the 7th Squadron operating from Kiev remained active. When, on May 28 air reconnaissance confirmed that the Bolshevik units were trying to cross the river Dniepr at Rżyszczew, the CO of the 3rd Army ordered the 5th Wing of Maj. Kossowski to take counteraction. On May 28, Poles managed to intercept a Bolshevik dispatch indicating that on the 30th a Bolshevik attack was planned from Rżyszczew in the direction of Witaczów and Tripolje. On May 30 at 3:45 all the planes of the 3rd and 16th Squadrons and three crews of the 7th Squadron left for Witaczów. When they saw no signs of any Bolsheviks there, they directed the planes to the river landing facility at Rżyszczewo, where they surprised marine units full of equipment and soldiers, ready to cross the river. Corsi, Clark, and Cooper distinguished themselves in action. The participants in this expedition succeeded in destroying several navy units on the Dniepr River. One of the Bolshevik ships was directly hit by a bomb and sank, and one of the monitors, escaping fire, ran aground. The tank was loaded with ammunition and its explosion killed a large number of soldiers on board. The rest tried to save their lives by jumping into the river.[32]

The airmen's expedition stopped the crossing at Rżyszczew, which finally was abandoned by the Bolsheviks due to heavy losses inflicted from the air. Ultimately, the crossing was prevented by an air attack the next day by the 5th Wing of Maj. Kossowski. Bolsheviks suffered significant losses of both men and marine equipment. From then on their attention was directed north of Kiev, where their troops had gathered near Okuninowo at a crossing by the Dniepr, this time with the aim of encircling the northern wing of Gen. Śmigły-Rydz's army. On the afternoon of June 1, Cooper and Corsi took off once more for the east and their reconnaissance led to the discovery of the advanced construction of a pontoon bridge on the Dniepr, which they bombed effectively. The bridge suffered permanent damage.[33]

The same day Cooper and Corsi took part in the *Breguet* Squadron's expedition, under Maj. Kossowski's command, to a Bolshevik heavy artillery position near Dymirki bridgehead. Cooperation with Kossowski's bomber planes brought excellent results. All positions were silenced and a few artillery pieces were destroyed. The next action in which Corsi participated was an attack by the *Breguet* group on an armored train near Borysław on the same day. The train was destroyed.[34] On the next day, June 2, Cooper again accompanied a one and a half hour expedition by Maj. Kossowski's *Breguets*. Then the expedition came across a flotilla of at least four steamers and a monitor of transporting soldiers. Three vessels were sunk and a fourth was seriously damaged. These were the last actions of the Kościuszko boys in Kiev. The changing situation around the city led to an order for the pilots to abandon the city, and they joined the squadron at Koziatyń. Clark was not among those returning. He had contracted a serious lung infection with bronchitis, and he had to go to the hospital. His illness was so serious that he never returned to the squadron. It was the next painful weakening of personnel.

The pilots of the 7th Squadron were about to face an extremely demanding test. Sunday, May 30, and the next day, remained forever in the 7th Squadron's book of glory. In the space of 48 hours, Fauntleroy performed a number of acts which in the eyes of the superiors deserved to be rewarded by the Virtuti Militari, the oldest and most respected Polish military decoration.

On Sunday the 30th an order was issued by the 13th Division for Maj. Antoni Szylling's Group, consisting of the 44th and the 40th

Infantry Regiment, to carry out a counterattack to fill gaps in the front-line between Napadowka and Pedosy. That breach directly threatened Koziatyń. The vital link in this operation's success was communication with the 26th Infantry Brigade, which had been cut off in Lipowiec. Fauntleroy carried out the assignment independently and so did an HQ courier by car. Fauntleroy's first flight began at about 4:30 A.M., Shrewsbury also took off and during the day Rorison took off as well. This time overwork caused Rorison, returning from action, to make an error while landing that destroyed his controls. Seeing the enormous exhaustion of those under his command, Fauntleroy ordered a few hours rest (sleep) in the wagons.

Just at that time, a Bolshevik plane flew over the squadron's airfield and dropped several bombs from an altitude of over 2,000 m. It caused no damage, but the pilot immediately went back east. Before the Americans could take off, the Bolshevik airmen were already far away. Their chase failed and the opportunity to compete with the enemy was lost. On Monday, May 31, Fauntleroy took off at 4:30 A.M. in a southeast direction from Koziatyń along the road to Lipowiec. His objective was to establish communication with the Polish 25th Infantry Brigade near Pohrebyszcze. Fauntleroy dropped orders from the air and reported on the enemy position and strength. During his return flight, he shelled the enemy with machine gun fire. After he had reported the situation at the 13th Division HQ, he took off again at 8:00 A.M., this time with Lt. Chess. Meanwhile the Brigade prepared for battle with 1,000 soldiers against the Bolsheviks, whose numbers were estimated to be 2,500. The imbalance was levelled by the presence of the two airmen, whose machine gun fire caused confusion and significant losses of the enemy. Unfortunately, after his return to the airfield, Chess seriously damaged his aircraft, and Fauntleroy was forced to take off on the next flight alone. Around 4:30 P.M. he checked the southeast direction again, where the Polish units had efficiently repulsed the enemy. Then he flew northeast from Koziatyń, where he noticed around 2,000 of Budenny's cavalrymen about 20 km from the city. They had broken through Polish positions and were moving in the direction of Koziatyń. What more, flying lower Fauntleroy observed that the Bolsheviks had mined the railway line between Koziatyń and Fastov on the part between Zarudince and Roś railway station. It was an important artery for transporting troops to the frontline. The Bolsheviks took up positions on both sides of the tracks in expectation of the arriving train. The ambush would have undoubtedly led to huge losses if the train had encountered a mine or been the object of heavy shelling. Mindful of the possible consequences, Fauntleroy flew west towards Koziatyń to check if there was any train coming from that direction. In the near distance he spotted a trace of smoke signaling the Polish army transport approaching from Koziatyń. In the space of a few minutes he was already flying over the train, which was transporting a battalion of the 19th Infantry Regiment and the accompanying units, 1,000 soldiers altogether.

For the sake of historical precision, it should be noted that the train was not transporting several thousands of soldiers, as some authors maintain. Only the soldiers of the 19th Infantry Regiment were directly threatened. Another matter is that after that transport, another larger one followed.[35]

Appalled by the possible consequences, Fauntleroy made dramatic efforts to persuade the machinists to stop the engines. He tried to cut off the train's course in front of the engine, gesticulated, flew back and forth the whole length of the train, until at last it came to a halt. Fortunately, he found a strip meadow nearby where he could land, and in a few minutes he was able to explain to the Polish officers the magnitude of the awaiting danger. There is even an account that after Fauntleroy had reported to the Polish officers, he fainted for a moment from emotion and exhaustion. Anyway, the infantry was regrouped and immediately dispatched to attack the ambushed enemy. Fauntleroy not only saved the lives of hundreds of soldiers, but also thanks to his immediate action the Bolsheviks suffered significant losses.[36]

The superiors quickly evaluated the importance of that action. One of the officers noted details from "Faunt's" identity card and the deed was the basis for the recommendation for the Virtuti Militari. There was praise for the whole squadron in the 13th Division report dispatched to Gen. Listowski:

> The American airmen, despite their exhaustion, are fighting like possessed. They are carrying out excellent intelligence work. Lately, during the attack by our division on the enemy, their commander attacked the enemy and roasted the Bolsheviks. Without the help of the American airmen, those devils would have taken us long ago.[37]

Several days later, Lt. Col. Tadeusz Kurcyusz from that division's HQ wrote in an order which summarized joint operations:

> From the first minutes of the 7th Squadron's arrival at Koziatyn, Budenny's movements ceased to be a secret for us. The precision and

6. In the Kiev Offensive

orientation excellence of the reconnaissance carried out by the efficient Americans was amazing. However, it was not only their reconnaissance, but the 7th Air Squadron's combat activity. They seriously made the Bolshevik Regiments' lives a complete misery. From a low altitude they dispersed long enemy columns through attack and machine gun fire, they helped the offensive of our infantry, they transported orders, which they delivered wherever necessary. They worked indefatigably and heroically. If the division units have in this heavy battle maintained their own positions — this is due, to a great extent, to the cooperation of the 7th Air Squadron.[38]

Fauntleroy and Shrewsbury took off that day and their action completed the activities of the 7th Squadron in May. Altogether, the squadron carried out 147 combat sorties, that is nearly 5 flights a day, including days with bad weather and not including transportation from one airfield to another and the flights taking reports to the HQ.[39]

On June 1 Fauntleroy again distinguished himself, this time in the vicinity of Murowana and Morozowka, where a Bolshevik cavalry column, extending for as far as 7 km (!) tried to breach a trap set by the Polish units. Fauntleroy spotted the Bolsheviks during a morning flight, when they had left Murowana at full trot and crossed the nearby railway track. Fauntleroy, "flew his plane extremely low and relentlessly attacked them with his machine guns, he flew the length of the column sowing panic and destruction. The whole column fell into disarray in the nearby fields."[40]

The immediate action of the Polish infantry and General Jan Sawicki's cavalry cut off the Bolshevik return route. Yet again, the squadron airmen caused Budenny to be defeated locally. On June 2, the indefatigable Rorison carried out two three-hour flights. Famous for his excellent reconnaissance of ground targets, he was chosen to carry out a reconnaissance flight on HQ orders. He racked up a similar flight to his account the following day. On June 3 he took off with Lt. Kubala and Capt. Bastyr, one of the heroes of the 1918 defense of Lwów. His flight was regarded as one of the 7th Squadron's. On June 4 Cooper took off on a flight that lasted 2 hours and 20 minutes, and Corsi and Chess were also in the air and dropped four 12 kg bombs. That flight lasted 2 hours 45 minutes. Apart from the bombs, they dropped specially prepared propaganda leaflets in Russian. One of them directed specifically to Budenny's cavalry, was entitled *Cossack Brothers People from the Don and Kuban Region*, another *Brothers*. They both encouraged Bolshevik servicemen to desert. As time showed, they were to a certain extent effective.

On the 5th of June Gen. Listowski noted the desertion of two Bolshevik airmen, who admitted that Budenny's cavalry suffered serious losses because of the Polish attacks.[41] Some of those losses had been inflicted by the hardworking 7th Squadron.

On June 6, Corsi carried out two flights. During the first he dropped one 12 kg bomb. The second flight lasted one hour and 15 minutes. Chess carried out a flight of similar length that day, but Cooper's flight was two hours.[42] On the next day Cooper, Corsi, and Chess attacked and shelled an 800-man Bolshevik cavalry. In addition, Fauntleroy was also in the air; however, in compliance with the 13th Division HQ orders, the Squadron ceased flying that day.

On June 5, despite the relentlessly rainy weather, Corsi and Chess carried out the HQ orders to reconnoiter the neighboring fields. Over Dzionka they spotted 1,500 of Budenny's cavalrymen, who they treated to four bombs and machine gun fire. As the result of a strong wind the shelling was of limited efficiency. Despite the difficult conditions, after their return to the landing strip at Koziatyń, an order blocked them from carrying out further reconnaissance. This time Corsi and Chess flew towards Skwira and the town of Antonów, but unfortunately there was no chance of any observational activities, and they returned to the airfield. Not until the third flight that day did Corsi notice a larger formation of Budenny's cavalry near Rużyn. He dropped two bombs and shelled them with some 200 rounds of ammunition.

A fundamental breakthrough was expected the next day — namely a decisive Polish counteraction against Budenny, but Budenny unexpectedly broke through the Polish position at Samhorodek and took the initiative.

A period of burdensome retreat lasting several weeks began for the Polish Army. The squadrons, sometimes in fewer numbers and with fewer planes, were still very active. The retreat in no way impeded the effectiveness of their service. A good example is June 6, when the 7th Squadron carried out at least eight flights. Corsi took off first, then Cooper, flying the length of the railway southeast of Koziatyń. Cooper chanced upon a Bolshevik unit near Rużyn, which he attacked with machine gun fire. Over the same place Corsi appeared after Cooper and dropped a bomb on the Bolshevik cavalry, which numbered 700 horses. He flew on to Bielówka, where he dropped a second bomb and shelled a 300-strong cavalry unit. His target was a formation of 50 rail wagons. Lt. Chess carried out the third flight over Rużyn and Bielowka, and he fired 150 rounds of ammunition at the enemy and dropped two bombs.

That day Rużyn was an important point. It was here that the Bolshevik armed forces advancing on Koziatyń were concentrated. Lt. Rorison also flew in this direction, and he noticed the blasting of a railway bridge near Bielówka and larger enemy units near Rużyn, at least eight columns numbering 12,000 people, which seemed to be advancing on Koziatyń from the north. It was not until Corsi's next flight that day that the true direction in which the Bolsheviks were advancing was discovered. They had unexpectedly turned in a northeasterly direction. It turned out that their aim was to cut off the railway line to Fastov. Corsi dropped two bombs and fired 100 rounds of ammunition. Chess took off in his wake towards Rużyn along the railway line to Berdyczew. On the way he noticed a road bridge had been blown up, and he shelled the enemy with 200 rounds of ammunition and dropped two bombs. Cooper set off after him, but his engine broke down shortly after take-off, forcing him to land about 5 km from Koziatyń. After the aircraft had been repaired, he took to the skies again, along the railway line towards Fastov. Corsi carried out the last sortie of that day, which was complicated by a heavy downpour and fog. Nonetheless, the pilot managed to note the movement of an enemy patrol to the northeast of Berdyczew.[43]

Meanwhile the Bolshevik movement threatened Koziatyń, which was defended by weak Polish forces. There was a danger that the Bolsheviks would take control of the 7th Squadron's landing strip, so Fauntleroy ordered the transport of the equipment to Berdyczew and then to Żytomierz. However, even Żytomierz was not completely safe. The situation was analyzed at HQ and Fauntleroy decided to work on precautionary measures in case of a sudden Bolshevik advance. The events of the following day speeded up his decision. Shortly after take off on the morning of June 7, Fauntleroy discovered that the Bolsheviks were already operating a few kilometers from Koziatyń. He returned immediately to warn the ground crew and to order an immediate evacuation. Fortunately the night before the mechanics had been sent west with part of the equipment. Now it was the turn of the pilots and planes. Weber and the pilots remaining on the ground carried out an immediate evacuation. It involved further loss of equipment, caused by unfortunate accidents and bad weather. In any case, Cooper, Shrewsbury, Chess, Rorison, Crawford and Fauntleroy managed to get to Nowogród Wołyński, which became the squadron's next airfield.

The weather on June 8 prevented practically any take off; nonetheless Rorison took to the skies to carry out reconnaissance in the direction of Berdyczew. Unfortunately the wind blew him off course to the airport at Połonne. The 9th Squadron was based there, with whom the Kościuszko boys had closely worked over the past few weeks. On the same day, Shrewsbury took off for Kiev and Weber after him. Both of them carried Piłsudski's orders for Gen. Śmigły-Rydz to leave the city. It was an unusually important mission that consequently decided what forces Piłsudski would have at his disposal in the battle for Warsaw. The Marshal was not concerned about staying in Kiev, but about having a reliable force with which to check the Bolsheviks when the time came. Gen. Śmigły, on the other hand, counted on a spectacular success, i.e., holding on to the city despite a siege. Gen. Listowski supported him, but he could not overrule specific orders signed by the Commander-in-Chief. Communication with Kiev was maintained via Gen. Listowski's HQ, who passed on Śmigły-Rydz's reports to Warsaw and orders issued in the other direction. Since it was difficult to maintain reliable radio communication, pilots always delivered reports, among them the 7th Squadron. The final abandonment of Kiev was completed on June 9 and 10, 1920.

On June 9 Fauntleroy took to the skies again. During this flight he discovered that the Bolsheviks had abandoned the plan to take Żytomierz and instead turned to the east again, with the aim of encircling the Polish troops around Kiev by a scissor movement of two major groups. Gen. Listowski noted that day:

> According to the 7th Squadron's report, today at 3:00 P.M. two columns of enemy drive in a general easterly direction, probably to Fastov.... The general number of both columns are about 12,000 swords and a train of from 600 to 700 horse carts with three people on each. As evident from movements until now, Budenny's force pushes on the length of rivers or by field and never by road.[44]

Fortunately for Gen. Śmigły-Rydz this movement had been badly calculated and the Polish forces managed to avoid ambush. On June 10 bad weather prevented effectual reconnaissance. Gen. Listowski even complained that he could not inform Gen. Śmigły of the Commander-in-Chief's next order. It was not until Maj. Kossowski's 5th Air Wing reached Nowogród Wołyński that the news of the evacuation of Kiev was confirmed. The Major also told of the destruction of bridges on the Dniepr and the evacuation of air units, which had destroyed the hangars and other equipment that could not be evacuated. On the other hand, the results of the reconnaissance flight on June 11 were consoling. They confirmed that Gen. Śmigły's trains had already reached Żytomierz, and that the withdrawal had been carried out without any major problems.[45]

Meanwhile the losses suffered in the course of air action were so serious that they threatened the execution of further orders by the Squadron at that point. Another plane was lost in addition to the two planes lost during the evacuation to Nowogród Wołyński. On June 12, during Corsi and Konopka's flight, Corsi's Balilla was shelled by the Bolsheviks and forced to land. During its descent to the ground the plane was damaged, but Corsi suffered only minor injuries. What was worse, Konopka's plane, which had accompanied Corsi, crashed into a tree during landing and was completely destroyed. Fortunately, Konopka did not suffer serious injuries.

On the 13th Cooper, Weber, and Rorison carried out five flights. The airmen, on Gen. Listowski's orders, searched for Budenny all day and tried to keep in contact with the units of the 3rd Army: "On the 3rd Army, which is withdrawing its forces we have only meagre news, only what the airmen see."[46] The conditions of retreat, the reduction in personnel, and the loss of equipment forced the 7th Squadron to take shelter in Lwów. This had to be done to replenish their equipment and to reorganize, and was conducted after a personal inspection by the Commander of the 2nd Army at the airfield on June 14. After a longer consultation between Gen. Listowski and Fauntleroy, it was decided that the 7th Squadron would retreat further to the west. Corsi and Weber, together with four mechanics, were to be seconded to Gen. Romer's Cavalry Division. Their task was to carry out reconnaissance flights from the airfield at Szepietówka. Since the formation was small, and due to the specific demands of the Cavalry Division HQ, both pilots' duties were strictly limited to observation. There were also days of bad weather, which forced them into a completely demoralizing inactivity. However, there were also extremely active days when they were airborne for 8 to 9 hours. For example, on June 19 both pilots carried out five sorties.

On June 23, both of them joined up with the 7th Squadron at Lewandówka. Meanwhile new Balilla planes had arrived at Lwów, which replaced the lost ones. A period of relative rest followed, allowing recuperation from injuries suffered during the previous campaign. The U.S. Military Attache took advantage of this time to analyze the actions of the 7th Squadron in a longer report dated July 3, 1920. His analysis accurately described the innovative use of the airforce in pursuit and during the retreat of one's own forces. Farman volunteered the thesis that the airforce had been used for the first time as rear guard in time of retreat.

Rorison, Fauntleroy and Corsi in rare moment of relaxation. (Courtesy of Dr. Tomasz Kopański, Warsaw.)

He also described new battle methods, joining the cavalry operations with those of the air force. He excellently stressed the value of reconnaissance of the advancing cavalry from the air, and the great mobility of the squadron, whose airfield was always near a railway line. Only a railway guaranteed a swift relocation of equipment in the event of an offensive or retreat. Farman also stressed the close proximity of these airfields to the battlefield; between 5 and 50 km. It made deeper intelligence possible in the enemy-held territory; however, it was also open to enemy threat. There had been several evacuations a few kilometers from the advancing enemy cavalry units. The Attache emphasized that the squadron crew consisted fundamentally of 80 people, whereas an American unit would number around 200. Despite weaker equipment and technical imperfections, the air force had carried out its mission in the campaign, namely to delay Budenny's advance:

> For this sort of warfare scout pilots of considerable skill are necessary as they must land on unimproved fields and must be capable of maneuvering their planes rapidly at extremely low altitudes.[47]

The lull in action permitted testing of new parts for the Balilla planes. They had turned out to be useful in the conditions so far, even though at the beginning there had been doubts as to their potential.

Several accidents, which did not pass the Kościuszko boys by, did not end tragically thanks to the advantages of the Balilla planes. After the first ten days of July, it was clear that Lwów would again be in danger. Since the armed forces were seriously overburdened, the fate of the city was again in the hands of the inhabitants, and also rather more than expected in the hands of the pilots. On July 11, an order arrived to relocate the squadron to Hołoby, northeast of Lwów, which was also the airfield of the 21st Squadron commanded by Maj. Rayski. There was a concentration of the two elite air squadrons for the decisive battle at the gates of Lwów. A situation similar to that in November 1918 was expected, when the city was cut off from the world and the air force was the only link with HQs and the Commander-in-Chief.

By the next day all the machines had already arrived at Hołoby. The squadron was replenished. Apart from Lt. Konopka, who had spent several of the last few weeks in the squadron, the 7th Squadron was reinforced by the return of Capt. Kelly, who had been on training for several months in Lwów and had finally earned his pilot's wings. Together with Konopka, Kelly replaced Clark and Shrewsbury, who had returned to the U.S.

On July 12, Crawford took off first and Rorison soon after. On the 13, after a longer break, Capt. Kelly reported for a combat sortie. He was accompanied by Lt. Stanisław Skarżyński of the 21st Squadron as an observer on a flight along the line of Lwów, Brody, Beresteczko, and Łuck. During the hour and a half expedition no larger enemy units were spotted. Fauntleroy and Senkowski carried out similar observations that day. Cooper also took off for Brody on the 13th of July. He had returned from Warsaw barely two days earlier with a new Balilla and announced his upcoming promotion. However, Cooper, to the great surprise of his comrades, did not return from his flight to Hołoby. It was not yet time to despair, since this had happened to other pilots of the squadron. More than once, the aircraft damage or lack of fuel had forced someone to land behind the enemy line and the pilot reached his unit after a few or a dozen days. Rorison himself experienced a similar fate. It was quite simply necessary to wait patiently for an explanation of Cooper's fate. Nonetheless, it weakened the squadron further, and his loss was more keenly felt because he was an experienced pilot.[48]

On July 14, Kelly carried out another flight, this time with Lt. Reptki in a German AEG. They spotted 1,500 cavalrymen near Targowica and bombed and shelled them with machine gun fire.

The number of personnel lost, so few in the first part of the campaign, began to increase. On July 15 Lt. Kelly took off with Lt. Skarżyński towards Łuck. Over Zwierowce, around 1 km north of the Łuck-Rovno road, the Bolsheviks effectually shelled the plane, which with great force nose-dived into the ground. The pilot was literally driven into the controls and the observer catapulted out of the cabin. They were both killed instantaneously. As if that was not unfortunate enough, Capt. Ciecierski was shot by the Bolsheviks on the same day. He had come to the 7th Squadron without proper orders assigning him to the unit, so Fauntleroy had sent him back to Lwów for the appropriate papers. Meanwhile the ambitious Ciecierski had taken off, not for Lewandówka, but for Łuck. His British SE5 scout plane was surprised by Bolshevik fire and the pilot had no chance whatsoever.[49]

Even such an experienced pilot as Fauntleroy fell into a Bolshevik trap the following day. Flying low, he flew into mass fire by Bolsheviks hidden in the forest. The main fuel tank was hit and the pilot was shot in the leg. Fortunately, it was not a serious wound, nonetheless the Major had to land at Łuck. He reached Hołoby the next day. On July 16 Rorison flew for over 2 hours. Weber, Konopka and Corsi also took to the skies. Their flight lasted 2 hours 15 minutes.[50]

July 18 saw a continuation of bad luck with the accident of Buck Crawford. He took off that day on an evening flight with Corsi towards the Horyn River. During the flight, both pilots found themselves under mass fire from Bolsheviks hidden in the forest, who managed to hit Crawford's main fuel tank. The pilot immediately reconnected the fuel from the small emergency tank. Unfortunately the flow was blocked in some way and Crawford had to land in the first patch of bare space. The Bolshevik cavalry had waited for this and moved towards the plane. Meanwhile Crawford had jumped from the aircraft, and without even switching off the engine, ran in the direction of the nearest forest. His chances of survival were less than zero as the distance between him and the pursuing Bolsheviks decreased with every second. Fortunately for Crawford, the engine started to turn its propellers again. Most certainly the fuel pipe, blocked by natural causes, had been unblocked by apparently supernatural causes, allowing fuel to reach the engine. Without any hesitation whatsoever, Crawford turned round and leapt into the machine, which he managed to get up into the air just ahead of the charging Bolsheviks. The machine was further damaged on take-off from hitting an irrigation ditch. Crawford managed, however, to take to the skies and land in Łuck. The next morning he reached Hołoby, where he found that two mechanics had succumbed to typhus.[51]

On July 19 Corsi and Konopka carried out combat flights over enemy territory and on July 21 Corsi and Konopka took off again, as did Chess and Senkowski.[52]

The resourcefulness of the airforce did not restrain Budenny. In view of the threat to Hołoby, on July 23 a decision was made to withdraw the 7th Squadron to Uściług, a small town on the eastern bank of the Bug River, near the town of Hrubieszów. The next day Corsi and Senkowski took off from this airfield. The former's flight lasted two hours and the latter's an hour longer. On July 27 Crawford, Corsi, and Senkowski carried out combat sorties. The following day Corsi and Senkowski took to the skies. Corsi was in the air for 2 hours and 35 minutes and Senkowski was airborne for ten minutes longer. All their activities were directed at Budenny's cavalry. On August 3 Weber was wounded again. This time his plane overturned during landing, which injured him in the head and the shoulder. After a few days in the hospital Weber returned to the ranks. In addition, there was an outbreak of typhus among the mechanics, which posed a further threat to the squadron. In August, because of this (not mentioning the bad weather) combat flights were relatively limited between the 5th and 9th. However, it was the proverbial calm before the storm.[53]

7 | An American Legion Again?

One of the consequences of the Polish retreat was the reactivation of the idea of a volunteer army and possibly even a foreign legion to help the war effort. The task of implementing a legal background for such a possibility fell on the shoulders of the Council for National Defense, a new body activated on July 1, 1920, which was to coordinate all the defense efforts. On July 7, the National Defense Council decreed the establishment of the Volunteer Army with Gen. Józef Haller at its head. Haller's troops quickly began to reinforce the frontline units. The National Defense Committees, functioning in towns, voievoidships and counties, began collecting money and material for the army.[1]

The situation worsened so quickly that the idea of using foreign volunteers was proposed again, even more so as sympathy for Poland was awakened in many countries. Besides declarations by heads of states, celebrities and organizations, there were also spontaneous offers of military aid. At the beginning of July 1920, approximately 200 Belgian officers reported to the Polish mission in Belgium, expressing their readiness to enlist in the Polish Army. In the memo of the Minister of Foreign Affairs in Warsaw, it was stressed that, "This is not an entirely new matter, since our mission in Brussels has for the last year informed us that volunteers have been reporting and inquiring about conditions of service."[2]

The volunteers from Belgium were certainly aware that the Polish Uprising of 1830 had prevented Tsar Nicholas I of Russia from intervening in Western Europe and had saved Belgian independence. In any case their motivation was not limited to historical considerations, anticommunism was also present in every application. On July 1 the Polish Military Attache in London reported that the Danish Captain Palludan proposed the organization of a machine gun unit to fight against the Bolsheviks on the Polish frontline. The Captain, who had previously fought in the Archangel region against the Bolsheviks, agreed to take the equipment and pay of the Polish government. His unit was to number around 100 soldiers. Pilsudski basically agreed to this proposition, recommending only that he provide further details and the foreseeable costs of the venture.[3]

Even some British were ready to volunteer to support the Polish Republic. It was a fundamental breakthrough, particularly in light of the trade talks of Krassin in London, and the withdrawal of British involvement in helping the Whites in Russia's south. The British General Crozier made a proposal to the Polish Military Attache in London that a British Legion be organized to fight the Bolsheviks. The General had previously been the head of the British Mission in Kovno, therefore he had firsthand knowledge of Russian matters. His proposal was communicated to Warsaw on July 12. Shortly after, the Chief of the General Staff, Gen. Stanisław Haller, asked the Attache in London about the organizational conditions of the Legion and its presumed size. Crozier's initiative was of an individual nature and remained without any connection to Foreign Office policy.[4]

Offers flowed in not only from the West. The nations of the Caucasus looked to Poland, as did many democratically minded Russians, since in the summer of 1920 it was the only significant force effectively fighting the Bolsheviks. Some of the Russians with the Socialist Revolutionary activist Boris Savinkov, the former member of the Duma Fiodor Rodichev, and the writer Dimitr Merejkovskij gathered in Warsaw. Thanks to their attempts with Pilsudski in summer 1920, plans to establish a volunteer army from anti–Bolshevik Russians and prisoners of war in Poland became a reality. White officers were also enlisted. They treated the venture as a second front assisting Gen. Wrangel's army on the Crimea, and counted on the possibility of the forces joining up.[5] Despite the favorable conditions, none of the Russian units, nor the Belgian, Danish, and British, arrived in Poland. The speed with which the Bolsheviks marched towards the Vistula River overtook any preparation whatsoever.

There was one more direction from which help could be expected, namely the United States, which was to supply not only volunteers but also credit to buy equipment and enlist a highly qualified air force cadre. This expectation was shared by the Polish military and political elements and an echo of this can be found in the diplomatic-military correspondence between Warsaw and the mission in Washington, where the air force's matters took up a disproportionate amount of space. Signals coming from several western states persuaded the Ministry of Foreign Affairs to outline the basis for accepting volunteers. In a document of July 20, 1920, the Ministry announced that the volunteer formations could wear special uniforms. It was not specified then whether they would be those of other countries or if they would merely differ from those of the regular units of the Polish Army. It was further stressed that the command of specific-country units was to be in the hands of an officer of that country, that they would take a Polish salary and would be subject to the Polish commander in chief in operational matters. It was foreseen that there would be a relative discount in duty, transport, and financial matters.[6]

On July 19 a decree was issued by the National Defense Council, which opened up the possibility of enlisting foreign volunteers to the ranks of the Polish Army.[7] The situation in regard to volunteers from America differed from other situations. The growth of isolation, the distance in relation to European affairs and the League of Nations, and the approaching Presidential elections made Polish attempts doubly difficult. In addition, Congress was in recess during the summer months, which paralyzed any discussion of credit for Poland. On the other hand, war on the outskirts of Europe began to make its way onto the front pages of newspapers. The fall of Poland was perceived to pose a threat to the stability of Europe, although there was no lack of critical commentary on Piłsudski and his eastern policy. The shift of the frontline into ethnically Polish territory enlivened the Polish community in America. An array of veterans of Gen. Haller's Blue Army announced their readiness to return to Poland, Polish diplomatic and consulate representations and the newspapers of the Polish community sounded the alarm that there were no guidelines for handling these potential volunteers. There were organizations that helped volunteers, such as the Committee of National Defense in Chicago with Professor Tomasz Siemiradzki, and the American Committee for the Defense of Poland, with Jan F. Smulski and Col. Franciszek Fronczak at the head, and on the continent, the Provisional Committee for American Military Help for Poland was founded in Warsaw. These organizations carried out propaganda and lobbied for American-Polish cooperation and military aid for Poland.[8]

Meanwhile the enlistment of volunteers posed many problems to overcome. This concerned the U.S.'s attitude to war and Polish policy in the east, which had undergone no fundamental change since 1919.

Gen. Zygmunt Brynk, the Polish Military Attache in Washington, expressed the hope that the occupation of Kiev by the Poles would influence the crystallization of the policy of Wilson administration in regard to Poland and Eastern Europe. "The instability and lack of definition in policy up until now must give way to a firm declaration either for or against Polish action." In another part of the report the Attache wrote that he expected an explanation of the situation in connection with an $8,000,000 line of credit to buy military material: "Does the opinion prevail that it is necessary to help Poland with the strongest forces as the only country to have defeated the Bolsheviks, or will our offensive be considered as an unaided action, which ought not to be supported in the thought often put forward against Poles, that of Polish imperialism and excessive territorial appetites — currently it is still difficult to reply."[9]

On May 25 the envoy of the Republic, Prince Casimir Lubomirski, placed a memo on the subject of previous agreements for military purchases in the hands of the Secretary of State, in the hope of a positive explanation.[10]

By June 10 the previously agreed purchases were canceled due to resistance by the Treasury Department.[11]

There were attempts to overcome these obstacles in a variety of ways. Polish representatives appealed to traditionally friendly ties and the input of the Americans to Poland's current military effort. On July 5 Lubomirski, in a pompous speech, mentioned it in the following words:

> ...Hundreds of American men are today fighting in our Army. Thousands of Americans who emigrated from Poland have returned to take up a gage of battle. Over our swaying lines fly the volunteers of the Kościuszko Esquadrille, full-blooded Americans, translating into action the ideals of their ancestry. These noble young crusaders have more than repaid the debt of Kościuszko and Pulaski.... Like the Polish heroes who came to aid Washington, these Americans came in greater numbers to the aid of Poland.... We are proud and grateful for these spirits, but we do plead for America's understanding, for America's material support and for America's voice to help us make the peace that will prevent further sacrifice....[12]

In the situation that existed at the time, all help was eagerly received, although undoubtedly the priority was to obtain equipment and highly qualified volunteers. Polish missions and consulates reported an ever-increasing flow of volunteers, which could not be enlisted without suitable legal conditions and the agreement of the Administration. On the other hand they did not want to squander this enthusiasm. On July 14, 1920, Gen. Zygmunt Brynk reported from Washington: "A large number of expert officers are continuously reporting for the Polish Army, and many Poles and Americans are reporting as soldiers. The envoy intends to begin enlistment action and is awaiting the decision of the Foreign Office. Poles importunately demand enlistment in the army."[13] Lubomirski also confirmed that mood, indicating that airmen were also involved.[14] Meanwhile the State Department maintained a policy of not entangling the U.S. in the Polish-Bolshevik conflict. In a later dispatch, Lubomirski lamented, "The position of the administration, which is not issuing weapons, is preventing the enlistment of volunteers and it is even difficult for airmen to get passports."[15]

At the beginning of August, the shift of the front to the vicinity of Warsaw assumed all the characteristics of defeat. On August 5 Farman reported that he had dispatched part of his staff and equipment out of the capital.[16] In desperation, the Polish authorities sought outside help. They seized every opportunity to strengthen their own forces. On August 6, Prince Eustachy Sapieha, Minister of Foreign Affairs, sent a dispatch to Prince Lubomirski demanding that certain decisive steps be taken with the aim of organizing volunteer artillery regiments, air squadrons, and armored units (tank units).[17]

On the same day the Polish High Command sent a long report to its Military Attache in the United States about the conditions that had been offered to the volunteers. They declared that the volunteers would be paid according to their rank and the standards accorded them in their own countries. The salary was to be paid in Polish currency at a rate set once every ten days. The families of those who fell would be provided with help under the same conditions as the soldiers and officers of the Polish Army. It was expected that the volunteers would declare their service until a signing of a peace treaty with the Bolsheviks. As far as organizational matters were concerned, the structure of command would be based on the organizational principles of the given country, using commanders from that country. The Polish government announced the possible covering of the organizational costs and propaganda. Moreover, the Poles expected that the U.S. administration would give its agreement to the purchase of weapons, ammunition, and uniforms at their wholesale price.[18]

These stipulations were undoubtedly the result of the experiences of 1919, when the question of finance and a lack of the implementation of western organizational standards were some of the obstacles in getting volunteers to Poland. This time it was decided to fly in the face of expectations as much as possible. Since the military situation was critical, following a dispatch from Piłsudski and the Minister of Military Affairs, Gen. Kazimierz Sosnkowski sent a dispatch to Gen. Brynk to use all available resources to send to Poland "as many complete air force squadrons, together with pilots, as you can muster. The number of aircraft and people is unlimited. The squadrons are to be a fighter group for bombardment, completely equipped with a sufficient amount of ammunition, at the moment at least for six weeks."[19]

It was the first time that the positive echo of the airforce contribution in the Kiev Expedition was present with such force, with indirect and enthusiastic evaluation of the American pilots.

Up against the wall, Lubomirski decided to renew contact with Col. Harry Howland, who in July 1920 had taken off his uniform and taken up residence on Wall Street. On August 9, Lubomirski telephoned Howland, asking him about the feasibility of enlisting volunteers and the organization of a volunteer legion. On the next day the envoy received a lengthy report about the feasibility of the whole project. Knowing Howland's involvement in Polish affairs, it was difficult to suspect him of a lack of goodwill; nonetheless his answer was in the best case cautious, if not negative. Howland set forth a range of obstacles for Lubomirski. Firstly, the support of the U.S. government had to be guaranteed. Anticipating the resistance of the administration, the Colonel concluded that it was necessary to obtain:

> assurance from the American Government that it would not object to the enrollment of Americans or Polish Americans in a military force to be sent to Poland. It is certain that some official consent, whether it be written or simply verbal, must be obtained from the American Government before any steps can be taken.

In his opinion, the Polish mission ought to have probed the State Department in this matter, and about the possibility of obtaining passports. Nonetheless, in Howland's opinion, time was an important factor; in other words, in the light of the dramatic situation near Warsaw, was there enough time for the volunteers to be appropriately trained and transformed into a coherent military formation, not to mention transporting it across the Atlantic. The next obstacle was money, and how to guarantee the flow of funds. Fundamentally, assuming that the administration in Washington would not supply them and that the government in Warsaw did not have them at its disposal, Howland came to the conclusion that the only chance would be to invite tenders for loans from the Polish community in America. This in turn would have demanded the activation of all the territorial organizations, which would have prolonged the time taken to achieve this. The matter of the volunteers' provisions, uniforms and salaries, in Howland's opinion, ought to be based on American standards. He further considered that, similarly to 1919, the best candidate to conduct the organization process and to command the volunteer legion would be Gen. A. W. Bjornstad. Thanks to him, he wrote, "I am sure that it would go by leaps and bounds, and that it would have the Polish-American Military Contingent in Poland within the least practicable time."[20]

There was no sign whatsoever that these obstacles would be overcome swiftly. What's more, the contact made between Lubomirski and Howland coincided chronologically with the diplomatic note of Secretary of State Bainbridge Colby from August 10, 1920, whose meaning was decidedly unfavorable for Poland.[21]

Repetitions of Lubomirski's appeals brought no results, neither did pressure by Polish-Americans. The American Committee for the Defense of Poland organized on August 15 a range of meetings in various American towns, with the participation of local politicians, congressmen, and city Mayors. Most of them overwhelmingly passed a resolution, which a delegation made up of 300 activists took to Washington. On August 18, it was handed over to Colby and Joseph Tumulty, the Secretary of the sick President Wilson. A head of the delegation, a very well known doctor and veteran of WWI named Fronczak gave a spirited appeal on Poland's behalf, but in reply he heard only words of sympathy and no concrete obligations.[22]

Lubomirski and Gen. Brynk did not wash their hands of this matter. On August 13 Lubomirski sent a copy of the plan of the High Command of the Polish Armed Forces to Gen. Bjornstad together with his own commentary. He contacted the General twice more about the matter. On August 14 the envoy addressed Colby about credit to equip three air force squadrons with ten planes each and purchase 500 machine guns, 120 artillery pieces and equipment for ten divisions with an appropriate amount of ammunition. It was the quantity for a legion if one had to be organized, or for reinforcements of forces already fighting on the Vistula.[23]

At the same time the mission tried to find a solution to the question of passports and visas for the volunteers. Gen. Brynk thought up a way to circumvent the objections of the State Department. Since it was virtually impossible to obtain a passport for a direct trip to Poland, the volunteers would declare their destination as France. Brynk intended to prepare a letter of recommendation, which the volunteers were to present in Paris, and the Polish mission there was to facilitate the issuing of Polish visas on the spot. The Attache also left with a project aimed at overcoming the financial shortcoming. It depended on inviting tenders for large loans among the Polish population in America under the slogan "Help for the Polish Army." Brynk expected that American *Polonia* would raise $1,000,000 in three weeks, the next million or two in the next few weeks. Polish organizations that raised large sums of money could expect to have a particular air force squadron named after them, and the same went for individual donors. A noble rivalry was expected for the right to an indirect presence on the Polish-Bolshevik frontline. Gen. Brynk planned to assign resources raised in this way to purchases for the squadron that had been officially ordered by the Polish High Command. Through this procedure, they counted on breaking the connection between the mission and the effort to build a volunteer legion, at least as far as the State Department was concerned. The planes purchased in this way were only to be given a crew of volunteers from America after the transaction had been made. After these stages had been completed, they planned to finalize the pilots' journey to France. From there, they were to fly directly to Poland without passports.

Gen. Brynk's plans developed in the middle of August. Before the Attache put them into action, the war on the approaches of Warsaw underwent a dramatic turnaround of Poland's fortune. News of the breakthrough in the battle reached Washington on August 18, 1920.[24]

Although the "official" path taken by the mission brought no tangible result, it would have been a misunderstanding to say that the position of the State Department towards Poland mirrored that of American society. Many newspapers saw the need to help, and many put forward matter-of-fact arguments for this. The *Baltimore Sun* wrote, for example, that if Poland won the war, she would become a powerful state, but if the Bolsheviks won, then it would be a catastrophe for Europe and the world. In both cases, the paper concluded, it would mean a departure from the conditions of the Versaille treaty. In both cases, it was argued, America's inactivity was harmful. There were also biting ripostes. On the demands for the Polish Army to stop at the ethnic border, a commentator at the *Evening Mail* reminded readers that the American Expeditionary Forces had not had any such hesitations in relation to Germany two years before. Why then was Poland supposed to stop at the eastern ethnic border, which was impossible to defend?[25]

The project to establish a volunteer force somehow leaked to the public to the extent that people who could supply practical help began to report to Lubomirski. On August 18 Lubomirski received a letter from the sculptor Gutzon Borglum, who in his time had supported the efforts of Paul Baer. Baer, as is well known, had promised Paderewski in the autumn of 1919 to organize another squadron. Borglum wrote that in connection with the plans for a legion for Poland he was ready to hand over his large country estate near Stamford, Connecticut. The advantage of this was that during the years of the Great War, the premises had served as a training camp for Czecho-Slovak volunteers. There were barracks that could accommodate 1,000 men and serve as a training camp or as recruitment center. Borglum sent a copy of his letter to Colby.[26]

Another, less feasible, idea was the project to send a flotilla of submarines to Poland, which according to the architect of the project, Maj. Gen. Daniel Appleton, could operate in waters of minimal depth. No less feasible, although this time not for technical reasons, was the appeal by an individual by the name of Poray, who in a telegram to Lubomirski demanded help in transporting several hundreds of volunteers to Poland, whom he had managed to organize in one of Pittsburgh's suburbs. After visiting Pittsburgh, the representatives of the Polish Consulate confirmed that the said neighborhood was populated mostly by Italians and Greeks. They were not even able to locate the address where the volunteers were to be meet. Both matters, despite their impracticability, characterized the prevailing mood of those days.[27]

Characteristically, just as in 1919, the lack of cooperation of the Administration did not dampen the efforts of many friends of Poland in American society. The head of the American Flying Club, Col. Benjamin Castle, made persistent attempts on behalf of the 7th Squadron. In summer, he launched a major propaganda campaign. The Club was used as an information point and recruitment center for those interested in service in Poland. Here he posted bills for airmen visiting the Club who might join the Squadron. On July 2 Castle received a dispatch from Fauntleroy with an appeal to send reinforcements. After this, he decided to send a telegram to President Wilson requesting the withdrawal of objections by the State Department and for an exception to be made for 23 airmen who had decided to go to Poland. He invoked the bravery of those who had already resisted the Bolsheviks, and the example of the Lafayette Escadrille. However, he received no reply.[28]

Failure in this did not diminish his activity. On July 9, 1920, he expressed his opinion in the *Evening Telegram*, summoning the youth of

America to join the ranks of the Kościuszko Squadron. He himself would have joined, he wrote, but for ill health.[29]

Appeals of that sort touched upon a sensitive, romantic strand of the American psyche and were emotionally charged in the sense that they contained a call to help a newly reborn pro–American democracy in faraway Europe. It also suited those who sought combat experience unavailable in peace-time America. Undoubtedly it was thanks to Col. Castle that the 7th Squadron received so much publicity and the lion's share of reinforcements during the war. In reality the only form of aid that reached Poland from the United States was half a dozen volunteers.

8 | In Defense of the City of the Lion

Neither personnel nor materiel reinforcements arrived during the general battle waged near Warsaw, nor was there any aid for Lwów, which was facing its own battle of life and death. At the very beginning of August 1920, when the Bolsheviks occupied the Brest fortress, the road to Warsaw seemed to wide open and defenseless. The fall of the Polish capital appeared to be inevitable. Foreign missions, with a few exceptions, began to evacuate from Warsaw, the world press began to write about the fall of Poland. On August 11 the *Universal News Service* reported from Washington that the Secretary of State recommended the U.S. legation move to Grudziądz. Other sources confirmed the information.[1]

Piłsudski took full responsibility for the preparation of a counteroffensive. At first his plan depended on a concentration of forces under the cover of the fortress at Brest. When the fortress fell on August 1, his plan had to be completely rethought. The French advisor to the Polish General Staff, General Maxime Weygand, opted for a concentration of forces around Warsaw and a linear defense along the natural lines. Waygand envisiged only a limited counterattack. Rozwadowski, who from July 22 was the Chief of General Staff, proposed a counterattack with a force concentrated near Garwolin. None of these plans gained full recognition by the Commander in Chief. It was on August 6 that Piłsudski prepared the basic idea of his maneuver. It established a broad pincer movement from the south, striking the Bolsheviks' left wing engaged near Warsaw and closing off their retreat path to the east. Piłsudski simultaneously issued an order dividing the armed forces into three fronts: the Northern, Central, and Southern. The 7th Squadron was assigned to the

Southern Front in the area bordered by the line between Włodzimierz Wołyński, Hrubieszów, and Zamość, all the way to the Romanian border. At the same time, the Marshal recommended a concentration of troops in the vicinity of Puławy, under the cover of the Wieprz River, south of Warsaw. This was to be established from the 1st and the 3rd Infantry Division Legions, the 21st Mountain Division, the 14th *Wielkopolska* Infantry Division and other smaller units. These units had been delegated to carry out the main strike. The key to success was that designated units were to swiftly isolate themselves from the Southern Front, while at the same time effectively defending their right wing in order to prevent Bolshevik units operating in the Lwów area from taking part in battle. The next crucial element for the success of operation was to maintain the complete secrecy of the plan and to guarantee maximum surprise by attacking at the very moment of the full engagement of the enemy near Warsaw. Piłsudski personally led a counteroffensive in the morning hours of August 16 on the Wieprz River. His presence among the units, as Gen. Maxime Weygand wrote, transformed morale, which had been shaken after a retreat lasting a few weeks. The Bolsheviks were completely surprised; they did not expect the Polish armed forces to be ready for a greater offensive. Their defeat was more complete because the day before Piłsudski's counterattack, the 5th Army under the command of Gen. Władysław Sikorski gained a local success in action north of Warsaw along the Vistula. On August 18 the Poles' success was already evident. The Bolshevik *Mozyr* Group, which approached Warsaw from the southeast, was smashed, as was the 16th Army, which attacked Warsaw from Mińsk Mazowiecki and Radzymin.[2]

By August 25 the Bolsheviks had lost 25,000 killed and wounded, with 66,000 taken prisoner and over 231 artillery pieces, 1,023 machine guns, and a huge amount of military equipment captured. The 3rd, 4th, 15th, and 16th Bolshevik Armies found themselves in a panic retreat. The battle was swiftly baptized as the 18th decisive battle in world history. It was already clear that Piłsudski had halted the Bolshevik advance into the heart of Europe.[3]

The Air Force played a role in the battle, though not as great as in the defense of Lwów. In the first case, it was used mainly for reconnaissance of the direction of the advance and determining the size of the enemy concentration, whereas at Lwów it played an independent role, and in the days from August 16 to 18 even a major strategic role, stopping the march of the Bolshevik *Konarmia* on Lwów.

At least ten air squadrons were engaged in the defense of Warsaw, with nominally 80 planes at their disposal.⁴ Two squadrons worked directly with Piłsudski's operation on the Wieprz. The 3rd Squadron operated directly on behalf of the High Command HQ, and the 10th led reconnaissance in the areas of Garwolin, Żelechów, Stoczek Łukówski, Międzyrzec, Siedlce, and Łuków, advancing in the wake of Piłsudski's counteroffensive. On August 19 both squadrons were assigned to the 4th Army and were ordered to go to the airfield at Siedlce. By the 22nd of August they had already moved to Warsaw, and then they were moved closer to the front, this time to Biel airfield near Małkina. In general, two thirds of the Polish air force took part in the Battle of Warsaw, yet the outcome of the battle was not decided in the air.⁵

In Lwów the situation was completely different. On August 11, at the moment when the Bolsheviks were approaching Warsaw, the Southern Front, led by Gen. Wacław Iwaszkiewicz, consisted of the 6th Army and the allied Ukrainian Army under the command of Gen. Pavlenko, which defended the extreme southern wing to the east of Stanislawow. Opposite the Ukrainians, who defended the key railway line linking Poland with Romania, the 14th Bolshevik Army was stationed. To the north of the Ukrainians, were the 12th and 13th Infantry Divisions and the 6th Army and the 6th Division of the Polish Army. These units defended Lwów from Budenny's *Konarmia*, Jakir's Operational Group and the 11th Bolshevik Army. The Southern Front Air Force was based on the 3rd Air Force Wing (*Dyon*), made up of the 5th and 6th Intelligence Squadrons, the 7th Kościuszko Squadron, and the 3rd Mobile Air Park. These units were nominally stationed at Lewandówka airport, near Lwów. Beside the 3rd *Dyon*, the 15th Fighter Squadron were also stationed there. The Southern Front Air Force had 32 planes for combat, but almost half of these were not fit for combat. The Intelligence Squadrons were equipped with Haviland DH 9 planes and even obsolete German two-seater Gotha aircraft. The Fighter Squadrons, for example, the 15th, flew Fokker D VII and Albatros BII aircraft. Only the Kościuszko Squadron had new Ballila or Albatros D III aircraft. Only a small number of planes were equipped with machine guns, and generally there were no means of communication. The technical state shortly after the end of the battle near Lwów was confirmed by the reports covering the period between August 10 and 25. On August 25 the 5th Squadron had barely one functioning aircraft and five directed for general repair. The 6th Squadron had three functioning aircraft, two in need of repair, and the 7th Kościuszko Squadron had five aircraft, two temporarily not functioning and three being repaired (of those one was in general repair). The 15th

8. In Defense of the City of the Lion 143

Squadron had four functioning aircraft, one undergoing minor repair and six in major renovation. Thus the 3rd *Dyon* had only 13 planes that could take off on combat action. At the height of battle in Lwów, and in the space of barely one day, the Southern Front Air Force numbered 19 aircraft.[6]

From August 9 to 10, 1920, Maj. Cedric Fauntleroy commanded the 3rd Squadron, and on August 18 he was entrusted with command over the whole air force of the Southern Front, while at the same time fulfilling the duties of the Head of the 6th Army Air Force.[7]

In the first Fauntleroy replaced Stefan Bastyr, who died on August 6, 1920, and in the second he replaced Capt. Camillo Perini, who had been promoted to lead the Air Force Section of the High Command. Lt. George Crawford took over Fauntleroy's place at the head of the 7th Squadron. These appointments occurred at a critical moment in the war, which confirms the great trust with which the foreign volunteers were treated, and Americans in particular.[8]

When Fauntleroy took charge of the 3rd *Dyon*, Budenny was carrying out maneuvers near Beresteczko, Brody, Toporów, and Chołojów. The initial battle against Budenny from July 26 to August 6 ended with a undecisive outcome. The *Konarmia* tried to stop the three Polish Infantry Divisions and two Cavalry divisions. After they had drawn away from the Poles, the *Konarmia* concentrated itself from August 8 to August 10 in the region between Beresteczko and Kozin, where they had a rest for several days. The 3rd *Dyon* kept in constant contact with it, plaguing the *Konarmia* with bombardment and airborne fire. Every day between three and four hours of raids were carried out, and the American pilots played a significant role in this. On August 12 Budenny moved on Kamionka Strumiłowa and Busk. The direction of his march was detected by the air force. On August 11 Maj. Fauntleroy was at work in the air, and his flight lasted one hour and 45 minutes. Lt. Crawford was in the air for two hours and 55 minutes, and Sec. Lt. Senkowski's flight lasted two hours. The next day, one of the longest flights, which lasted exactly two hours and 55 minutes was carried out by Crawford.[9]

On the basis of the reports obtained in this way, the Polish Operational Group of Gen. Paweł Szymański received the task of cooperating with Col. Juliusz Rómmel's Cavalry Group in the area of Toporów-Stanisławczyk. On August 13 the 3rd *Dyon* carried out intelligence to determine precisely the enemy's intentions in the areas of Toporów, Szczurowice, Retków, Beresteczko, Stojanów, and Radziechów. Pilot Paweł Tysler navigator Lt. Kazimierz Kubala reported that in Toporów there

Top: Fauntleroy behind controls of his aircraft. *Bottom:* Balilla aircraft of the Kościuszko Squadron at Lewandówka. August, 1920. (Courtesy of Dr. Tomasz Kopański, Warsaw.)

8. In Defense of the City of the Lion 145

Balilla of the 7th Squadron near Lwów. (Courtesy of Dr. Tomasz Kopański, Warsaw.)

were 60 horse carts of the Polish Infantry, and by Zabłotów there was an active artillery battery. Bridges over the Radostawka River had not been destroyed. In the region of Majdan Nowy, Monastyrki, and Ohladów they noticed a group of *Konarmia* horse carts numbering between 120 and 600 and a similar amount of cavalry. Somewhat less of the armed forces were observed in the vicinity of Kolonia Mytnica (around 60 horse carts) and Beresteczko. In Burkacze and the vicinity there were around 70 horse carts parked in Strzemilcza and the surrounding area. On the road from the Wygoda estate in the direction of Uwina they counted 40 carts, from Uwina to Radziechów the presence of 80 horse-carts was confirmed. Then in the area around Sebin around 900 carts were camped together with 400 cavalrymen, and between Niemilów and Środopolce around 600 cavalry and 50 carts. Air force intelligence confirmed the direction of the *Konarmia* march, despite increasingly effective camouflage.

The mentioning of these very small places, which were difficult to find on a map, confirms above all the preciseness of the reconnaissance. However, the arrangement of the information on the ground was not easy. The Bolshevik cavalry most often marched forward at night through large areas of forest or along rivers, skillfully taking advantage of what the terrain had to offer. They swiftly learnt how to dismount from the panic-stricken horses and how to fire on the planes from the ground in a more organized manner. At this stage Budenny ordered *tachanki*, or horse carts with machine guns mounted on top of each, to be positioned at the front and rear of the marching column. The *tachanki* had the same fire strength as a nest of heavy machine guns, and fulfilled additional functions of observation and anti-aircraft weapons.

On August 13 Capt. Corsi distinguished himself in the air by dropping 24 kg of bombs during his almost two-hour flight, as did Senkowski, in the air for 2 hours 35 minutes, and also the less well known temporary member of the crew of the 7th Squadron, Kubala-Tysler and Meissner-Jabłoński, who carried out flights of almost two hours.[10]

On the basis of the reports obtained, the command of the Southern Front issued an order to Gen. Szymański's Group and Col. Juliusz Rómmel's Cavalry Group to shift the 38th Infantry Regiment, reinforced with an artillery battery, armored train and sentry battalion, from Brzuchowice to Sokal. On the same day at 12:50 P.M., the 7th Squadron sent two planes into the air. At the same time Maj. Fauntleroy ordered the whole of the 15th Fighter Squadron to commence battle against the enemy cavalry. Four planes carried out this task. After they returned to the airfield and lodged their reports, the Southern Front Command addressed the High Command in Warsaw. Their proposal was to leave the 15th Fighter Squadron (which were thought to be best prepared to fight the cavalry) under the direct tactical supervision of Maj. Fauntleroy. The Command of the Front wanted to group together the two most efficient and experienced air force units, with a greater number of planes equipped with machine guns. However, the 7th Squadron had barely two. The High Command gave permission for the use of the 15th Squadron to this end, but this was not an immediate solution to the problem of reinforcements, which depended on supplies from abroad. Very little reached Poland, considering strikes in factories, West European ports, and Gdańsk shipyards.

At 11:00 P.M. of August 13 the Southern Front Command ordered an organization of the defense along the line of the Rivers Bug and Strypa. It indicated the movement of the enemy cavalry in the region of Beresteczko, through Łopatyń in the general direction of Lwów. Once again, it ought to be stressed that this was the result of Air Force intelligence.[11] On August 14, the Polish 6th and 15th Infantry Divisions retreated to the line of the River Bug, and Gen. Szymański's Group remained in the region of Toporów. The 7th and 15th Squadrons carried

8. In Defense of the City of the Lion

Balilla's repair at Lewandówka. August, 1920. (Courtesy of Dr. Tomasz Kopański, Warsaw.)

out a few flights, during which they attacked the enemy cavalry, and the 5th and 6th Squadrons led intensive reconnaissance sorties. Crawford and Weber distinguished themselves that day.[12] The next day (August 15) brought further battle for Gen. Szymański's Group and Col. Rómmel's Group. Gen. Szymański withdrew his units to the western bank of the River Bug; however, Rómmel effectively put a stop to the Bolshevik attempts to press on to the Bug north of Lwów. The air reconnaissance from that day discovered an enemy concentration in the region of Poburzany and Derewlany. The 15th Squadron took off twice. In the evening it suffered severe losses, as Sec. Lt. Rozmarek was wounded for the second time in few days and his plane was forced to land. Three days later Rozmarek died of loss of blood. In addition, also from the 15th Squadron, Lt. Józef Hendricks' plane was forced to land, but the pilot managed to return to his airfield and shortly after he carried on flying. In general, the day brought increased airborne activity. Of the 7th Squadron, the following carried out combat flights: Capt. Corsi dropped 24 kg of bombs, Lt. Chess bombed the enemy with a similar amount, and Corsi, who flew again that day with Chess, dropped another 48 kg of bombs. It was clear that Budenny's approach led to the ultimate fusion of intelligence, fighter and bombing functions by all the squadrons defending access to Lwów.[13]

The most hard-fought battles with Budenny took place in the region between Busk and Kamionka Strumiłowa and near Chlojów. The furious 15th Squadron, with the help of the 7th Squadron, attacked the first of the concentrations mentioned. To a certain extent, effective action was made more difficult by uneven terrain and numerous forests, which facilitated better camouflage. Despite that the cavalry suffered serious losses. Reconnaissance missions that day reported a new tactic used by an enemy column. At the first signal of the approaching planes, the columns turned around with lightning speed and marched away from the frontline. This was observed several times by Sergeant Piątkowski, who was an observer and flew several times with Fauntleroy. Budenny's next trick consisted of delegating smaller units of the cavalry to simulate the march of a major unit, galloping over a large area, kicking up dust and capturing the attention of the Air Force. In the uneven terrain the Bolsheviks arranged machine guns positions and opened fire on the surprised crews. The Bolsheviks had also learnt not to react to the presence of the airmen if the territorial conditions allowed it, for example in the forest. In that way they forced the airmen to lower their altitude and fall into the trap, and when this happened they opened heavy machine gun fire, which was very effective.[14]

The activity of the Bolshevik Air Force was much in evidence during those days. According to M. Strojev, a Bolshevik air-force officer and the author of the book *The Air Force with the Cavalry*, the Bolsheviks had eight functioning planes, well trained pilots and mechanics in that area. The Southern Front Command, because of this, issued an order for an immediate report of the number and direction of the enemy flights. In the event of spotting an enemy plane, they were ordered to immediately interrupt *Hughes'* communications and with highest possible speed to inform the 3rd Operational Section of the Front HQ. The High Command was concerned about organizing an appropriate air force counter-action.

However, it was difficult to note enemy air force activity, despite repetitive alarms here and there. It was extremely obvious that the Bolshevik airmen avoided combat engagement in the critical days of battle.

On the night of August 15, under cover of dark, more of Budenny's detachments succeeded in clearing the Bug River. The air force reconnaissance carried out in the morning of August 16th confirmed a cavalry

8. In Defense of the City of the Lion 149

crossing in the region between Busk and Kamionka Strumiłowa. The cavalry immediately attacked energetically in a western and southwestern direction. The situation of Lwów became critical. In persistent battle, the 12th and 13th Polish Infantry Divisions maintained the line of the Rivers Strypa and Bug as far as Krasne, but the 5th and above all the 6th Infantry Divisions did not manage to keep the Bug in the area of Busk and Kamionka, exposing the same road to Lwów. There was a gap the width of 50 kms, and the enemy units had poured into it. Budenny was around 40 kms from the city. Polish Air Force estimated that around two cavalry divisions together with artillery and armored cars had crossed the Bug River.

Intelligence carried out in the early hours of that day by the 5th Squadron included the areas of Lwów, Zadwórze, Lisko, Niesłuchów, Streptóv, and Milatyn. In Streptóv the position was still held by the Poles, but on the road from Milatyn to Niesłuchów, the movement of around 300 Bolshevik cavalrymen was confirmed, on whom they dropped four bombs. This flight lasted from 8:25 to 9:45 A.M. The second flight began at 10:10 A.M. and lasted for one hour and ten minutes. The presence of the enemy cavalry was confirmed, numbering around 200 horses, in the forest south of Kozłów, where the bombardment had been carried out. However, the Fighter Squadrons received assignments to attack the enemy in the region of Lwów, Wierzblany, Poburzany, Streptów, Żelechów, Rzepniów, Kozłów, Niesłuchów, Jakiniów, and Dziedziców. At 9:20 A.M., first to take off was Lt. Bartowiak's crew from the 15th Squadron. The pilot observed enemy movement in the direction of Lwów from Wierzblany, through Miroszyn, Poburzany, Rakobuty, and Rzepniów and immediately attacked the column, inflicting heavy losses and causing dispersal of the column. The presence of Bolshevik armored cars and an armored train in the region of Krasne and Busk was something entirely new. At around 9:45 A.M., Lt. Dziembowski, the commander of the 15th Squadron, took off in a Fokker D.VII 511 and Sec. Lt. Lewandowski in a Fokker D.VII 505 with the task of attacking the Bolshevik cavalry crossing in the region of Derewlana and Busk. On the road from Jabłonówka to Busk, the airmen attacked a column of 1,000 cavalry with horse carts, causing heavy losses. Then they bombarded the Bolshevik sappers attempting to repair the crossing over the Bug by the village of Poburzany. In the 7th Squadron Lt. Weber's combat action lasted from midday until 2:20 P.M., and he bombed a column of 100 horse carts. Maj. Fauntleroy, together with Sergeant Piątkowski, took off at 7:10 P.M. and confirmed the approach of a mass cavalry column in the direct vicinity of Lwów.

Balilla of the 7th Squadron over Lwów. (Courtesy of Dr. Tomasz Kopański, Warsaw.)

Cavalry and wagons could be seen on virtually every road leading into Lwów from the east and the northeast. That day, among others in the 7th Squadron who carried out their assignments, was Capt. Corsi, who was in the air for two hours and ten minutes, during which he bombed the enemy with two bombs.[15]

The fatal threat posed to Lwów did not paralyze its inhabitants, but rather mobilized them. An atmosphere of responsibility and preparation for the defense could be felt all around. Some inhabitants, and mainly those who were not able to serve or work for the military, gathered on *Unia Lubelska* Square to support the airmen flying off into action. The citizens of the city counted every returning plane and cried over every loss.

It was really a crucial moment. On August 16 the greatest battle began between the air force and the cavalry. Polish and American pilots attacked using tactics based on previous experience, with some corrections forced by preventive measures the Bolsheviks had begun to use. Since there was more than one squadron based at one airfield, the planes took off in strict order to avoid accidents during take-off and landing and to save extremely precious time. In this way, there were always several planes in the air at any given moment. After completing his sortie, the pilot returned and lodged an oral report at the airfield while the ground crew replenished the fuel, bomb and ammunition supplies. Budenny and his cavalry experienced it as a constant mass bombing, although there could be only between four and five aircraft in the air at a time, and that day barely 16 aircraft overall participated in the action.

The attack on the cavalry columns was preceded by the occupation of a suitable air position. If possible, they hid in the sun, to prevent effective observation and anti-craft fire from the ground. The attack was begun by single aircraft, which took their turns bombing from a height of between 700 and 800 meters. Antiaircraft fire was of little effect at that altitude. The bombardment almost always threw the enemy column or formation into disarray and panic. Just after the bomb load had been released, the planes came again and attacked the shifting columns from a ceiling of between 200 and 300 meters, with machine guns. The effect of such an attack was virtually always crushing. The horses were not used to planes and panicked, the column was further torn apart, and the advance was further disrupted.

On that day, the 15th and the 7th Squadrons effectively attacked the horse carts and cavalry near the village of Kupcze, near Kozłów, Rzepniów, Milatyn, and Kędzierzawice. The Polish Intelligence even received information that Budenny himself had been injured by shrapnel during one of the attacks. The Polish Air Force suffered no losses, but a number of aircraft had been shot and required repairs. The actions of the 3rd *Dyon* were highly appreciated by the Southern Front HQ:

> On the 15th and 16th of August, the 15th Fighter Squadron under the command of Lt. Dziembowski distinguished itself in action against Budenny's cavalry army, but on August 16 the whole of the 3rd Air *Dyon* (the 15th and 7th Kościuszko Squadron and the 5th and 6th Reconnaissance Squadrons) under the command of Maj. Fauntleroy, distinguished itself by bombing the enemy, attacking with machine guns, causing a great loss of enemy horses, and carrying out intelligence operations. On August 16, the 3rd *Dyon* carried out 49 flights over the enemy with 16 aircraft.[16]

In order 3403/III from August 16, the Command of the Front stressed: "Today the famous 3rd Air Force *Dyon* took part in action against the Bolshevik cavalry. Today, it carried out about 40 sorties over the enemy, with whom it fought extraordinarily effectively with bombs and machine guns."[17]

The airmen's action kept back the Bolsheviks but did not stop them altogether. Two divisions had already crossed the Bug, and between 4,000 and 6,000 enemy horse carts were now preparing to cross. On August 17 the Polish troops received orders to take up position in the vicinity of Lwów before the Bolsheviks got there. At the same time, it was recommended that the supply station of the 3rd Air Force *Dyon* be relocated from Lwów to Przemyśl. The duty of patching up the front was mainly up to the airmen. They received orders to attack the *Konarmia* with all possible force, and to support the offensive by their own armed forces north of the railway line between Krasne and Busk. An additional problem stemmed from the fact that the Bolshevik forces had encountered the 6th Infantry Division, who they surrounded along the road from Nawosiołki to Zadwórze. Zadwórze itself was defended by Polish volunteer formations made up of high-school boys, students, and older men officially unsuitable for bearing arms. On that day, few people realized that Zadwórze would become known as the "Polish Thermopylae," and that it would become an inspiration to artists and writers, a role model for training soldiers and scouts.[18]

A variety of documents differ in their evaluation of the forces at the disposal of the 3rd Air Force *Dyon* that day. Estimates range from 14 to 19 aircraft. Most probably there were 19, which had been brought up to flying capability with much effort the previous night. That day 69 sorties were carried out, about 4,000 kg of bombs were dropped, and 25,000 rounds of ammunition fired. Of course, in the light of contemporary standards the numbers are not impressive, but one must remember that the equipment was improvised, and the planes were not often equipped to carry bombs or to carry out bombing missions.[19]

The intensity of flights far exceeded the normal limits of equipment and crews, who were used to carrying out, at the most, one long or two short sorties daily. August 17 passed into history as one of the most active days in the war between the Polish Air Force and the Bolsheviks. Capt. Corsi took off at 4:05 A.M. on an hour-long sortie. After a short break he took off again at 6:10 A.M. on a flight lasting until 7:20 A.M. He flew again between 8:00 and 9:15 A.M. and then lastly between 12:45 and 1:35 P.M. Lt. Weber registered combat action from 5:20 to 6:20 A.M., on another two sorties before midday, then between 3:30 and 4:40 and from 6:00 P.M. to 7:00 P.M. Five sorties during the day demanded huge physical and psychological energy from the pilot and also a lot from the machines. The 15th Squadron participated in similar record-breaking actions. Lt. Dziembowski carried out four flights that day, as did Sec. Lt. Lewandowski. The flyers fully appreciated the burden of responsibility resting on their shoulders and, as time showed, passed the examination with flying colors. The airmen kept back Budenny, who only in rare instances moved as much as three kilometers forward, and that not until the end of the day when the bombing subsided. At Zadwórze Budenny managed to overcome Polish volunteers from the railway station and reached the line of the forest south of it. Battles in that region were exceptionally hard fought, and the air force constituted for the defenders of that small place the only real reinforcement. The atmosphere that day was described in the memoirs of one of the participants:

> At last help arrived. Three planes approached from Lwów and they are helping us from the air with machine guns and bombs. Real Hell. The enemy batteries are beginning to play again, it was raining a hail of shells from everywhere. The air was full of smoke, so there was no way of determining from which direction the enemy was attacking. The deafening noise of firing, the explosion of bombs, the noise of savage units was so effective that one could lose one's feeling of life and senses. In this hell, we are fighting with the remainder of our strength against a six thousand cloud of attacking wild forces. More and more of them are surrounding us.[20]

On August 16 and 17 the airmen of the 7th Squadron single-handedly stopped the advance of the 6th Cavalry Division of Budenny's *Konarmia*. It was a success of great strategic importance, since the fall of Lwów would threaten the entire Polish front and release the Bolshevik forces for a swift advance on Warsaw. This feat was more momentous because it coincided with the beginning of Piłsudski's counterattack on the Wieprz.

A communiqué from the Polish Army GHQ of September 1, 1920, proudly announced: "The 5th, 6th, 7th Kościuszko, and 12th Squadrons under the command of Maj. Fauntleroy, Chief of the Aviation of the 6th Army, on the days of the 16th and 17th of August carried out 129 sorties during which they dropped 7,700 kg of bombs and fired 16,700 rounds of ammunition."[21]

There is no better proof of the effectiveness of the air force than Budenny's dispatch to the High Command of the Red Army, intercepted by Polish Intelligence. At 3:00 P.M. of August 18th, he wrote:

In recent days the enemy has widely used airplanes in battle and in this way they have compensated for rather thin forces. On the 16th and 17th of August, enemy squadrons with up to 9 planes have flown in circles over the attacking columns of the *Konarmia*. The bold enemy planes flew low and strafed and bombed our units. The armed forces were attacked from the air no less than three times a day, and suffered huge losses in both men and horses. On August 17, in the 6th Cavalry Division alone, 100 men and 100 horses were either wounded or dead. One of the attacks on the 6th Division was conducted solely by planes. Please issue an order to immediately send one anti-aircraft (zenith) artillery battery (ZPT) for my disposal, which would follow the Army.[22]

On the same day Izaak Babel, then an officer and war chronicler of Budenny's *Konarmia,* wrote in his diary: "We are standing on the edge of the forest, the horses are chewing, and the hero of the day was the plane. The raids continually escalated. The planes are flying non-stop, five or six at a time. Bombs are falling every 100 steps."[23]

The effort made in such a short time had an impact on the technical conditions of the 3rd *Dyon* planes. At least five aircraft were seriously damaged, some reportedly — and it seems rather improbable — as a result of collisions with the Bolshevik riders. Kościuszko men and Poles of the 3rd *Dyon* flew at lethally low altitudes. The U.S. Military Attache confirmed that they flew at a ceiling of between 10 and 20 meters above the enemy columns. Besides Farman's reports, this fact was also confirmed by the recommendations for the "Virtuti Militari" decoration (see Appendix).[24]

Some of the airmen were suffering from extreme exhaustion and injury, yet on August 18 the 3rd *Dyon* continued to serve as efficiently as on the previous day. The first task of that day was to find and establish contact with the 12th and 13th Infantry Division and the allied Ukrainian Army operating to the south of Lwów. An additional assignment was to define the size of the gap in the defense line that had arisen as a result of the movement and withdrawal of the Polish units. And last, just as formerly, they carried out sorties to fight against the Bolshevik Cavalry. The 7th Squadron carried out a concentrated attack on Budenny that day. At 1:15 P.M., Capt. Corsi took off, followed five minutes later by Lt. Weber, and at 1:45 P.M. by Lt. Senkowski.[25] In all the 3rd *Dyon* carried out 72 flights with 14 planes that day, in other words an average of over 5 flights per aircraft.[26]

Apart from the losses inflicted on Budenny, the squadron's expedition led to the precise establishment of the direction of the movement of the main columns of the *Konarmia*. This was reflected in the order issued at 6 P.M. that day by the Polish Southern Front Command. It specified that Budenny had advanced towards Lwów with three columns. The North fought with Col. Rómmel's Cavalry Group (mentioned earlier) and Gen. Szymański's Group, the central column engaged the Polish 13th Infantry Division in battle east of Winniki near Kurowice, and the south, after the capture of Przemyślany and Bóbrka, turned in a southwestern direction. The airmen discovered a formation of around 600 Bolshevik infantry advancing westwards from Kniazie to Rozdoły. At the same time, because of the threat to the city, the Front Command issued an order to transfer the 3rd *Dyon* from Lwów to Przemyśl, which was around 80 km away. Only Maj. Fauntleroy and his HQ remained in the City of the Lion.

On the next day the air force continued their action, but the number of sorties carried out by the 7th Squadron was limited by the distance from the frontline, bad weather, and the wear and tear of the aircraft. The 15th Squadron did not hang around. Its commander, Lt. Dziembowski, carried out four flights: from 7:56 to 8:35, from 11:02 to 11:45 A.M., from 2:54 to 4:08 P.M., and from 6:44 to 7:45 P.M. Lt. Hendricks also distinguished himself. After he had been shot and wounded few days before, he miraculously returned to his own airfield and carried out four flights over enemy positions: from 7:56 to 8:35 A.M., 9:31 to 10:03, 10:30 to 11:28, and 2:58 to 3:58 P.M. Reconnaissance carried out by the airmen confirmed at around 10:30 A.M. at least 400 of Budenny's cavalrymen on the move from Remenów to Żółtańce, and around 1,000 cavalrymen in the vicinity of Borszczowice and Pikulowice. Half an hour later, order L.3475/III of the South Front Command confirmed the reconnaissance of a 2,000-strong Bolshevik cavalry on the march from the railway station at Borynicze via Brzozdowicze and Olechowicze, to Mikołajów. At 6:30 P.M. the air force scout confirmed the movement of a 500-strong cavalry around 25 km southwest of Lwów.[27]

That day was in any case the beginning of the breakthrough for the defenders of Lwów. From dawn Gen. Rómmel's Cavalry Group began a counterattack near Żółtańce. The *Konarmia* did not manage to break through the defense line around Lwów, and what is more, the Polish 12th Infantry Division withdrew to the city periphery reinforcing its defense. The inhabitants of Lwów received a second, more favorable piece of information from the General Staff in Warsaw. It reported the breakthrough in the Battle of Warsaw, the collapse of the Bolshevik forces and their panicked retreat from the capital suburbs. It was as if the defenders' strength had been renewed. Meanwhile, on the other side of the front frustration was increasing. Izaak Babel noted on August 18:

> The battle is constant, I am living like a soldier, I am completely exhausted.... The Poles are defending themselves mainly by air force action. The planes are becoming dangerous. To describe the raid: far, just as a slowing clatter of machine guns, panic in the camps, nerves. They constantly carry out flights, we hide from them. There are new ways of employing the air force.... Captain Fauntleroy took off from Lwów.... Mortal danger.[28]

Typical of this note is that most of the attention is devoted to the effectiveness of the air force. Its action appears to be more threatening than the actions of the Polish cavalry or infantry. The battle with the cavalry and infantry was equal and natural, but the Bolsheviks had no remedy to the air force, and the losses inflicted from the air were painful. On August 19, when Budenny was barely a dozen kilometers from Lwów, he was ordered to immediately withdraw from the city and to march in the direction of Włodzimierz Wołyński. It was already too late for any form of cooperation in attacking the Polish capital, but still the Bolshevik HQ counted on a reversal or at least on limiting the scope of defeat inflicted by Piłsudski. Budenny's march in the direction of Zamość relieved Lwów from immediate danger and gave the air force an exceptional opportunity to again pursue the large body of enemy cavalry. Budenny's rear was defended by Jakir's Group. The main task of the air force on August 20 was to determine the precise route of the enemy's march to the north. Order L.3518/III from 4:40 P.M. that day provided information obtained thanks to the air force. On the basis of this it was established that some units of the Bolshevik 8th Cavalry Division, concentrated in the region of Mikołajow, Rozdół, and Brzozdowica, had crossed the Dniestr River and were heading in the direction of Żurawno. The next report filed by the airmen facilitated order number L.3520/III, issued at 6:00 P.M. This order noted the movement of another Bolshevik cavalry group from Dalnicz to Baliatycze. At least 1,000 cavalrymen were said to be moving in that direction. A hour later, the movement of 1,000 horses and 400 horse carts was discovered on the way from Podchoryszcz to Mikolajow, the movement of a further 1,000 cavalrymen in the vicinity of Czarnuszowice and Zadwórze was spotted, and finally, 1,000 cavalrymen were spotted on the way from Borszczowice to Chreniow. This information allowed the ground forces to take appropriate

8. In Defense of the City of the Lion 157

action. At the same time, the 15th and 7th Squadrons carried out several sorties against the 8th Cavalry Division advancing on Stryj.

On August 21 there was only one operational sortie in the direction of Stryj. However, preparations were made to return from Przemyśl to Lwów. On August 23 and 24 the 3rd *Dyon* reported again at Lewandówka. At the same time, the Russians were continuing to suffer severe losses at the hands of the air force. On August 23, when elements of the *Konarmia* were at Sokal, there was a raid during which "Troop Leader" Trunov, the commander of Isaac Babel, was killed. In *Red Cavalry* Babel reconstructs the chain of events leading to Trunov's death. Once again, the Polish Air Force, and specifically American Pilots, are the culprits. Trunov anticipates the upcoming raid when he notices four small specs in the sky — four bombers sailing in and out of the swanlike clouds, Kościuszko planes, which climb to their maximum ceiling and then suddenly slide down, opening fire at 300 meters above the ground. The most difficult obstacle for the defense is the fact that Fauntleroy has covered his planes behind the sun. Trunov is killed almost immediately, together with another machine-gunner. His face is punctured with bullets and his tongue ripped out. None of the shots fired by Trunov and his comrade harm Americans.[29]

It is worth emphasizing here that Babel described the 7th Squadron as a Bomber Squadron.

The battle of Lwów was finished. One of the most interesting aspects of the war was the testing of limits of the air force's potential, which it passed with flying colors. The pilots of the 3rd *Dyon* not only managed to locate and engage the cavalry advancing towards Lwów, but also, particularly between the 16th and 18th of August, effectively restrain their mobility. This action was appreciated at all levels of command. Praise rained down upon the airmen, and both Polish and foreign newspapers wrote about them.[30] In the commendation order issued by the Command of the 6th Army for the 3rd Air Force *Dyon*, in whose formation the 7th Kościuszko Squadron fought, we read *inter alia*:

> In the battles with Budenny's *Konarmia*, the constant and tireless activity of the 3rd Air Force *Dyon* logged one of the glorious pages in battle annals of the air force. It was our airmen who first discovered Budenny's marching columns and from that moment did not take their eyes off them for even one day, as far as the weather allowed, providing the command with excellent intelligence. Their heroic deeds in the region of Koziatyń, Berdyczew, Połonne, Szepietówka, Dubna, Brody, Krzemieniec, Podwołczyska, Tarnopol, Kamionka Strumiłowa, and Busk

displayed more than once how effective the air force action was at paralyzing the advancing enemy cavalry. In the moment, moreover, when the enemy converges on Lwów, wishing at any cost to take the city, the airmen of the 3rd *Dyon* with Maj. Fauntleroy at the head and 14 aircraft attacked the advancing columns of enemy cavalry, from dawn to dusk, for three days in a row. They effectively stopped the enemy's activity by bombing and machine gun fire, causing serious losses. One of the most active pilots, Sec. Lt. Rozmarek died of his wounds. Then the 3rd Air Force *Dyon* accomplished equal feats, working with 18 aircraft, with the unusual number of as many as 72 sorties over the enemy in the space of one day. At last Budenny retreated from Lwów in a northerly direction and even then our airmen did not rest, but carried on further with their work, cooperating in the battles of Zamość and Komarów, carrying out continuous intelligence and effectively fighting the enemy with bombs and machine guns.... For that efficient work and heroic deeds, I express my highest respect for Maj. Fauntleroy, Lt. Kubala, Lt. Hendricks, Sec. Lt. Turbiak, Sec. Lt. Bartkowiak, and all the officers and ranks of the 3rd *Dyon* in the name of service to the homeland. This order is to be read out to all the units at the frontline.[31]

From the air force perspective Budenny's withdrawal was significant in the sense that the squadron took part in the defense of Lwów and immediately thereafter in the relentless pursuit of the *Konarmia*, showing remarkable flexibility and adaptability to changing combat situations. A few days later it supported the pursuit of Budenny by the forces of 6th Polish Army and a few days later supported the action at Uściług and Hrubieszów, where the Polish Cavalry came to face Budenny. The 3rd *Dyon* then operated from the outpost airfield at Korczów, on the railway line from Uhnów to Bełż. The airmen attacked cavalry columns in the region of Zamość, Komarów, Tyszowiec, Werbkowice, and Hrubieszów.

At the small village of Komarów, at the end of August and beginning of September, the greatest cavalry battle of the war took place. Budenny suffered defeat and was forced to retreat. In the first phase of this battle the 7th Squadron carried out a range of flights against elements of Jakir's Group. At 1:40 P.M. on August 25, Lt. Chess took off, followed at 2:20 P.M. by Lt. Senkowski and at 2:40 by Corsi. In the evening, Lt. Weber carried out his air assignments. Crews from other squadrons also took off, among them those of the 15th, with whom the Kościuszko Squadron had previously worked with such good results. On the next day Lt. Chess's flight is documented. In all from the 19th to the 26th of August, the squadrons of the 3rd *Dyon* carried out 23 combat sorties. On August 29 Lt. Senkowski's sortie is confirmed, and on August 31, that of Lt. Weber.[32]

This does not mean that the squadron's activities were limited to those noted in the flight reports and statistics. Given the conditions of a constantly changing situation, and with some airmen delegated to assignments from other airfields, and moreover in a situation when, with administrative duties, Lt. Weber himself carried out a range of flights, there is no doubt that some of the flights were not included in the reports sent to the superiors. The assignments of the airmen of the 6th, 7th, and 15th Squadrons in the cavalry battle at Komarów and Zamość were made easier by the cooperation of the 2nd Air Force *Dyon,* consisting of the 8th, 9th, and 14th Squadrons, stationed at airfields in the vicinity of Lublin and Chełm.

However, the American and Polish units of the 6th Army and the Southern Front attacked the Bolsheviks near Uściług and Hrubieszów. Just as at Lwów, the men of the Kościuszko Squadron worked tightly together with the 15th Squadron. On the 1st of September, Lt. Crawford, Sec. Lt. Bartkowiak, Capt. Prosiński and Lt. Lewandowski twice, all from the 15th Squadron, apart from Crawford, carried out combat sorties. On the next day, Lt. Weber took off; on September 3, Senkowski; the following day Crawford; and on September 5, Weber.

Here we are mentioning only the action of the 7th Squadron. The most important objective at this point was the battle with Budenny's cavalry, which after the defeat at Komarów, drained away to the east. Around the middle of September the terrain that had been the site of the battle for the previous two months had already been cleared of Bolsheviks. Limited combat action was carried out by Senkowski (September 11), Crawford (September 13), Weber, Konopka, Chess, and Crawford (September 15–16). Crawford, the commander of the 7th Squadron, took off again on September 18, and Weber took off on September 20. The last combat flights in the Squadron were those of Crawford (September 21), Konopka (September 22), and Corsi. The last flight on September 23 ended the squadron's combat epic.[33]

A few weeks before this date, the 7th Squadron was reinforced with several volunteer pilots from abroad. Capt. John Stanley McCallum, who was from Canada but serving in the Royal Air Force, reported to the Polish Military Attache in London with a proposal to serve as a volunteer. Invoking the rules that were already in existence, on August 6th, Rear Admiral Wacław Kłoczkowski provided him with a letter of recommendation to the Chief of the 2nd Intelligence Bureau of the High Command

Decoration of the pilots of the Polish 3rd Air Group in Lwów. September, 1920. (Courtesy of Dr. Tomasz Kopański, Warsaw.)

in Warsaw, with which McCallum succeeded in reaching Warsaw at his own cost and risk. He arrived there before August 11, according to the date of the request from the 2nd Intelligence Bureau to the Air Force Inspectorate to complete all formalities and to facilitate his entry into service. Admission into the ranks of the Haller's Volunteer Army, together with a referral to the 7th Squadron, occurred on the basis of Maj. Jasiński's decision the next day. The bureaucratic procedure was so limited that not even a formal contract, similar to those signed with McCallum's predecessors, was signed. The Captain went straightaway to Lwów, where he reported for duty on August 24.[34]

On the last day of August, McCallum tried to familiarize himself with the *Balilla* aircraft, which was completely unknown to him. During the training flight McCallum suddenly crashed to the ground. His death was a painful blow, in particular because it happened behind the frontline, shortly after his admission to the squadron. It is not surprising that it widely reverberated and was also covered in the news of the Associated Press and other press agencies.[35] Paradoxically, the squadron sustained more losses during training flights than in actual combat sorties.

8. In Defense of the City of the Lion

Debris of Lt. McCallum's aircraft. Lwów, August 31, 1920. (Courtesy of Dr. Tomasz Kopański, Warsaw.)

A curiosity is also the fact that the deaths of Graves and McCallum spanned the squadron's combat activity in Poland. A cease-fire with the Bolsheviks was approaching. Not everyone believed that it would be a lasting one, so when several new pilots were enlisted into the squadron in the summer of 1920, they were received with relief. Apart from McCallum, the pilots were Lt. Thomas H. Garlich, Lt. John Inglis Maitland, John C. Speaks, Earl F. Evans, and the later chronicler of the squadron's history, Kenneth Malcolm Murray. History treats only these newly arrived pilots as full members of the squadron. Several others also came, but due to the termination of hostilities they almost immediately left Poland. The volunteers who remained in the squadron possessed very solid backgrounds, which were excellently confirmed by their records. The first three of the airmen named above had served in the Royal Air Force. Lt. Garlich was born on December 23, 1898, in Philadelphia, and enlisted in the American Army on August 1, 1917. For the next four months he attended the Officers' School. From December 1, 1917, until March 1, 1918, he was trained in a Pilots' School, and was promoted to Lieutenant on March 16 that year. He was referred to the Higher School of Pilotage in

August–September, 1920. Recent arrivals among the regular officers of the Squadron, from left to right: Władysław Konopka, Kenneth M. Murray, Jerzy Weber, Antoni Poznański, Zbigniew Orzechowski, Edward Corsi, George Crawford, John C. Speaks, Elliot W. Chess, Earl F. Evans, John Inglis Maitland, Aleksander Senkowski, Thomas H. Garlich. (Courtesy of Dr. Tomasz Kopański, Warsaw.)

England, and after he graduated from there, he served as an instructor for two months. After the cease-fire, he served in Germany in the 119th Air Squadron. He racked up 102 flights to his credit. He formally reported to the Polish Armed Forces on July 1, 1920, in England, served in it until May 20, 1921. His superior, Capt. Crawford, evaluated this period extremely positively, writing: "A very conscientious and diligent officer, a good pilot."[36]

Lt. Maitland was born on February 12, 1894, in Toronto and joined the military on June 1, 1917. On November 1 that year he graduated from Pilots' School and then until July 1, 1918, he improved his qualifications in Pilots' School in Scotland. He also undertook training in machine gun skills and a communications course for senior Air Force officers — both of these courses in France. He was promoted to Lieutenant on April 1, 1918, and until October of that year he served in the 80th and 54th Squadrons in France. Up until he was demobilized on August 20, 1919,

8. In Defense of the City of the Lion   163

he declared to his credit 200 combat sorties. He was admitted to the Polish Armed Forces on August 21, 1920, and served until May 1921. "A very serious and conscientious officer. A very good pilot." This was the opinion issued about him during his service in Poland.[37]

Lt. Speaks was born on February 17, 1896, in Columbus, Ohio. He was the son of a Brigadier General, who after the World War I became a congressman from his hometown district. Speaks Jr. served from June 1, 1917, in Officers' School and from August 1 until September 30, 1917, in Pilots' School. After he graduated he became an instructor at the latter school until May 1, 1918. He served in the 56th Squadron as second-in-command and was promoted to the rank of Lieutenant on October 1, 1918. He carried out over 200 sorties before he was discharged. When he heard about the possibility of serving in Poland he came forward to volunteer and then on August 21, 1920, he was assigned to the 7th Squadron. His superior, Capt. Crawford, wrote about him: "A young, very conscientious, and disciplined officer, an excellent and experienced pilot."[38]

In a certain sense Kenneth Murray, who came from New York and who was enlisted by Col. Castle, was an exception. Murray had served in the British Royal Air Force and transported his own aircraft, a Sopwith Camel, to Poland. The aircraft was formally purchased by the Polish Purchasing Bureau in New York and was transported to Lwów through that agency.[39]

Earl F. Evans came from El Paso, graduated from the University of Texas, and then enlisted in the U.S. Air Service. He fought in France as pilot of the 49th Squadron. Apart from these pilots, a few others joined the squadron, among them, Charles E. Hays of Memphis, Tennessee, and S.T. Kauffman and Richard Allen of Kansas City. However, these last two did not stay long and left Poland immediately.

The announcement of reinforcements, as well as the generally positive opinion about the squadron, was echoed in a report sent to Washington on September 21, 1920. The U.S. Military Attache wrote:

> Kościuszko Squadron. Twelve aviators formerly in the American service, several of them in the Lafayette Escadrille. One has been killed, two are missing, presumably dead, several have returned or are returning to America. Recruiting is being carried on in America, through Colonel Castle, formerly Aviation Attache, American Embassy, Paris; eight aviators have been secured and will shortly join. Four of the original 12 remain with the squadron. Commander, Major Fauntleroy. The organization has done brilliant work and has been the chief element in

securing recognition by the Polish Staff of the importance of aviation in this warfare.[40]

The Attache considered Kelly and Cooper as lost. He did not know at that time that in reality Kelly had been killed in action, but Cooper survived and had been captured by the Bolsheviks.

9 | CAPTAIN COOPER'S ODYSSEY

The day on which the commander of the squadron was captured turned out to be the beginning of one of the most dramatic odysseys experienced by an American in Russia. The only event that possibly bears any resemblance to this was the 20-year journey of Father Walter Ciszek, who carried out secret priestly duties both in and outside the Gulag Archipelago.[1]

The loss of Cooper was interpreted as death in action, and this phrase was in one of the reports by the American Military Attache in Warsaw. From another source, however, all communications permitting the supposition that he was still alive were seized upon. The Associated Press reported, for example, that based on the report of Lt. Noble in Paris, that it was impossible to definitely establish the fate of the lost pilots. It was certainly true in the case of Kelly and Cooper. In another report by the same agency, based on the evidence of Bolsheviks captured in Poland, was the news that one of the missing American officers was working as a cook in a Bolshevik regiment. Unfortunately, there was no confirmation of that either. What is more, the lack of food for prisoners in Russia was one of the most difficult barriers to survival. Cooper did not escape this experience.[2]

It was not only the remaining airmen based at Hołoby who took part in the search on the day after Cooper went down, but also Polish Intelligence. It was rightly feared that in the event that Cooper had been captured by the Bolsheviks, there was the possibility that he would be shot on the spot. Due to this fear, even his closest family was not informed that he was missing. It was not until August 4 that Fauntleroy carved out a little time to write to John C. Cooper, Sr., the pilot's father, who lived in Jacksonville, Florida. He reconstructed the course of the events that had preceded the transfer of the squadron to Hołoby on July 12 and the events of the next day. He also tried to console him with the lack of positive news:

> To my mind, this is a good sign; because in the case of every pilot heretofore killed or captured by the Bolsheviks, the news came back almost immediately.... Everyone in the squadron confidently expects Merian to come back safely. We have pilots return after being reported missing for a period of two months. Owing to the size of the country and looseness of the warfare, it is entirely possible for a pilot to land behind the Bolshevik lines, burn his plane and live with friendly peasants, without being able to cross the lines or get news of his whereabouts back to his friends.... I am at a total loss without him. If the proposed armistice or peace with the Bolsheviks comes off in the near future, I shall immediately set out with a motor car in search for him.[3]

Fauntleroy kept his word. After the Bolsheviks had been repulsed from Lwów in the middle of September, he searched in the region of Dubno, Rovne, and Łuck. He confirmed the death of Sec. Lt. Jakubowski and corporal Antosz of the 21st Squadron, and also succeeded in establishing the circumstances of the shooting down and further fate of a few other airmen. Among those were Capt. Ciecierski and Capt. Kelly, who died July 15 near the village of Zwierówka. This was about 1 km to the north of the Łuck-Rovne road. Both airmen were buried on the site of the catastrophe. After identifying the remains, Fauntleroy recommended the exhumation and transportation of the remains of both pilots to Lwów. Fauntleroy also succeeded in establishing the circumstances of Cooper's shooting down. Cooper's plane was forced to land on the fields of the village of Didycze, near the small town of Ołyka, around five kilometers to the north of the Łuck-Rovne road.

The Bolshevik Cavalry immediately captured him and took him to the HQ of the 2nd Brigade of the 6th Division of Budenny's *Konarmia*. Peasants who managed to see the events gave an exact description of the airman's appearance, and on the basis of this, Fauntleroy identified Cooper.[4]

As it happened, the plane was damaged during the landing and Cooper himself lost consciousness. When he came round, he found himself surrounded by Budenny's cavalrymen. At that moment, the wounds and burns he had suffered in action in September 1918 were his succor.

9. Captain Cooper's Odyssey

One of the basic Bolshevik practices towards prisoners and people of the captured areas was to seek out the "representatives of the Bourgeousie." One of the most popular tests of class membership was an analysis of their hands. The so-called "white hands" signified a man who had never done any manual work and therefore was an "enemy of the people." However, Cooper's hands were burnt. His second lucky break was his army discharge underwear, which he had on that day. The underwear was stamped with the name of the previous owner, who was Corporal Frank Mosher. Both lucky events allowed Cooper to maintain that he was in reality a corporal of that name who had been enlisted into the Polish Armed Forces. Of course, the Bolsheviks did not entirely believe that story, because even within their ranks the names of the American pilots were known. Apart from that, Cooper had some incriminating documents in his pocket, such as notes addressed to Fauntleroy and, even worse, his memo to Col. Castle regarding the importance of the air force. Its content was unambiguous. Cooper wrote that through their participation in the war, the airmen of the squadron were gaining experience of the role of the air force in a war of maneuvers in geographically wide-open country. This experience, he noted, could have significance in the event of a revival of the war with Mexico. He also summarized his thoughts on the subject of the air force combat effectiveness against the infantry and cavalry. They were certainly not commensurate with even the most sharp-witted corporal.[5]

Cooper was transported to the Division HQ, where he was interrogated by the *komdyw*, or Division Commander, Timoszenko, who was later to become a Soviet Marshal. They tempted him with the proposition of service as an instructor of the Bolshevik Air Force, but he consistently refused. Even a five-day visit to the Bolshevik Air Squadron did not help to change his mind. Early in his captivity, Cooper attempted to escape. Unfortunately after two days he was caught and imprisoned with a heavy guard. He found himself in Moscow, where in all he spent as much as ten months in various penal facilities. Prison food rations consisted of barely half a pound of black bread per day — and not always. Years later, he recalled his experiences in a reply to a letter from Capt. Marek Mażyński, a Polish airman of 303rd Squadron who in the first years of World War II was also a Soviet prisoner. The men compared notes on prison conditions in the 1920s and the 1940s. Cooper wrote:

> For a week in Moscow, nobody had a bite of eat — nothing. One of the prisons I was in was fairly good. The second one was just about as

you describe. The third was rougher and tougher than any you describe; there was a good reason for this as my imprisonment was during the starvation period of 1920–1921, where for one week in January (as I have already said) there was absolutely no food in Moscow. Not only had the transportation broke down, but this was the first time the peasants refused to give food to the city workers.... Nothing is more terrible than the breaking of the human spirit by torture, starvation, and the sadistic questioning by "Cheka." I want to say that in the toughest prison I was in, where men died every night from lack of food and typhus, there were two prisoners who kept other prisoners from complete disintegration. One of the men had lost all his teeth while working in the coal mines of Siberia; he was a 30-year-old baker who had only one tooth. He was from Łódź, Poland. The other man was a man who spoke only a little Polish. This, of course, was me. I take no credit, but credit only the tough training I had at the United States Naval Academy in Annapolis.[6]

The prisoners' situation was saved by food parcels from "Amcross" and one of the English charitable organizations. The living conditions in jail were also severe for other reasons. Cooper recalled gaining permission from the prison authorities to hold prayers in the presence of a priest on Christmas Eve. It was an evening when companions in misery were people of differing confessions and nationalities, including prisoners related to the richest American families. On that day they were joined in prayer, although not all of them were believers. The prisoners' prayers cemented the Bolsheviks' hatred towards them as representatives of the social order that they had vowed to destroy.[7]

The last prison that Cooper was in was Vladykino. Here with two Polish officers he decided to escape. This time he succeeded. In a way he was forced to escape by his Polish counterparts. In his report filed after reaching Warsaw, he wrote that the two Polish prisoners managed to brake into the prison office in order to forge a few documents for the escape. At this point there was no return. Cooper was very well aware that not only the two direct perpetrators might be shot dead on the spot. He, after all, was considered to be a dangerous anti-revolutionary and enemy of the people.

The escape must have happened at the beginning of March, 1921.[8] Since Cooper himself did not know Russian, he pretended to be mute, and on the long march from Moscow to the Latvian border, Lt. Stanisław Sokołowski and Corporal Stanisław Zalewski facilitated everything for him. They marched in the direction of Wielkie Łuki with Latvia as their general destination, which was then, as through the entire inter-war period, the most efficient crossing point between the workers' paradise and the outside world. It was through this very border that Boris Savinkov, the famous terrorist, returned to Russia, lured by the mirage of the great anti–Bolshevik conspiracy. Food was obtained by exchanging the clothes they had received in the Amcross packages. The escapees brushed with arrest several times. They were, after all, moving across completely unknown territory with neither a compass nor a map. Cooper recalled that he spent one night up to his neck in water. In any case in an expedition covering over 800 kilometers, the sympathy, or at least indifference, of the local population had to play a crucial role. The last five days of the route to the border was on foot through mud and swamps. At the last minute, a smuggler they had engaged tried to betray the escapees by refusing to lead them across the border. Only threatened with death did he decide to fulfill his part of the contract. The border was crossed at 2:00 A.M. on April 23, 1921. "We came to 'Amcross' in rags and without shoes, hungry and completely fatigued," as Cooper wrote in his first dispatch from Riga.[9]

The shoes were payment for the smuggler who had led them across the border. Cooper would not have been himself if he had not immediately expressed his gratitude to Amcross and brought attention to the need for better care of the American prisoners still held by the Bolsheviks. He wrote about this a few weeks later, to Hoover among others, including a few practical hints. He brought attention to the still existing legal avenues of action by Western charitable organizations in Russia, he stressed the attitude of the two Polish officers and the local population. As an eyewitness, he was also a credible source of information about the conditions prevailing under the communist rule in Russia: "Cooper, a prisoner in Russia, states that Russia is full of propaganda against United States, France and Great Britain; people are told that these countries are responsible for all trouble in Russia. German influence is strong and popular."[10] In another report he confirmed the level of control by the new regime. "Absolute control of Bolsheviks, either they will stay in control or anarchy."[11] This experience of the nature of the communist system, gained through direct contact with the iron hand of terror, remained with Cooper throughout his life. He became an unrelenting opponent of the system, and he intended to write a book about his experiences.[12] However he never fully realized his intention. The only fragments were included in his book *Things Men Die For*.

It is worth mentioning here the durability of the anti–American propaganda, whose influence is present even in contemporary academic

Merian Cooper with Lt. Stanisław Sokołowski and Corp. Stanisław Zalewski after crossing the Soviet-Latvian border, April 1921. (Courtesy of Dr. Tomasz Kopański, Warsaw.)

works. Simonenko, already mentioned in these pages, states in an article about the Kościuszko Squadron that after the signing of the Polish-Bolshevik peace in Riga, Cooper was most ordinarily released from prison and arrived to Poland without any problems. He does not say, however, why he had to overcome the boundless Russian territory in rags and on foot, nor why he crossed the border illegally.[13]

Meanwhile, the Polish authorities and the squadron airmen awaited the miraculous rescue of their comrade. His journey from Riga to Warsaw began on April 29, his train reached the capital on May 3, the day celebrated by Poles as Constitution Day. As a witness to the event recalled, "he received a great ovation." It so happened that this was the first time that Constitution Day had been celebrated without a major war being waged, although the borders had not yet been officially recognized by the Conference of Ambassadors. It is true that in Silesia the third uprising had broken out against the Germans, but Poland was not officially involved in that conflict. Help was provided to the insurgents unofficially using paramilitary organizations such as the Polish Military Organization. Thus, the 3rd of May in 1921 was celebrated solemnly and in an atmosphere of peace, as the new constitution was declared in March and a peace treaty was signed with Russia.

That signified the end of the squadron's war mission. There was no need to extend their contracts. Cooper made it to the discharge ceremony of the Americans and to their farewell. On May 8 he discovered that during his absence he had been promoted twice, the first time shortly after he was shot down on July 13, 1920, and the second time, to the rank of Lt. Col. at the end of the war. In the same way as other officers, he was awarded the *Virtuti Militari*, the oldest Polish military decoration. It was presented in the courtyard of Belvedere Palace by Józef Piłsudski himself. Later on *Pole Mokotowskie* airfield General Józef Haller awarded the Haller Cross, which commemorated, their nominal service in the ranks of that General's Army. In the evening there was a farewell in the Air Force Mess. On May 9 General Haller issued a warm farewell order to the airmen.[14]

One of the privileges of a Knight of the *Virtuti Militari* was the automatic assignment of a plot of land. This was also the case with the Americans. They, however, foreswore their privilege and decided to join their plots of land and to create a convalescence center for injured or recovering Polish soldiers. It was repayment for the deeds of Kościuszko, who had refused to accept the plot of land offered to him by the U.S. Congress, recommending instead the buying out of Black slaves.[15] On May

Top: Gen. Józef Haller (in front, stepping down the stairs) with American officers. Warsaw, May 1921. *Bottom:* Cooper and Rayski in May 1921. (Courtesy of Dr. Tomasz Kopański, Warsaw.)

10 Maj. Stanisław Jasiński, the commander of the Air Force, issued a farewell order in which he wrote:

> At the time when Poland was surrounded by a ring of enemies in the bloody struggle for its independence, nine American officers came to Poland to fight arm to arm in line with the old Polish battle cry "For Your Freedom and Ours." Modest by nature, brave in the battlefield, under the command of Col. Fauntleroy they wanted to let the World know that Poland is rising and regaining its independence in the bloody battles.... Today, after victorious war, after accomplishing deeds that Kościuszko himself was trying to achieve, young Eagles of free America are leaving us today. For their sacrifices paid in blood, for their endurance in the hour of trial during the war, in the name of the Polish Air Forces I offer my most sincere thanks to: Col.-Pilot Cedric E. Fauntleroy, Lt.Col.-Pilot Merian C. Cooper, Maj.-Pilot George M. Crawford, Capt.-Pilot Edward Corsi, Capt.-Pilot Carl Clark, Capt.-Pilot Harmon Rorison, Lt.-Pilot Kenneth Shrewsbury, Lt.-Pilot Elliot Chess, Lt.-Pilot Kenneth Murray, Lt.-Pilot Earl F. Evans, Lt.-Pilot Inglis Maitland, Lt.-Pilot John Speaks; Lt.-Pilot Thomas H. Garlich

And for those who sacrificed their own lives for Poland — our eternal tribute and appreciation.[16]

There was one more token of appreciation, this time from a fellow officer of the 7th Squadron. On May 9, 1921, Capt. Zbigniew Orzechowski, who served as adjutant of the Squadron, filed a memo at the Polish Ministry of Military Affairs requesting promotion for Lt. Col. Fauntleroy to the rank of General. Orzechowski was arguing not only in favor of Fauntleroy's military exploits, but pointed out his contribution to the Polish cause during his trip to America in late autumn, 1920. Eventually, Orzechowski's request was partially granted. On May 15, 1921, Fauntleroy was promoted to the rank of full (bird) Colonel.[17]

10 | WARTIME AIR FORCE EXPERIENCES

Virtually the day after the end of the war, discussion began about the air force contribution to the war effort and the future role of this branch of the military. This discussion was carried out in the military periodicals, among the experts, in the headquarters, and in and outside of Poland's borders. On the basis of 1939, when the German Luftwaffe gained a decisive advantage in the air, some military historians have felt that appropriate conclusions were not drawn from the Polish-Bolshevik war. Such an opinion is not justifiable. In 1939 the German potential was incomparably greater, and we have to bear in mind that the Third Reich equally quickly suppressed a first rank power such as France. There are enough indicators that in 1920 the value of the air force was quickly perceived in reconnaissance and intelligence, in maintaining communication, in direct combat with the infantry and cavalry, and in destruction of fortifications. The war of 1919–1920 was also attentively watched by foreigners, including the French, Italians, Germans, and, of course, the Americans. The most complex was the presence of the French, who had the most influence on the organization, training, and armament of the Polish Air Force. The French Military Mission in Warsaw had a separate Air Force section, at the head of which was Lt. Col. de Vergnette. Overall, 127 French officers and 37 instructors trained the Polish pilots. The presence of the Frenchmen in such numbers was connected to a certain extent with the transfer of the air force units of the Haller Army in 1919 from France to Poland. Apart from 88 Polish pilots and cadets, three observers, three technical officers, and 110 mechanics, a lot of French officers also served who then took on instructors' duties and sometimes line duties in the Polish Air Force. The French also conducted the highest level of training in the air force schools in Poland. It was not until August 1, 1920, that the Air Force Schools passed formally into Polish hands.[1]

To complete the picture it is necessary to add the preponderance of French battle methods and equipment. This influence was visible in a briefing that was obligatory in the Polish Air Force prior to combat. In 1919, under the auspices of the Center of Artillery Studies, *A Lecture on the Military Air Force* was published: "The Combat Air Force *(l'aviation de combat et la bombardement)* task is to prolong the activity of artillery and in crucial stages of the battle to carry out long range expeditions to prevent the activity of the enemy chaser air force from the battlefield itself."

The same briefing stated that the task of the Air Force Group on the Army level was to follow the enemy beyond the front, to defend the intelligence squadrons, and to carry out intelligence. The depth of the reconnaissance was defined as between 20 and 60 kilometers.[2] The relatively passive nature of duties and separation of responsibilities of the Reconnaissance and the Fighter Air Force is very characteristic and did not survive the Polish-Bolshevik war.

While taking advantage of the broad experience of the French, the Poles attempted to avoid any dependency. Therefore, they welcomed a limited competition from the Italians, in particular as concerned the supply of aviation equipment. Capt. Camillo Perini played a huge role in tendering mutual relations between the countries. The Italians supplied the highly valued Balilla aircraft, which the Americans flew. They tried to build a plane factory in Lublin, which evoked a great deal of dissatisfaction among the French. The Italian Military Mission in Warsaw, with Gen. Romei in charge, had in its ranks an Air Force officer, Maj. Stabile, who also had a Polish brevet, the insignia of a Polish pilot. The English, less interested in direct investment in Poland had limited presence in Poland, but sold to the Poles tens of planes.[3]

The American Attache devoted a lot of attention to the air force. His report of September 21, 1920, gives an analysis of the state and the potential of the Polish Air Force. The number of trained pilots who had completed the Officers' School was estimated at 250, the number of observers (navigators) at 100, and the whole air force personnel numbered 4,000 people. After an analysis of the individual qualifications of the highest commanders, Farman concluded that the greatest problem remained the fluid organizational state caused by the war. The airmen's pay was low: "Pay in the Polish Army is by no means adequate, but is based on the normal value of the mark. Even if the mark were not immensely depreciated, it would hardly be sufficient. To meet the situation in part, the Army is paid wages every 20 days."[4]

In a further part of the report the Attache stated that discipline in the air force was extremely strong; he praised the "elan" of the air forces, particularly, in comparison with other branches of the armed forces. He emphasized their persistence: "the Poles are physically tough, and will endure an enormous amount of hardship." In "Racial characteristics" he stated: "The Poles are at times stolid, at times temperamental and easily disconcerted. Flying ability is fair, with some pilots who are excellent, chiefly Posnanians, German trained." He moderately praised their mechanical skill. He also gave an analysis of the quality of airfields, which with the exception of a few situated in larger towns (such as Poznań, Warsaw, Toruń, Lwów) left a lot to be desired. The situation was similar regarding hangars and the ground infrastructure.[5]

A report written at the end of the war reflected the situation at the end of September 1920. The cease-fire had not yet been signed, although the activities of the air force, on the front near Wilno, where the great Battle of the Niemen River took place, had gradually decreased. More interesting were the observations about new battle methods and the conclusions reached as to the future. That the war was of a rather different character to that observed in the years 1914–1918, was apparent to everyone who had come into close contact with it. One of the squadron volunteers, Lt. Charles E. Hays, returned to the United States after a short stay in the 7th Squadron. On the basis of his reports, the *Evening Post* wrote that in the Polish-Bolshevik war, the air force had played a far greater role than on the Western Front.[6]

Lt. Col. Farman's observations from July 1920, after the Kiev Expedition, are interesting: "The value of these operations lies in the fact that the warfare on the Polish-Bolshevik front is similar to that which would be encountered in Mexico, viz., Long lines thinly held, rapid movements, large cavalry forces, unimproved fields, preponderance of aviation on one side and difficult supply." The Attache noted that it was essential to position the airfield at a distance of between 5 and 50 kilometers from the front, near railway lines, which made evacuation and relocation easier:

> During the retreat of the Polish Army from Kiev from June 11, 1920, to June 24, 1920, aviation was used probably for the first time in the rear guard of an Army. Previously the use of aviation for this purpose

was considered impracticable due to the great technical difficulties in constructing suitable flying fields, and the danger of capture of all aviation material.... During this operation the squadron had eight pilots and 14 single-place scout aeroplanes carrying two 24-pound bombs each. After locating the column the pilot would fly well out of range to a point about one half a mile behind the rear of the column and then at a height of about 300 meters would fly back over the rear of the column. Here among the wagon trains and the rear of the cavalry the two bombs would be dropped. After dropping the second bomb the pilot drives upon the troops and at the height of 100 meters opens fire with both machine guns. It was most important to withhold the opening fire until within 100 meters of the ground. The aviator would continue the dive to as low an altitude as possible, firing continuously, and then pull out of the dive, ceasing the fire at the same time. At this period of the attack the wagon trains and the rear of the cavalry would commence scattering in all directions, and with a number of killed and wounded men and horses the confusion is very great. The pilot now being in position at the rear of the column would open his motor full so that the roar would have a frightening effect on the horses. Flying directly down the line by elevating and lowering the nose of the plane a very slight degree while at a height of 10 to 15 meters above the column machine gun bullets could be sprayed through the entire length of the column thus causing casualties and creating great disorder and confusion. By this method one squadron was able to check the advance of 20,000 cavalry for several hours every day. This method of attack was adopted by all the pilots as best and safest. Attempts to attack the column from the flank resulted in the plane being subjected to heavy and accurate fire and was extremely dangerous. Attacking from the head of the column was not effective and also more dangerous.[7]

Since the experiences of the war were in a way similar in character to the activities on the American-Mexican border, Farman recommended better preparation for American Reconnaissance Pilots and American Air Force observational planes to drop bombs from lower altitudes.[8]

The members of the Kościuszko Squadron returned to the problem in their memoirs. Merian Cooper discussed the role of the air force in the following words: "During the offensive we were the first to come into contact with the enemy, we were the avant-garde of the forces moving on Kiev—[then] we were the rearguard, protecting our forces' retreat from the sudden and unexpected enemy attacks."[9]

Cooper further wrote that during the battle of Koziatyń in May 1920, the 7th Squadron developed a new method of engaging the enemy based on reconnaissance of the terrain from 600–800 meters. After the enemy column had been located, they attacked first with a bomb and then with machine guns along then length of the column. A single-bomb attack was to serve as an estimate of the accuracy of the bombardment. After the attack had ceased they returned to base, refuelled, rearmed and went back into action according to the plan.[10] Kenneth Murray, who in reality did not take part in battle, wrote on the basis of other pilots' reports:

> Fighting in the rear-guard, as they were, against the greatest horsemen on earth, it was inevitable that hitherto undreamed tactics should be born: Budenny's wild hordes soon saw that they must avoid all roads and open country if they did not wish to be annihilated from the air — and the pilots in turn, were forced to hunt them out in the rugged, steep-sided waterways, rocky hill lands and thick, impenetrable forests; often flying within 50 or 60 feet of the ground for the sole purpose of drawing the fire of the hidden forces. When, in this fashion, such groups were sighted, the little ships would whirl away out of range, climb quickly to 1,500 or 2,000 feet, return and let go a bomb or two, then pull up in a stall, throttle their motors and drop like a plummet from the blue, their machine guns spitting a double stream of lead in the demoralized mass below. Yet even then the Cossacks were known to bravely hold their ground and return the fire with carabine and pistol, as may be seen.[11]

Of course, the part that imputes that Budenny's Cossacks avoided the main roads because of the presence of the Polish Air Force is not true. The Cossacks acted in this way long before entry into battle on the Polish front.

The air force tactics described also developed independently in other squadrons. One of the most famous airmen of the war, Lt. Col. Tadeusz Prauss, writes in his memoirs that observation of the terrain was carried out at around 800–1,000 meters altitude, and the attack began at around 500 meters and was completed at 30 meters above the enemy column. Prauss indicated that machine gun fire was conducted both by the pilot and the observer.[12]

Another participant in battle brought further attention to the necessity of the precise planning of the order of attack on the column. The concern was the maintenance of constant pressure on the enemy through an organized attack by three to five planes using established signals for retreat and communication. He stressed the necessity of attacking "from the sun," starting at 500 meters and flying along the length of the cavalry column to as low as 50 meters above the ground.[13]

10. Wartime Air Force Experiences

Map of Poland within 1921–1935 borders. (Courtesy of Mariusz Kędzierski, Cracow.)

Lt. Turbiak, who fought with the 15th Squadron, confirms the method of attack described above, and even draws conclusions for the future:

> At Lwów, in battle with Budenny's cavalry and even earlier in the Polish-Ukrainian conflict, in battle with the infantry at Kulikowo, at Wapniarka, in battle against armored trains, infantry, and artillery, and even in battle against a flotilla on the Dniepr River, the Polish Air Force performed in completely different conditions than the West European

air force during the Great War. The Polish Air Force for the most part acted independently against the armed forces on the ground. This type of air force could be termed as an "assault air force." In the organization of the French Air Force during the Great War, there was no air force of that type, but the Germans had them in their formation. Our General Staff concentrated most of its attention on the "assault air force," working on its organization, tactics, and weapons....[14]

Staff officers also took part in examining the air force's role. Major Adam Brzechwa-Ajdukiewicz, a later General and in 1920 Head of the 3rd Operational Section of the HQ of 6th Army, prepared a report entitled *Our Air Force and Its Activity*. In it, he discussed the activity of the 5th, 6th, 7th, and 15th Squadrons. In discussing reconnaissance and intelligence, he stressed that the scout missions were decisive, more than once flying in excess of 500 km, with flight times of four or five hours. These missions often concentrated on railway junctions and main roads as opposed to the frontline itself, which often did not exist. The problem with which they had to contend was the lack of precise maps and neglect from their own units in putting up identification signs. To summarize, Maj. Brzechwa-Ajdukiewicz asked:

> What were the results of this intelligence? My answer is one word only — fantastic! Quite simply I cannot imagine how the Operational Section could have functioned had it not been for the daily air force reports. All calculations, decisions, and orders were based on them. When the 2nd Bureau (Intelligence) had not given me any news about the enemy apart from the Bolshevik radio dispatches and information about whether our own units are being attacked or not — unable to say anything about the formation and strength of the enemy, then the one and only help for me was the airmen, providing, quite simply, priceless reports about the formation and movements of the Bolshevik Armed Forces.[15]

Discussing the activity of the fighter squadrons, Brzechwa-Ajdukiewicz theorized on the functions of particular branches of air force: "We had three types of air force and a dozen or so types of plane — reconnaissance, fighter, and bomber — but all of them more or less "served all purposes." Therefore, they had to carry out all the missions that came up.[16] Given the sparse activity of the Bolshevik air force, the main task of the fighter squadrons was to fight the enemy cavalry, armored trains, and communication junctions. The fighters were equally as efficient as infantry: "During the 2nd Army attack on Berdyczew in April 1920 the

7th Fighter Squadron chased off whole Bolshevik infantry units with ease."[17]

Those who participated in this war did not shun predictions for the future. One of the pilots said that in future conflict every large unit ought to have its own air force and appropriate training in defense against the enemy air force: "The air force can inflict heavy losses on ground forces, it can paralyze them and virtually destroy them. The air force can efficiently haunt and delay large ground units, but the air force cannot defend territory."[18]

Maj. Pilot Marian Romeyko, a participant in the war and later the Polish Military Attache in Rome, suggested appropriate organizational preparation and a unification of equipment, if possible on the basis of domestic production. As concerned the tactical analysis of the battle during the war, he stressed the relatively (for that time) large areas of air force reconnaissance, which stretched for hundreds of kilometers, and their direction right along the communication lines leading to the front: "The necessity of using reconnaissance sorties ordered equally to *link* reconnaissance with the bombardment and the attack of units on the ground...."[19]

It was the same regarding the squadrons nominally known as bomber squadrons, which also carried out observational tasks. In Romeyko's opinion, the organization of a few squadrons with the aim of carrying out specific orders was important, exactly what had been observed in the area of Lwów in August 1920: "One of the momentous experiences that the Polish-Bolshevik war gave us the use of the bomber air force, was the use of the air force in pursuit. That type of air force activity was used during the retreat of the Bolsheviks at Warsaw." A similar type of pursuit was applied through the deployment of the 7th and 15th Squadrons in the vicinity of Lwów. For Romeyko, the conclusions drawn from the Polish-Bolshevik war were so important that he did not hesitate to write:

> Even our meager experience indicates forcibly that aerial bombardment will be widely applied in future warfare. *This fact imposes the condition that equipment should be introduced into the air force that is rather more mobile* [the emphasis is Maj. Romeyko's].

He wrote further:

> *Air force maneuvers will be of immense importance in future warfare* [the emphasis is Maj. Romeyko's], that is why today also through peace work we ought to consider and remove those factors which were barriers to the use of these extra characteristics.[20]

Romeyko precisely anticipated the role of the air force in future conflict, that is, the heavy bombing of roads, communications and water crossings. Of course a range of other military experts discussed the role of the air force in future warfare, including Col. Sergiusz Abżółtowski and the later Commander-in-Chief of the Polish Armed Forces during WWII, Gen. Władysław Sikorski. Their views are much better publicized, so no further presentation of their ideas is needed here. The conclusions drawn and presented here concerned not only American pilots. There is no doubt, however, that they contributed heavily to the development of those new methods.

Beyond Poland no more attention was paid to the military experiences of the Polish-Bolshevik war. The fact that another conflict could have a dynamic mobile character with the use of a swiftly moving cavalry, substituted in time by the panzer/tank formations, was disregarded. The need for speedy development of multifunctional planes was for some time overlooked.

One of the officers who put the experience from 1920 into some sort of order and brought it to life in another world conflict was Merian Cooper. He participated in the creation of an independent American air force in China with 500 fighters and bombers and at least 100 transports. Let us not forget that he carried notes about the significance of the air force when he was apprehended by the Bolsheviks on July 13, 1920.[21]

New experiences also fell to the lot of the successors of the 7th Squadron, who took on the first attacks of the Luftwaffe in September 1939.

11 | THE SQUADRON'S ODYSSEY

The arrival of the Americans in Poland in 1919 and Cooper's wanderings through the Bolshevik Russia was not the last odyssey that airmen bearing the insignia of the 7th Squadron were to endure. A dozen or so years later, during World War II they had to defend not only their own territory but also the French and English skies. Poland was the first to experience the *Blitzkrieg* from the Third Reich, and the Polish airmen were the first to test themselves in the air against the German pilots. The war, from its very inception, brought a range of new air tactics. None of the enemies of the Third Reich had any knowledge on that subject in 1939.

In the Squadron's odyssey throughout Europe the Polish pilots cooperated again with American airmen, who this time learned the new air battle tactics from their Polish comrades in arms. One of them was Lt. Francis Gabreski, an American of Polish origin, who during his career shot down 37½ planes to his credit. Prior to the U.S. full involvement in Europe, Gabreski served in the 317th Polish Squadron of the RAF. He stressed more than once how much he had learned from the Polish pilots.[1]

Before the war began, Poland had lived through 20 or so years of a peace. After the 1920 war, the 7th Squadron was under the command of Capt. Jerzy Weber, and from May 31, 1921 it was stationed at the *Mokotów* airfield in Warsaw. As time passed, the equipment was modernized. Italian and French planes were replaced by modern aircraft, designed and constructed on the basis of Polish plans. The squadron also underwent a few reorganizations. In spring 1925 it was renamed the 121st Fighter Squadron, and three years later, on an order issued on August 2, 1928, it was renamed the 111th Fighter Squadron. It lasted until the outbreak of the Second World War. The orders did not change the insignia at all, which remained as designed by Lt. Elliot Chess. Apart from training work, the squadron kept in contact with the American veterans, who tried to help Poland and visited the country several times. Just a few years after the 1920 war Fauntleroy tried to facilitate the purchase of American trucks for the Polish Army. In 1930 Merian Cooper and Edward Corsi visited the squadron at *Mokotów*. In the same year the Polish movie director Leonard Buczkowski made a film about the 7th Kościuszko under the title *The Starred Squadron*.

One of the most spectacular occasions was the September 1933 victory of the Polish crew on the *Kościuszko* balloon in the Gordon-Benett Cup in Chicago. It was accompanied by many press articles, radio broadcasts, and a range of celebrations. On September 25, 1933 Corsi arrived at the Polish Consulate in New York to congratulate the victors, Capt. Hynek and Lt. Burzynski. When they left the U.S. on October 2, Corsi said goodbye to them by the "Kościuszko" ocean liner hull. The Polish balloon navigators took back a number of copies of Corsi's newly published book, *Poland. Land of the White Eagle*, with dedication notes for his old pals and official personalities. The same officer was involved in the work of a committee preparing the Polish pavilion at the New York World's Fair in 1939.[2]

Unfortunately, neither Corsi nor any of his colleagues could help the Poles in the subsequent war, although some of them tried. In spring of 1939, under the ever-increasing threat of war, Col. Fauntleroy reported to the Attache Militaire of the Embassy of Poland in Washington, DC, offering his services once again. The Attache sent a communication on this subject to the General Staff in Warsaw on June 23, 1939. In reply of June, 30, Brig. Gen. Stanisław Ujejski requested clarification of the Fauntleroy's involvement. It turned out that Fauntleroy had no specific plan, but was ready to go to Warsaw to discuss details and to adapt his role to the demands of the Poles. It was a valuable offer, which could have been used in any propaganda campaign.[3] Besides the official channels, Fauntleroy contacted his old friend Gen. Rayski. *The New York Herald Tribune* of August 27, 1939, quoted Faunt as saying that he would "be glad to serve any time [Rayski] may call me." Asked by the newspaper if Poland could turn back Nazi invasion, Fauntleroy said, "That's a difficult question to answer without knowing the full circumstances, but you can quote me ... that from the standpoint of courage and general morale the Polish Army is the finest in Europe and that under all conditions the Poles will put up a hell of a fight."[4]

The outbreak of war prevented the use of Fauntleroy's offer.

11. The Squadron's Odyssey

On September 1, 1939, the 111th Squadron was part of the 3rd Air Division and an element of the Pursuit Brigade defending Warsaw. Unfortunately, technical and numerical superiority was on the enemy's side. Poles used their own fighter planes of P.11c type production, which could not match the German Messerschmitt Me. 109 nor the Messerschmitt Me. 110. Despite this, the Pursuit Brigade noted a range of spectacular victories. Some of the first German losses in the air during World War Two were suffered at the hands of the 111th Squadron. Battles in the skies over Warsaw lasted six days, then the Brigade, together with the 111th Squadron, retreated to the east, continuing the battle for another 11 days. Unfortunately, the crossing of the Red Army into the eastern territory of Poland, dashed any chance of effective resistance. In general the Luftwaffe lost 260 aircraft over Poland and the same number were damaged. It was a fantastic result, which significantly exceeded the entire strength of the Polish air force. What is more, three planes of the 111th Squadron, with around 98 planes of other squadrons and 48 training planes, were rescued and transported to Romania. In all 10,000 officers and personnel of the air force and 2,100 employees of the aviation industry left Poland. Some of them, e.g., the cadet group of the "Young Eagles School" in Dęblin went on foot to Romania under the command of its instructor and later ace of the Battle of Britain, Witold Urbanowicz.[5]

At the beginning of 1940 there were as many as 8,678 Polish airmen and personnel in France. As the result of earlier negotiations with the French and British governments, 300 airmen and 2,000 technical servicemen were sent to the British Isles. The rest underwent training in new equipment and were enlisted into French units. The airmen of the former 111th Squadron found themselves at the Lyon-Bron center. The second part of this squadron was in the French "Grouppe de Chasse I/55." That group was commanded by Maj. Zdzisław Krasnodębski, one of the heroes of the September Campaign of 1939. Not all of the Poles were assigned to combat duties because the French Headquarters was plagued with disarray and disorganization. There was not enough equipment for the rest, nor were there appropriate orders. The Polish commander in chief had to fight serious campaigns with the French HQ about assigning a greater number of airmen to front-line duties. The French, however, distrusted the Poles, remembering the September Campaign of 1939. Due to these circumstances only 145 Polish airmen took direct part in air operations over France. Those who went into action quickly changed the perceptions of the French. Not only the HQ but also the press praised their exploits on the front pages. The first clash in the air in which they participated was a great success. On June 2, 1940, the pilots of the Kościuszko Squadron shot down five German planes over Rouen, among them a Messerschmidt Me.110. Unfortunately, France's capitulation two weeks later did not allow them to fully exploit their presence. In total the Polish pilots in French campaigns shot down at least 52 enemy planes, and probably another 10, and they damaged 7, accounting for as much as 16 percent of losses inflicted upon the Luftwaffe over the skies of France.

After the capitulation of France, the only lifeline was Great Britain. The Polish Tadeusz Kościuszko 303rd Squadron began to form on July 15, 1940, in Blackpool, within the Royal Air Force. On August 2 they were transferred to Northolt, near London, which became the squadron base during the Battle of Britain. The 303rd included pilots from the 111th and 112th Squadrons from the 1940 war in France. At the beginning there were only 14 officers and 135 N.C.O. and a few Englishmen. On August 31 the Squadron was considered not ready for action. Then during a training flight, Lt. Ludwik Paszkiewicz spotted some German Dornier DO.17 with whom the British Fighters were engaged. He broke off from the formation and shot down one of the enemy planes. It was the beginning of the most unusual triumphs of the Squadron, which during the Battle of Britain turned out to be the best in the whole Royal Air Force, notching up as many as 126 aircraft shot down. The contribution of the 303rd was confirmed on September 11, when it shot down 17 aircraft from the total of 89 brought down by the RAF that day. The Squadron was a mascot for the press, Royal family and high-ranking officials. It was visited by King George VI, the Duke of Kent, Winston Churchill, and the Ambassador of the United States, who in 1942 received the badge of the Kościuszko Squadron. The visit of King George VI on September 26, 1940, was typical:

> His Majesty talked with the pilots and then saw them take off to hunt enemy riders. He had to leave before they came back, but asked that news of their day's work should be sent on to him at Buckingham Palace. An elated officer a few hours later telephoned to say that the Squadron had bagged 14 without any own losses reported.[6]

All in all the Poles from all the flying units shot down 203 and a half enemy aircraft, that is 9 percent of the total Luftwaffe losses during the Battle of Britain. It was barely the start of their action. In recognition of the 303rd in December 1941 its best airmen, Lt. Witold Urbanowicz,

M. Feric, Zdzisław Henneberg, and Jan Zumbach, were awarded the highest decoration of the RAF, The Distinguished Flying Cross.[7]

When the direct threat of danger subsided, the Fighter Command transferred Squadron 303 to the airfield at Kirton in Lindsay, combining it with the Second Wing. For about half of 1942 the Squadron had the opportunity to work with the 94th American Air Force Division. On August 1, 1942, on the anniversary of the outbreak of the war, a congratulatory telegram arrived from China from Merian Cooper, with wishes for "Good hunting."

The Squadron did not limit itself to protecting the British Isles. In 1943 the best Polish airmen formed the so-called "Skalski's Circus" in North Africa. They were assigned to the 145th British Division as the "Polish Fighting Team." During their two-month assignment the Poles shot down 25 enemy aircraft and probably three more, and in addition they damaged nine aircraft. Their own losses were counted as barely one aircraft shot down.[8]

After their return to the British Isles and following reorganization in October 1943, the Squadron, together with the Polish 316th and 317th Night Squadrons, joined the 3rd Wing Air Defense of Britain. During Operation Overlord, the 303 took part in cover operations for the invading forces, then in extremely exhaustive fighting action against the V-1 and V-2. In the second case it meant action against the launch position situated on the continent. In the final phase of the war, the Squadron's main tasks were to escort large bomber expeditions. The last combat action in the war was the escorting of the 225th Lancaster Bomber Squadron to Hitler's quarters in Berchtesgaden.

Throughout the war, Polish airmen fighting as part of the RAF shot down and damaged 754 enemy aircraft, dropped 14,700 bombs, and carried out 105,300 sorties. Nineteen hundred pilots died in battle, from a total of 17,000 who served in the RAF. Equally in the Battle of Britain and in the remaining stages of the war, the 303rd distinguished itself in particular. It was dissolved on December 9, 1946, at Hethel airport, when Maj. Witold Łokuciewski, the last commander, removed the Kościuszko insignia from the planes. The Squadron ceased to exist. In the Polish People's Republic, for understandable reasons, the unit was not recreated. The very genesis of the squadron relating to American-Polish cooperation against Soviet Russia prevented any idea of this sort. Anyway, the Moscow puppets in Warsaw regarded all the pilots of the Polish Armed Forces in the West as traitors. In addition after the loss of independence and the eastern territories that were after 1945 annexed to Ukraine,

Belarus and Lithuania, the airmen of the 303rd had nowhere to return to. Those who attempted to return faced long imprisonment and often death. The death penalty was the verdict handed down on one of the most outstanding aces of the WWII, Col. Stanisław Skalski, who returned to the Polish People's Republic. It was only the thaw after Stalin's death that saved him from the implementation of that sentence. At that time a whole range of officers on whom the sentence had not yet been carried out were discharged from prison. In many other cases, sentences were shortened or partially annulled. Skalski left jail April 20, 1956.[9]

Anyway, those who decided to return were a negligible percentage. The overwhelming majority of airmen remained in the West. One of the remaining tasks was to maintain their readiness for combat should there be another conflict. For a few years it seemed that an armed clash between the East and West was unavoidable. It was not until after the death of Stalin and the following thaw in 1956 that it was possible to concentrate on the fostering of the traditions of the unit. This duty fell to the Polish diaspora. A large group of the Kościuszko men had immigrated to the United States. One of the commanders of 303rd and one of the greatest aces of WWII, Witold Urbanowicz, had fought from 1943 in the United States 14th Army Air Forces in China. He concluded his air force career with 28 German and Japanese planes shot down to his credit, not counting other damaged equipment. After the war he worked for American Airlines, Eastern Airlines, and Republic Aviation.[10]

Col. Zdzisław Krasnodębski, the Commander of the 111th Squadron in August of 1939 and CO of a squadron in France and in Great Britain, also found himself on the American continent. He lived in Toronto for many years. Fate also led Col. Witold Kołaczkowski, who had been the Commander of the Squadron from November 1941 to May 12, 1942, to the United States. In a certain sense one can say that it was ordained that after many years of living in New York he should end up in Florida, in the very state where Merian Cooper was born.[11]

The task of keeping alive the memory of the Squadron fell upon these officers. Their attempts fell on fertile ground also among American veterans of WWI. It was not just about maintaining contact with Polish associations and membership of veteran organizations, as in the period before WWII.[12] The outbreak of WWII advanced it much further. For the Americans, the 303rd remained a continuation of the tradition of the 7th Squadron. Cooper quickly received news of the squadron's achievements. On March 9, 1942, he sent a congratulatory dispatch to the CO of the 303rd with the following words of praise: "The

American officers of the Kościuszko Squadron during the Polish War of 1919–21 extend to you their highest praises and congratulations for your wonderful record."[13] Attached to the dispatch was a modest gift, a silver cigarette case with the engraved names of the airmen who had served in Poland between 1919 and 1921. Lt. Bieńkowski replied to the congratulations on May 22, and on May 30, 1942, the same officer wrote to Cooper with a request to send him his recollections about the inception of the 7th Squadron and his diary from those times:

> I am writing this letter also because it is my earnest wish, and I think that of all my fellow pilots, to renew your association with our squadron. We remember with pride your magnificent and brave work in the early days of its history. We can never forget the unselfish motives which actuated you in your fight against our enemies from 1919 to 1921, and now that the fame of the Kościuszko Squadron is established for all time, we do feel that we owe our greatest debt to you for what you did and for what you created. The Polish Air Forces grew from that nucleus of the Kościuszko Squadron, and your names will always be remembered when any history of the Polish Air History is written.[14]

The wartime conditions and the fact that Cooper, who was then Chief of Staff to the American Armed Forces in China (China Air Task Forces), was then serving so far away, meant that his reply was dated as late as September:

> I will be delighted on my return to the United States to send you all the records I have concerning my services with the Polish Air Forces from 1919 to 1921 and to write you a description of the very founding of the Kościuszko Squadron, which actually was started by me in Lwów early in 1919....

In a further part of the letter, Cooper again congratulated them on their achievements, and asked by the way if the 303 used the Kościuszko Squadron's insignia on its planes:

> We bore it with pride on ours in Poland, and I know each and every American who served in Poland would be proud to have that insignia stand for the friendship of the United States and Poland throughout the pages of history.[15]

The insignia of the Squadron retained its identification and connection with the past, and it was even more valued in light of the recent achievements of the Squadron. On June 3, 1944, at Horne, the landing field of the 303rd, three American veterans of the 1919–1920 war were presented with "Polish Pilot's Wings" and the insignia of the 7th Squadron. Capt. Elliot Chess, who during the Second World War served in the "A" Troop Carrier Group of the Ninth Air Force, was the most moved. "I designed this insignia 20 years ago and I never expected to receive it, nor that someone would remember me," he said in thanks for the decoration. Apart from him, General V.H. Strahm, Chief of Staff of the Ninth Air Force, and Maj. Thomas J. Cummings of the Ninth Air Force Command also received the decorations.[16]

Officers of the Polish Armed Forces participated in the ceremony, among them the most famous aces of the Squadron: Urbanowicz, Zumbach, Krasnodębski, and also high-ranking English and American officers. Unfortunately, neither the founder nor the commander of the squadron was present. The former was serving in China, the latter was in Salt Lake City. Military duties prevented Cooper from fulfilling his duty to Bieńkowski, even during his holiday in the United States, which he took in early autumn 1943. His wife justified it, writing to Bieńkowski on October 2 that despite his attempts, her husband had not had time to find the documents nor to write, as she described it, his resume of the first period of the Kościuszko Squadron's history:

> Although he is fighting on the other side of the world, I know he has and always will have a deep affection for Poland and the Kościuszko Squadron. He is happy that Americans played a part in the conception of the Squadron and takes great pride in the brilliant record of the Squadron's gallant members in this war.[17]

After the end of the war, there was no difference in his attitude towards the squadron. After he left military ranks in 1953, Cooper renewed contact with Squadron members who were living in the United States. One of them was Capt. Marek Mażyński, who during a visit to Cooper's home in Pacific Palisades, California, returned to the need to write a book about the squadron. Cooper had thought about it for many years, and had even considered making a film on the subject. He was then already a renowned filmmaker, producer of *King Kong* and in 1952 the recipient of of a special Oscar for his contribution to the art of motion picture.[18] A movie on the Kościuszko Squadron would definitely make the headlines. This idea, however, was buried in a stream of everyday duties and "more important" matters. Then others began to show an interest in the squadron. At Cooper's request, Marek Mażyński helped the authors

11. The Squadron's Odyssey

of the first monograph about the squadron. In his support of the authors Robert Karolevitz and Ross Fenn, Cooper continued to keep in touch with the veterans. He was seen at the veterans' ceremonies and gave his patronage to conventions of the Association of Polish Airmen, which took place in the United States. In the last years preceding his death, he became patron of the *Lwów Circle* in California and instigator of the plan to erect a Remembrance Plaque to the *Lwów Eagles* in the Smithsonian Institution in Washington, DC. However, death prevented the realization of that intention.[19]

His emotional link to Poland is probably best illustrated by his request for the honorary "Orleta" decoration preceding the wedding ceremony of his daughter in 1965. On July 26 of that year the "Dzienik Polski Dziennik Żołnierza" reported that the former hero of the battle for Lwów somehow lost this decoration, but wished to have one on the wedding day planned for summer of that year. He wrote to the Polish Library in London for help and received the last remaining copy of this very special medal.[20]

No less moving was the meeting arranged on the 1,000th anniversary of Christianity of Poland on June 17, 1966. Several Generals of the American Armed Forces, among them, Merian Cooper and Gen. Ludomił Rayski, who came from London, met at the hotel Beverly Hilton, in Beverly Hills. It was the first meeting between Cooper and Rayski in about 40 years.[21] Capt. Richard Cooper, the son of the squadron founder, also attended the celebration, straight from Vietnam. The participants of the academy wanted the next generation to maintain the tradition of Polish-American cooperation and the memory of the 7th Squadron. Certainly very few believed then in a swift victory over communism; only a small number of veterans from WWII, and unfortunately none of the squadron airmen from the period of battle under the Lwów skies, lived to see it. Until 1989, when Poland regained her independence, the guardian of the tradition and the graves of American heroes who sacrificed their lives for Poland was the *Guard of the Graves of Polish Heroes* in Lwów and the "Defenders of Lwów Cemetery."

12 | THE DEFENDERS OF LWÓW CEMETERY

The 1914–1920 war imprinted such an indelible mark on the Polish psyche that the administration of Lwów decided to honor the memory of its fallen defenders in a proper fashion. That more or less is the genesis of the famous Defenders of Lwów Cemetery — called sometimes *Orleta*, Young Eagles, or *Dzieci Lwowskie*, Children of Lwów cemetery,[1] names derived from the fact that in 1918 Lwów was defended by an unprecedented number of students and schoolchildren.

At the cemetery, organized after the Polish victory over the Bolshevik onslaught, a place of honor has been designated for the graves of U.S. airmen. The first impulse to emphasize the airmen, even before the establishment of the cemetery, was to a certain degree the funeral of Edmund Graves in November of 1919. In Graves' funeral procession the propeller from his aircraft was carried behind his coffin, and so a tradition began of placing a propeller on the graves of airmen fallen in the city's defense. The propeller, in addition to the cross mounted on the airmen's graves, created an atmosphere deeply impacting the minds of contemporaries.

The deaths of the so-called "first threesome" of airmen who in 1918 defended Lwów has been a huge incentive in creation of the legend surrounding the airmen. First in the group was Stefan Bastyr, killed on August 6, 1920. His death occurred during a training flight over Lwów airfield in a newly assembled Fokker D VII. His funeral took place four days later, when Budenny's cavalry was approaching Lwów. The shock of Bastyr's death prompted the idea of erecting an imposing memorial to him. A citizen's committee was formed, which appealed to the city inhabitants for donations. Among the first signatories of the appeal was

Cedric Fauntleroy. Before the project had a chance to be implemented, however, another of the legendary defenders of Lwów perished. Stefan Stec died May 11, 1921, and then Lt. Col. Władysław Toruń was killed over the Warsaw *Pole Mokotowskie* (Mokotów airfield) three years later.

These deaths caused an alteration in the plan of individually memorizing the hero-pilots. After deliberations, a concept of a collective tomb at the *Orleta* cemetery prevailed. The idea was implemented in 1935.

Orleta occupied a distinguished place in the Polish national mythology between the two World Wars. The Polish Airforce Pilot Training School adopted the name *Young Eagles School*. Some of its graduates distinguished themselves during their service in the Polish Wings serving in the Royal Air Force during World War II.[2]

The enshrining of the American pilots took place much earlier. On November 10, 1921, the remains of Edmond Graves, Arthur Kelly and J.S. McCallum were laid to rest in a collective tomb. At the same time a committee for the memorial erection was established. It was joined by distinguished citizens of Lwów, veterans, high-ranking officials and the city administration. Squadron officers also joined, including Capt. Władysław Konopka and Capt. Jerzy Weber, who together with American pilots contributed the initial funds. The memorial project gained momentum, and as early as Memorial Day in 1922 a flower-placing ceremony took place at the *Orleta* Cemetery. W.H. Gwynn of the U.S. Humanitarian Mission to Poland took part, as well as representatives of the city administration, veterans and youth organizations.

On the following Polish All Saints Day, which happens to be on November 1, and the following Memorial Day, celebrations were held at the cemetery, giving another impetus at popularization of the American Flyers contribution to the defense of Lwów. At the same time a competition was announced for the memorial. Józef Różycki and Józef Starzyński were the winners. Their project featured a flyer with spread wings and an inscription reading: "In Memoriam of the U.S. Airmen Fallen in the Defense of Poland in the Years 1919–1920. Pilot Officers of the Kościuszko Fighter Squadron: Edmund P. Graves, Lt. of the Polish Army, born 1891 in Boston, died November 22nd, 1919 in Lwów — Arthur H. Kelly, Capt. of the Polish Army, born in Richmond, Virginia, died July 16th, 1920, near Łuck — J.S. McCallum, Lt. of the Polish Army, born in Detroit, died August 31st, 1920, near Lwów."[3]

The memorial was erected with major financial contribution of the Polish National Alliance of Chicago, IL. The unveiling took place on Memorial Day, 1925. The ceremony was attended by prominent citizens and administration officials of the city of Lwów. Also in attendance was the U.S. envoy in Warsaw, Mr. Paerson. The keynote speaker was Leon Piniński, the ex governor of Galicia and the mayor of Lwów, who said,

> We who are living here in Lwów remember most vividly the days five years ago during the spring of 1920. We were then fighting against Bolshevik Russia — every moment the danger was more terrible — the new Polish State might have been crushed by the invasion of the half-savage Russian red army. The American help at that time was for us really like help from heaven. The brilliant part played then by the so-called Kościuszko Squadron and splendid American flyers can be, without exaggeration compared with those legendary medieval knights of the Grail congregation who appeared unexpectedly when it was necessary to fight for truth and justice to defend oppressed virtue.... The American squadron had for Poland not only a very great moral value, it brought us also an exceedingly efficient support in war. We had in our scarcely formed young army almost no aviators at all, and the American flyers were quite prodigiously plucky and skillful. When the result of the war after enormous difficulties and dangers was at last favorable for us, it was certainly in a considerable part their merit. If there had been at all any debt of gratitude to be paid, Americans certainly paid it during the wars and afterwards in a most generous and splendid way.[4]

The memory of the exploits of U.S. airmen was kept alive till the outbreak of WWII in 1939. Annual memorials were observed on Polish and American national holidays and on the anniversary of the 1918 siege of the city. Roll calls of the fallen as well as wreath laying ceremonies took place. Many were attended by representatives of the United States: Military Attaches in Warsaw as well as by envoys and ambassadors and the U.S. advisors to the Polish government. The Americans have repaid the homage by remembering the Poles who sacrificed their lives defending ideals of freedom and democracy. On the 10th anniversary of Polish independence, the U.S. Military Attache in Warsaw reported:

> On Memorial Day the graves of American Aviators in Lwów were decorated with American flags and flowers. A religious service was held, attended by Army and school children. Mr. Dewey placed a wreath on the grave of the Unknown Soldier in Warsaw.[5]

In 1935 Fauntleroy paid tribute to the memory of Jozef Pilsudski upon his passing away. In 1935 the U.S. Military Attache in Warsaw commented on this as follows:

I may add, in this connection, that at the annual services this year in Lwów — in commemoration of the death of Major Fauntleroy's three officers, in Poland's service, I took occasion to announce publicly his tribute to the Marshal, and I am sure it will be gratifying to him to know that the impression was that of deep appreciation.[6]

On several occasions the officers of Squadron 121 and 111 — both units have inherited the Kościuszko Squadron tradition — took part in ceremonies commemorating the American participation in the war against the Bolsheviks, sometimes risking their own lives. On May 29, 1936, Lt. Józef Drogoń perished during the "Honor Guard" flight of the 111th squadron from Warsaw to Lwów to attend a wreath-laying ceremony at the memorial of the fallen U.S. airmen.[7] His death was similar to that of Graves because it also happened during an air show.

The history lesson enveloped in lives of the airmen buried at the cemetery was present in the education efforts of the Polish authorities until they were abruptly interrupted in the fall of 1939, when Stalin's troops occupied Lwów. Borderlines were shifted, Lwów after 1945 was incorporated into the territory of the Soviet Ukraine. Any display of respect towards the defenders of Poland's independence became absolutely impossible and punishable. For decades the Polish population of Lwów, via a series of underground activities, tried to maintain the integrity of the cemetery. An organization by the name of the *Guard of the Graves of Polish Heroes* was active but due to the circumstances was limited to clandestine activities. Their members fought for the right to eternal peace for the fallen soldiers and officers. All in vain. From the day of WWII the cemetery was an object of systematic and vicious devastation. As early as the 1950s, at the height of the anti–American propaganda campaign, the memorial of the U.S. airmen was wrecked, and in the 1960s the cemetery was converted into a garbage dump. Another part of the cemetery was utilized as a truck parking lot with some ugly utility structures erected on the ground. As if it was not enough, a plan was devised to dynamite the cemetery. The plan was abandoned only because of the proximity of housing surrounding the cemetery. To add insult to injury an asphalt highway crossing the cemetery was laid by the communist authorities. The crowning point of barbarism came on August 25, 1971, when Soviet tanks leveled the cemetery to the ground.[8] These barbaric acts were met by widespread outrage. Despite the fear of reprisals, many Polish survivors of the 1918–1920 war protested in Poland, including Gen. Roman Abraham and Gen. Mieczyslaw Boruta-Spiechowicz. To commemorate the Lwów defenders a number of commemorative plaques were unveiled in Polish churches. Later the clandestine press picked up the subject, editing articles, books, postcards, stamps and other memorabilia. The protests of the emigree press were distributed in Poland. The Polish-Canadian Congress dispatched its protest to the Soviet Ministry of Foreign Affairs. The president of Pilsudski Institute of America for Research in the Modern History of Poland stated in a letter to American Battle Monuments Commission:

> This cemetery is considered in Poland as a sort of Sacred Pantheon. It was from this cemetery that a body of a soldier with an unknown name was transformed to Warsaw and deposited in the Cenotaph of the Unknown Soldier in the capital City of Poland. The cemetery also contains the graves of American and French officers who in 1919–1920 volunteered for the defense of Poland in its struggle against the Bolshevik onslaught and gave their lives to protect Europe from the Communist invasion of that time. As far as the Americans are concerned, they were the flyers of the glorious "Kościuszko Squadron" a voluntary unit spontaneously organized by U.S. Major Fauntleroy and Captain-Pilot Merian C. Cooper (later Brigadier General, USAF)....
>
> The graves of these brave Americans, who decided to reciprocate in Poland the traditions of Thaddeus Kościuszko and Casimir Pulaski in America 150 years ago, are located in the place of honor at the cemetery, with the Memorial Monument bearing the inscription in Polish and in English: To American Heroes Who Gave Their Lives for Poland 1919–1920.... We sincerely trust that you will take immediate and effective action to save graves of these American officers and that, in doing so, you will also demand the cessation of the systematic devastation and profanation of the Polish soldiers graves and insist upon the restoration of all damage already perpetrated.[9]

The matter has also been recorded in the U.S. Congress. Representative John Dingell introduced on February 18, 1972, a resolution passed by the Polish American Congress, Michigan Division, which stated:

> We request the Honorable members of the United States Congress to instruct the Secretary of State [in the] initiation of a vigorous protest in the name of the United States of America directed to the Ambassador of the Soviet Union in Washington and also instruct the United States Consular Authorities in the Soviet Union to voice similar protest with the Foreign Office of the Soviet Union — to halt immediately the systematical and methodical destruction of everything that reminds one of the Polish character of the City of Lwów, and especially stop the barbarian destruction of the "Dzieci Lwowskie" (Children of Lwów) cemetery.[10]

12. The Defenders of Lwów Cemetery

This resolution was also based on the presence of U.S. graves at the cemetery. On March the 1, 1972, a committee for the defense of the *Orleta* cemetery was established in the state of Connecticut. On May 17, 1972, the committee appealed to President Richard Nixon asking him for an intervention. The U.S. Embassy in Moscow confirmed after an on-site inspection the condition of the cemetery. The President brought up the problem in a conversation with Soviet Foreign Minister Andriej Gromyko, but all the appeals were stonewalled by the communist administration.

The second half of the 1980s brought about the weakening of the Polish government. In the year 1989 a few announcements by the Polish Minister of Culture resulted in reemergence of the *Orleta* cemetery affair. Almost parallel with the finalization of the round-table negotiations between *Solidarity* and the government, which put an end to the era of communist domination in Poland, a decision was reached on June 9, 1989, about the establishment of a joint Polish-Ukrainian commission to put under its patronage the Łyczakowski as well as adjacent Defenders of Lwów cemeteries. Even before the above date first restoration work had begun. This took place thanks to the initiative of the "Energopol" company, a Polish company working on a number of construction projects in the Ukraine. The management as well as the employees volunteered their weekends and free time to restore the cemetery. Their work was not restricted to the graves of Polish and American heroes. Side by side with Americans laid the last remains of other Allied officers, including French. After the Ukraine declared its independence in 1991, the matter was "officially" recognized and was included in the agenda of Government delegations. Poland started to finance a complex plan of restoration and renovation of the cemetery. The city government of Lwów was presented with no less than three reconstruction programs. One of the projects filed in August 1997 was rejected by the City Council's Commission for Military Memorial Affairs in December of the same year. It took the joint appeal by the presidents in January 1998 to obtain the approval of the Mayor of Lwów, Vasyl Kubijda, to start the reconstruction work. On the Polish side the activity and negotiations were conducted by Andrzej Przewoźnik, the Secretary General of the Council for Preservation of Monuments of Struggle and Martyrdom in Warsaw. Mr. Przewoźnik efforts were crowned in the Spring of 1998 by the initiation of the work for grave reconstruction and general cleaning of the cemetery surface. The predicted time limit called for four years. Much to everybody's amazement the bone of contention included the inscription on the U.S. airmen memorial. The Ukrainian side demanded that it should read that they fell in a Polish-Ukrainian war, not indicating which side they had been fighting for. The objective of this manipulation was to implicate the U.S. volunteers into an anti–Ukrainian venture in which they did not participate. Finally after a clarification by the Polish authorities, the city government changed its mind.[11]

It was planned that as early as November 1, 1998, i.e. on the 80th anniversary of the outbreak of the Polish-Ukrainian conflict, the festive inauguration of the cemetery would take place, with the participation of the Ukrainian and Polish presidents. Unfortunately some of the city council members voiced their opposition. To add insult to injury, before the projected date of the inauguration, Ukrainian nationalists changed the Polish language inscriptions at the cemetery. The historical breakthrough has not materialized.[12]

Official pronouncements published after the visit of Ukrainian president Leonid Kuchma to Poland in January 1999 indicated that the opening ceremonies, although less festive, would take place in May 1999. Alas this time also the opposition of the Ukrainian nationalists torpedoed any hopes. During a visit of the president of Poland to Ukraine, Ukrainians once again placed their own plaque at the cemetery, and in a very bad Polish. After an intervention of president Kuchma it was removed but the bitter after-taste remained. More so because it occurred during a inter-presidential conference attended by delegations from East-Central Europe deliberating about the ramifications of the Kosovo conflict for the region.[13]

In another bad turn for the cemetery the Ukrainian authorities requested in August 1999 that Energopol should stop its renovation work and leave the cemetery. Only after yet another intervention by the Polish side was this decision "frozen."[14]

Unfortunately, until this day Lwów is still awaiting restoration of the final resting-place for all its defenders, including those who in the spirit of lyrics of the Polish national anthem have crossed the ocean to fight "For Your Freedom and Ours."

Appendix: Service Histories and Commendations of U.S. Airmen in the Polish Military

This appendix details the service of the U.S. Airmen from the moment of signing the contract until the moment of discharge or death. Included are the commendations for Polish military decorations awarded to them for their deeds in the service of Poland. The appendix lists officers who arrived before the outset of the Kiev expedition in April 1920. Those who came after the conclusion of the battle of Lwów in August 1920 have been omitted because, by force of events, they did not participate in the military operations. The biographical data of those officers and the opinions of their superior officers have been included in the basic narration of the book.

The *Virtuti Militari* (equivalent of the British Victoria Cross and the U.S. Congressional Medal of Honor) is one of Poland's oldest and most prestigious military decorations. It was established for outstanding bravery in the battle of Zieleńce against the Russians in 1792. Among the first recipients were Gen. Tadeusz Kościuszko and Prince Józef Poniatowski, the future commander of the V Corps of Napoleon's *Grand Armée* during his Moscow expedition in 1812.

In 1832 Russia abolished the "VM" order. It was reactivated in independent Poland in 1919. The first meeting of the Orders Chapter in the resurrected Poland took place in January of 1920. The VM is divided into five classes, the first being awarded to victorious commanders-in-chief (among its recipients are marshal Ferdinand Foch and Józef Piłsudski), and the fifth for outstanding individual gallantry on the battlefield. The procedure of awarding the VM requires a verification and description of the heroic deed, certified by eyewitnesses and an opinion of the CO.

On the eve of the battle for Warsaw, August 11, 1920, a new decoration was instituted, the Cross of Valor. It was bestowed for courage at the front line. The cross could be awarded up to five times. The first time the decoration itself was awarded, followed by "bars" mounted on the original decoration if it was awarded for the second, third, forth and fifth time. One could wear up to four bars on his Cross of Valor.

Some officers who arrived from the U.S. also received the Cross of Polish Soldiers from America to commemorate their nominal service in General Haller's "Blue Army." The civilian decorations bestowed by the Polish government after 1921 have been omitted, as have those awarded by the Polish government in exile during the period of Soviet domination in Poland.

In the list below, the CO of the 7th Squadron is listed first, followed by the other officers in order of seniority in the Polish Army.

Polish officers who fought in the 7th Squadron, recipients of the VM, have been omitted here. Information on their service and decorations can be found in *Polski Slownik Biograficzny* vol. 1–38, Kryska-Karski, *Generalowie Polski Niepodleglej* and other sources.

Col. Cedric Fauntleroy, Pilot, Polish Air Force

As of Spring of 1919 served for 3 months in the Polish Military Purchase Mission in Paris under the command of Gen. Jan Romer. He was one of the principal Squadron organizers in Paris. Joined the Polish Armed Forces after signing a contract binding till February 1920, at the Polish mission in Paris. Commanded the 7th Squadron from October 18, 1919. As of July 1, 1920, Commanded the Polish-American Air Group, from August 10, 1920, commanded the III Air Group (*Dyon*) and became the CO of the Air Forces of the Southern Front of the Polish Armed Forces. Injured in action near Łuck on July 15, 1920, remained in the ranks, formally released from his contract on September 30, 1920, and subsequently signed a new contract on October 1, 1920. Promoted to the rank of Lt. Colonel and on October 8, 1920, granted a 4 month furlough to visit U.S. Discharged from Polish Armed Forces on May 15, 1921, as a full (bird) Colonel. The Chief of Polish Air Forces, Maj. Jasiński, has written in his opinion about Col. Fauntleroy: "An officer of unusual energy and elasticity. A person of outstanding intelligence — very devoted to the Polish cause. An experienced organizer. General qualification — an outstanding officer."

COMMENDATION FOR THE VM DECORATION

Maj. Fauntleroy while serving as a CO of a squadron has, in addition to his organizational skills, displayed as a pilot skills and valor in individual and formation sorties. Giving a shining example of allegiance to his duties and courage to all his subordinate officers of the 7th Squadron. As an example of his deeds we can quote the events of May 30, 1920. At 0500 hours he informed the HQ of the 13th Infantry Division that elements of their infantry Brigade had been cut off by the Bolshevik forces. At 0800 hours HQ delivered orders to the surrounded Brigade from 13th divisional HQ. He also informed them about their situation and displacement of the enemy, thus enabling the Brigade to overcome the enemy forces. Maj. Fauntleroy has engaged the enemy with his machine guns and inflicted many casualties upon them. At 1600 hours during a reconnaissance sortie he noticed the Bolsheviks planting mines under the railroad tracks in a spot which was being approached by two Polish infantry trains. Major Fauntleroy landed his aircraft by the train and warned them about the danger. At the same time he informed them about a 2,500-strong Bolshevik cavalry unit, which had broken through the front line and was approaching Koziatyń. This deed saved the infantry units and enabled the HQ to direct the attack at the proper destination.

On April 8, 1921, the recommendation for awarding the VM class V was approved. The awarding ceremony took place on May 10, 1921, at which Marshal Piłsudski personally decorated the Major in the Belvedere Palace. By the order of the Minister of Defense on April 21, 1921, he also received the Cross of Valor two times, and later four times (with 3 bars).

Lt. Col. Merian Cooper, Pilot, Polish Air Force

Signed the contract for volunteer service in the Polish Military granting him a rank of Captain in Paris August 3, 1919. Flight leader of the 7th Squadron and temporary Acting Commander of the same Squadron from April 10, 1920, to May 2, 1920, also from May 17 to June 3, 1920, when he commanded a detachment of the 7th Squadron in Kiev. On July 13, 1920, made a force landing in the vicinity of Didicze village

Virtuti Militari V Class, Cross of Valor with two bars and Haller's Cross of Polish Soldiers from America, all awarded to Merian Cooper. (Courtesy of the Piłsudski Institute, New York.)

not far from Ołyka, and became a Bolshevik POW. He remained in Soviet captivity until the Spring of 1921. After his escape with 2 Polish officers he found his way to Riga, and subsequently to Warsaw. Discharged on May 10, 1921, with the rank of Lt. Col.

COMMENDATION FOR THE VM DECORATION

Capt. Cooper has conducted reconnaissance sorties into the depth of enemy territory. He attacked the enemy from a very low ceiling. His merits include acting as a liaison between the Army HQ and cavalry units during the Kiev offensive. As a second in command during the absence of Squadron CO, Cooper conducted group operational sorties. Thanks to his composure and battlefield experience all the sorties have been crowned with success. In spite of enemy fire only one airman sustained an injury. Capt. Cooper was in command of 3 operational sorties on April 26, 1920. On that day Polish hostages were released from Soviet captivity at the railroad station in Berdyczew by Polish infantry. The infantry was kept at bay by heavy machine gun fire, which was silenced by Capt. Coopers aircrafts. On May 30, 1920, Capt. Cooper attacked enemy river vessels around Tripolje on the

Dniepr River. The result was crowned by sinking one and crippling another armored vessel.

Commendation for VM class IV was completed in Zwiahel on June 13, 1920. On April 8, 1921, the VM class V was confirmed. The presentation took place in Belvedere Palace on May 10, 1921. On May 7, 1921, Cooper received the Cross of Valor three times (with 2 bars).

Maj. George Crawford, Pilot, Polish Air Force

Recruited to Polish Military with a rank of Capt. on September 1, 1919, based on a six-month contract, which was renewed on February 1, 1920. As of August 1, Capt. Crawford acted as CO of the 7th Squadron. On August 28, 1920, Chief of Aviation of the GHQ proposed his nomination to higher rank; however, the regulations did not allow promotion of the contract officer at this stage.

Discharged on November 11, 1920, and re-recruited on the next day with a new contract, discharged on May 10, 1921, with the rank of Major. Fauntleroy wrote about him: "An outstanding fighter pilot, above average bravery, conscientious, compulsive officer, an excellent Squadron commander."

COMMENDATION FOR THE VM DECORATION

Lt. Crawford has displayed a great personal courage in conducting long range, individual reconnaissance into the depth of enemy territory. While attacking the enemy he also obtained vital information about them. During his second sortie on May 10, 1920, Lt. Crawford attacked, while being subjected to heavy enemy anti-aircraft machine gun fire, the largest of 7 Bolshevik vessels on the River Dniepr around Czerkassy. With his fire Lt. Crawford ignited the enemy vessel. As a result the soldiers jumped into the water. To bring precise information to his HQ Lt. Crawford extended his sortie, (and when he ran out of fuel, he made a forced landing 15 km away from his base. He notified without delay his HQ about the mission. In the time period from May 9 to 26, 1920, he conducted 10 similar sorties. On May 25, he attacked enemy cavalry in the area of Talnoje and inflicted heavy casualties.

Commendation for IV class VM submitted in Zwiahel on June 13, 1920. On April 8, 1921, VM class V was confirmed. In addition he received the Cross of Valor four times (with three bars).

Capt. Edward Corsi, *Pilot, Polish Air Force*

Recruited to the Polish Military with a contract dated September 1, 1919, with rank of a Captain, discharged from PAF with a rank of Captain on May 10, 1921. The CO of the 7th Squadron, Capt. Crawford, wrote in commendation for his VM: "Excellent pilot and officer, displayed proof of courage and devotion to duty."

COMMENDATION FOR THE VM DECORATION

Capt. Corsi has conducted long-range sorties into the enemy territory, frequently as a group leader. During his sorties he distinguished himself as a brave flier, skillfully attacking the enemy, using his bombs and machine guns. As a "Wing" CO he acted with experience, thus not paying attention to difficult conditions or enemy fire but always returned to base with excellent results and zero casualties. While conducting his assigned tasks during individual sorties, always supplied information about the enemy. On May 30, 1920, he took part in paralyzing and beaching of the second Bolshevik monitor (armored vessel on the Dniepr River). On the same day he attacked Tripolje. From April 9 to 14, 1920, in addition to reconnaissance sorties, Capt. Corsi conducted sorties to Berdyczew in order to deliver reports to 2nd Polish Army HQ. Regardless of bad atmospheric conditions he maintained exemplary communications.

Commendation for IV class VM submitted in Zwiahel on June 13, 1920, V class confirmed on April 8, 1921. In addition he also received the Cross of Valor three times (with two bars).

Capt. Charles Clark, *Pilot, Polish Air Force*

Recruited to Polish Military based on contract from September 1, 1919, with the rank of Lieutenant. On September 7, 1920, asked for summary discharge from Polish Armed Forces for family reasons. Discharge was granted on September 17, 1920, with promotion to the rank of Captain Clark's application for reenlistment to PAF from February 10, 1921, was rejected due to approaching peace treaty with Bolshevik Russia.

COMMENDATION FOR THE VM DECORATION

Capt. Clark distinguished himself during numerous operational sorties over enemy-held territory, with outstanding courage, while attacking various enemy branches of services. On April 26, 1920, despite a headache, Lt. Clark performed 3 operational sorties, 2 hours each. During the sorties he successfully attacked enemy columns and machine-gun emplacements near Berdyczew. During his attack, his plane sustained severe damage from enemy fire, thus one of his aircraft wings had to be replaced. Not paying attention to the above, Lt. Clark accomplished his mission and returned to the base after its completion. On May 30, 1920, he participated in a successful attack on enemy shipping on the Dniepr River around Tripolje. During the attack one vessel was sunk and the other (armored) was beached. We also underline the fact that during the 3rd sortie on April 26, 1920, Lt. Clark attacked with outstanding results the railroad station in Berdyczew, then subsequently a retreating Bolshevik column, inflicting heavy casualties upon it.

Commendation for IV class VM submitted in Zwiahel on June 13, 1920, confirmed for V class VM on April 8, 1921. In addition Capt. Clark received the Cross of Valor two times (with one bar) and the "Cross of Polish Soldiers from America."

Capt. Harmon Chadbourn Rorison, *Pilot, Polish Air Force*

Joined the Polish Military on the basis of individual permit allowing an 8-month service outside the borders of U.S. He signed the contract for enlistment into the Polish Military with a rank of lieutenant on November 27, 1919. On July 20, 1920, he requested a discharge from Polish Military in order to report in the U.S. He was discharged with a rank of Captain on July 31, 1920. The opinion about him attached to the VM commendation reads: "An excellent pilot and officer. In numerous and long-range sorties over the enemy lines he displayed boundless and uncommon courage and exemplary heroism."

Commendation for the VM Decoration

Distinguished himself with great valor and uncommon experience on performance of his operational sorties both solo and in concert with others. He frequently attacked cavalry and machine-gun emplacements, supply columns and infantry, inflicting heavy casualties upon the enemy. In spite the fact that he had not been assigned a specific theater of operations he conducted long-range reconnaissance sorties with excellent results. During one of those sorties an enemy bullet had blown away from his hand the only map in his Squadron possession. On May 15, 1920, during a reconnaissance sortie on Korsuń, Lt. Rorison attacked enemy heavy machine-gun emplacements. During his assault his main fuel tank was perforated by enemy machine gun fire, and he had to force-land his aircraft during his retreat. He landed 2 km from Korsuń. Chased by enemy peasant gangs he walked a distance of 45 km to his closest infantry positions. He delivered the results of his reconnaissance mission without delay. Immediately thereafter he returned and successfully recovered his aircraft. In spite the fact that he had no knowledge of local tongues (he speaks English only plus some German) he accomplished his duty.

Commendation for IV class VM submitted in Zwiahel on June 13, 1920; VM class V approved on August 8, 1920. The award ceremony took place March 14, 1921, at the Polish mission in Washington, DC with General Pershing and J.J. Paderewski in attendance. Rorison was also awarded the Cross of Valor four times (with three bars) and the Cross of Polish Soldiers from America.

Lt. Eliot Chess, *Pilot, Polish Air Force*

Recruited to Polish Military on basis of contract from September 1, 1919, discharged with the rank of Captain on April 30, 1921. In commendation for VM it was said: "Excellent pilot and officer, displayed proof of boundless courage and valor."

COMMENDATION FOR VM DECORATION

On May 21, 1920, during reconnaissance sortie conducted by Lt. Chess at an altitude of 100 meters in the direction of Taraszcze-Olszanica his aircraft received 14 hits. Attacking with machine gun fire he forced the enemy to disperse. Returned to base, where his aircraft was rendered temporarily unoperational due to serious damage. On May 31, 1920, with Maj. Fauntleroy, Lt. Chess worked through the night unloading spare ammunition from the transport in Koziatyń. After repair of his aircraft he attacked the enemy fighting against our forces along the Lipowiec-Nowochwastów line. Utilizing his machine guns and bombs he dispersed the enemy and facilitated our forces in occupying a natural stronghold. During the above attack, Lt. Chess has been shot in his leg.

Commendation for VM submitted in Zwiahel on June 13, 1920, for IV class; VM V class confirmed on April 8, 1921. He was also awarded the Cross of Valor.

Lt. Edwin Noble, *Pilot, Polish Air Force*

Recruited to Polish Military based on contract dated September 1, 1919, with a rank of second lieutenant Injured on April 26, 1920, by a "dum-dum" bullet in his right elbow. After a number of days in a field hospital, he had to be transferred to an American hospital in Paris, where surgery was performed. Formal discharge from Polish Armed Forces took place on September 23, 1920. Promoted to rank of Captain based on an order of Polish Ministry of Military Affairs on September 23, 1920, confirmed by Gen. Kazimierz Sosnkowski on October 5, 1920. On the commendation application for VM Fauntleroy stated: "Sec. Lt. Noble has displayed great courage and stamina in his struggle against the enemy, and for this reason I firmly support commendation for IV class VM."

COMMENDATION FOR VM DECORATION

During the preparation and the course of the Żytomierz and Berdyczew offensive Sec. Lt. Noble performed 13 operational sorties over the enemy territory, attacking the artillery, cavalry, infantry and supply column from the lowest possible ceiling. According to the testimony of the civilian population of Berdyczew he silenced the Bolshevik artillery by flying at very low ceiling and sniping with his machine guns. His plane has been shot numerous times. The enemy battery crew abandoned its position in panic. During a second sortie he attacked a Bolshevik column of a few hundred infantrymen marching toward Berdiczew. The column, including a number of supply wagons, was attacked by him an from an altitude of 20 meters. Soviet POW told Lt. Potocki, the Adjutant of the 2nd Polish Army, about a Polish aircraft which created a total confusion in their ranks, killing and injuring a number of soldiers during a third sortie on the same day. Lt. Noble attacked Bolsheviks in Berdyczew, flying in a group with three other pilots of the 7th Squadron. He facilitated the occupation of Berdyczew by Polish forces. He personally attacked three times an armored train at the Berdyczew railroad station. During that attack he was injured in his right arm by the explosive "dum-dum" bullet. Bleeding profusely from his wounds he returned 85 km to his base, performed a smooth landing in spite of loss of blood and severe weakness. The HQ of 2nd Polish Army announced as a result of this attack the Bolsheviks have scattered at the station, freeing the Polish POWs and hostages whom they intended to transfer from Berdyczew. They have been liberated by the Polish infantry. In addition to attacks he performed on that day, he always diligently carried out operational duties assigned to him. He was always an exemplary self-sacrificing flyer, disregarding personal danger.

Commendation for VM, IV class submitted on May 3, 1920, in Zwiahel and repeatedly on June 6, 1920. On August 8, 1920, V class VM was confirmed. Lt. Noble was also awarded the Cross of Valor two times with one bar, and also the Cross of Polish Soldiers from America.

Lt. Kenneth Shrewsbury, *Pilot, Polish Air Force*

Recruited in Polish Military on basis of contract dated September 1, 1919. On July 7, 1920, Shrewsbury filed for summary discharge for family reasons. Discharged on July 30, 1920. In a note to the Minister of Defense, the CO of the Polish Air Force stated: "The above mentioned is a very brave officer and a good pilot. That is why the Polish Air Forces HQ is parting from him with sorrow. However, the Polish Air Forces HQ is asking for a favorable resolution of the matter, in view of his merits in the recent fighting."

Commendation for VM Decoration

Lt. Shrewsbury has displayed uncommon valor during his attacks on all branches of enemy military and reconnaissance sorties at a low ceiling. He displayed uncommon valor and experience on April 24, 1920, when he performed in very adverse atmospheric conditions a reconnaissance sortie over enemy first line of defense. In spite of heavy artillery and machine gun fire returned to base with valuable intelligence. On April 25, 1920, Lt. Shrewsbury performed numerous attacks against the enemy retreating from Żytomierz and inflicted heavy material and human losses.

V class VM was presented to Shrewsbury in the Polish Mission in Washington, DC on March 14, 1921. He was also decorated with the Cross of Valor and the Cross of Polish Soldiers from America.

NOTES

Chapter 1

1. M.B. Biskupski, "Kościuszko, we are here?": American Volunteers for Poland and the Polish Russian War, 1918–1920, in: Stanislaus Blejwas, Mieczyslaw B. Biskupski, eds., *Pastor of the Poles: Polish American Essays Presented to Right Reverend Monsignor John P. Wodarski in Honor of the Fiftieth Anniversary of His Ordination* (New Britain, 1982), pp. 184–185. James C. White, "Newton D. Baker," *Free Poland* (Chicago), vol. III, no. 21, July 15, 1917, p. 14. Jacek R. Wędrowski, *Stany Zjednoczone a odrodzenie Polski. Polityka Stanów Zjednoczonych wobec sprawy polskiej w latach 1916–1919* (Wrocław, Ossolineum, 1980), p. 51ff.

2. Key Lundgreen-Nielsen, *The Polish Problem at the Paris Peace Conference. A Study of the Policies of the Great Powers and the Poles 1918–1919* (Odense University Press, 1979), pp. 143–145.

3. I. Paderewski to Col. House, January 4, 1919, no. 2067.41, WE 860c00/14, National Archive, Washington, DC, Record Group 165.

4. I. Paderewski to Col. House, January 12, 1919, in: *The Intimate Papers of Colonel House. Volume IV, The Ending of the War, June 1918–November 1919* (London, 1928), pp. 272–275. On American policy towards Paderewski's cabinet, see also: Mieczyslaw Biskupski, "Poland in American Foreign Policy, 1918–1945: Sentimental or Strategic Friendship" *"Polish-American Studies,"* vol. XXXVIII, no. 2, 1981, pp. 5–16. Mieczyslaw Biskupski, "The Wilsonian View of Poland: Idealism and Geopolitical Traditionalism," in: John Micgiel, ed., *Wilsonian East Central Europe: Current Perspectives* (Pilsudski Institute, New York, 1995), pp. 123–139. Jacek R. Wędrowski, *Stany Zjednoczone a odrodzenie Polski. Polityka Stanów Zjednoczonych wobec sprawy polskiej w latach 1916–1919* (Wrocław, Ossolineum, 1980), p. 100ff.

5. Col. House to President Wilson, February 23, 1919, *The Intimate Papers of Colonel House. Volume IV, The Ending of the War, June 1918–November 1919* (London, 1928), pp. 358–359.

6. I. Paderewski to J. Piłsudski, Paris, June 20, 1919, Jozef Pilsudski Insti-

tute for Research in the Modern History of Poland, New York, Adjutancy General of the Commander in Chief, vol. 57/2, doc. 1013/T4.

7. Appendix to Gen. Rozwadowski's Report, Paris, June 10, 1919, Central Military Archive, Warsaw, I 301.7.15.

8. Gen. T. Rozwadowski to J. Piłsudski, Paris, June 15, 1919, Central Military Archive, Warsaw, I 301.7.15.

9. Col. House to President Wilson, February 23, 1919, in: *The Intimate Papers of Colonel House. Volume IV, The Ending of the War, June 1918–November 1919* (London, 1928), pp. 484.

10. I. Paderewski to R. Lansing, Paris, July 18, 1919, *Archiwum Polityczne Ignacego Paderewskiego* [Political archive of I.J. Paderewski] (Ossolineum, Wrocław, 1974), vol. II, pp. 281–282.

11. Richard Ulrych, "General Tadeusz Rozwadowski and the Attempt to Establish a Volunteer American Legion within the Polish Army, 1919–1920," *The Polish Review* (New York), vol. XXXVII, no. 1, 1992, see also: Gen. Pershing Diary, June 27, 1919, Library of Congress, Washington, Gen. John J. Pershing Papers, Box 7.

12. Col. H. Howland to General Pershing, Commander in Chief, AEF, Paris, July 7, 1919, Archiwum Paderewskiego, Archiwum Akt Nowych [Archive of Modern History, cited hereafter as AAN] Warsaw, vol. 813, pp. 3–5.

13. Gen. Rozwadowski to J. Pilsudski, Report no. 50 (Secret), Paris, July 7, 1919, Pilsudski Institute, New York, Adjutancy General of the Commander in Chief, vol. 57/1, p. 54.

14. Cedric Fauntleroy's Audio Interview, June 3, 1962, Hollywood Race Track, Hollywood Turf Club, Inglewood, CA, Collection of *The Cross & Cockade. The Society of World War I Aero Historians*, deposited now at the Oral History Program, Air Force Historical Research Agency, Maxwell AFB, Alabama.

15. Col. S. Haller to Adjutancy General of the Commander in Chief, Warsaw, July 11, 1919, Pilsudski Institute, New York, Adjutancy General of the Commander in Chief, vol. 57/2, doc. 1103.

16. Col. S. Haller to Adjutancy General of the Commander in Chief, Warsaw, July 14, 1919, Pilsudski Institute, New York, Adjutancy General of the Commander in Chief, vol. 57/2, doc. 1122.

17. Maj. Gen. J.G. Harbord to Col. H.S. Howland, Paris, July 10, 1919, Archiwum I.J. Paderewskiego, cited hereafter as Paderewski Collection, AAN, Warsaw, vol. 813, p. 10.

18. Gen. Rozwadowski to High Command of the Polish Army, Paris, July 13, 1919, Central Military Archive, Warsaw, I 301.15.7.

19. Consolidated Memorandum of notes by General A.W. Bjornstad, United States Army, for Mr. Paderewski and General Rozwadowski, Paris, July 16, 1919, Paderewski Collection, AAN, Warsaw, vol. 813, pp. 12–14.

20. Col. H. Howland to I. Paderewski, Paris, July 16, 1919, Paderewski Collection, AAN, Warsaw, vol. 813, pp. 8–9.

21. R. Ulrych, "General Tadeusz Rozwadowski and the Attempt to Establish a Volunteer American Legion within the Polish Army, 1919–1920," *The Polish Review* (New York), vol. XXXVII, no. 1, 1992, 99.

22. Key Lundgreen-Nielsen, *The Polish Problem at the Paris Peace Conference* (Odense University Press, 1979), pp. 87, 179, 397. See also: Eugeniusz Romer, *Pamiętnik paryski 1918–1919* [Paris memoir] (Ossolineum, Wrocław, 1989), p. 289.

23. R. Ulrych, "General Tadeusz Rozwadowski and the Attempt to Establish a Volunteer American Legion within the Polish Army, 1919–1920," *The Polish Review* (New York), vol. XXXVII, no. 1, 1992, pp. 102–104.

24. M.B. Biskupski, "Kościuszko, we are here?": American Volunteers for Poland and the Polish Russian War, 1918–1920, in: Stanislaus Blejwas, Mieczyslaw B. Biskupski, eds., *Pastor of the Poles: Polish American Essays Presented to Right Reverend Monsignor John P. Wodarski in Honor of the Fiftieth Anniversary of His Ordination* (New Britain, 1982), p. 191.

Chapter 2

1. Robert Karolevitz, Ross S. Fenn, *Flight of Eagles. The Story of the American Kościuszko Squadron in the Polish-Russian War, 1919–1920* (Sioux Falls, 1974), pp. 15–16.

2. Merian C. Cooper to Marek Mażyński in Pasadena, CA, May 24, 1972, Mażyński File, Pilsudski Institute, New York.

3. M. Cooper to The Chief Signal Officer of the Army in Washington, DC, Mineola, Long Island, September 27, 1917, Merian C. Cooper Collection, Hoover Institution Archives, Stanford, CA, Appendix 8B.

4. M. Cooper to Adjutant General of the Army, War Department in Washington, January 20, 1917, Merian C. Cooper Collection, Hoover Institution Archives, Appendix 3.

5. M. Cooper to Adjutant General of the Army, War Department in Washington, January 20, 1917; Walter A. Harris to John Cooper in Jacksonville, Macon, August 27, 1917; Merian C. Cooper Collection, Hoover Institution Archives, Appendix 3. see also: R. Karolevitz and R. Fenn, *Flight of Eagles*, pp. 19–20.

6. Capt. James Murray to Col. Wilson B. Burtt, Aviation Section, December 23, 1917, Merian C. Cooper Collection, Hoover Institution Archives, Appendix 10.

7. Edward V. Rickenbacker, *Fighting the Flying Circus* (Frederick A. Stokes Company, New York, 1919), pp. 320–328.

8. Martin Gilbert, *The First World War; A Complete History* (Henry Holt and Company, New York, 1996), p. 457ff *"The Official Record of the United States' Part in the Great War"* (Washington, DC), pp. 118–125.

9. Lewis F. Turnbull, Headquarters, 20th Aero Squadron, Recommendation for the Distinguished Service Cross for M. Cooper, December 8, 1918, Merian C. Cooper Collection, Hoover Institution Archives, Appendix 15A. For Air Force role in those battles, see: *The Official Record of the United States' Part in the Great War*, pp. 120ff. Martin Gilbert, *The First World War; A Complete History* (Henry Holt and Company, New York, 1994), p. 454ff.

10. H. Hoover Address at the Polish Convention in Buffalo, November 12,

1919, reprinted in: George Lerski, ed., *Herbert Hoover and Poland. A Documentary History of a Friendship* (Hoover Institution Press, Stanford, 1977), pp. 84–90.

11. Alfred E. Cornebise, *Typhus and Doughboys; The American Polish Typhus Expedition 1919–1921* (Newark, University of Delaware Press, London and Toronto, 1982). Gaines M. Foster, "Typhus Disaster in the Wake of War: The American-Polish Relief Expedition, 1919–1920," *Bulletin of the History of Medicine*, vol. 55, pp. 221–232.

12. E. Farman to Military Intelligence Department (MID) in Washington, D.C. "Poland. Economic Factor," January 29, 1920, Report no. 591, E. Farman to MID, July 17, 1920, Report no. 882, "Poland. Economic Factor," National Archive, Washington, Record Group 165.

13. George Lerski, ed., *Herbert Hoover and Poland. A Documentary History of a Friendship* (Hoover Institution Press, Stanford, 1977), p. 4ff. M.B. Biskupski, "The Origins of the Paderewski Government in 1919: A Reconsideration in Light of New Evidence," *The Polish Review* (New York), vol. XXXIII, no. 2, 1988, pp. 157–166. Marian M. Drozdowski, *Ignacy Jan Paderewski, A Political Biography in Outline* (Interpress, Warsaw, 1981), pp. 142–144.

14. Rosa Bailly, *A City Fights for Freedom. The Rising of Lwów in 1918–1919* (London, no date of publication provided). Stefan Mękarski, *Lwów. A Page of Polish History* (London 1991). For accounts of military operations in and around the city, see: "*Obrona Lwowa 1–22 listopada 1918. vol. I–II, Relacje Uczestników* [Defense of Lwów, Testimonies of the Participants] (Lwów, 1933, 1936); Stanisław Nilski, Aleksander Kron, *Listopad we Lwowie (1918r.)* [November of 1918 in Lwów] (Warsaw, 1920).

15. [Merian C. Cooper], *Faunt-le-Roy i jego Eskadra w Polsce* [Fauntleroy and his Escadrille in Poland] (Chicago, 1922), pp. 60–61.

16. M. Cooper to Editor of *Chwila*, Dr. Gerszon Zipper, April 27, 1919, Merian C. Cooper Collection, Hoover Institution Archives, Appendix 15A. *Gazeta Lwowska*, vol. CL (110), no. 212, Lwów, September 17, 1920.

17. W.R. Grove to H. Hoover in Paris, Warsaw, May 20, 1919, Merian C. Cooper Collection, Hoover Institution Archives, Appendix IA-31A.

18. Letter of Lwów officials to Col. Grove, Lwów, May 16, 1919, Merian C. Cooper Collection, Hoover Institution Archives, Appendix 20C.

19. Elbert Farman, Parts of notes kept by Lt. Col. Elbert E. Farman, first Military Attache of the U.S. Legation in Poland — Spring 1919–June 1923, Elbert Farman File, Pilsudski Institute, pp. 9–10. On Farman's views regarding Galicia and the Polish-Ukrainian conflict, see: Władysław Żeleński, "Wojna polsko-ukraińska i bolszewicka w oczach pierwszego attache wojskowego USA w Warszawie" [Polish-Ukrainian War in the eyes of the first U.S. Military Attache in Warsaw], "*Niepodległość*" (New York, London), vol. 22, 1989, pp. 170–172 ff. For the French perspective of the same issue, see: Michał Budny, "Misja Generała Berthelemy w Polsce w relacji Romana Michałowskiego" [Gen. Berthelemy's mission to Poland as seen by Roman Michałowski], "*Niepodległość*" (New York, London), vol. 15 (1982), p. 184 ff.

20. Merian C. Cooper to Józef Piłsudski, April 29, 1919, Merian C. Cooper File, Pilsudski Institute, New York.

21. Cedric Fauntleroy's Audio Interview, June 3, 1962, Hollywood Race Track, Hollywood Turf Club, Inglewood, CA, Collection of *The Cross & Cockade. The Society of World War I Aero Historians*, deposited now at the Oral History Program, Air Force Historical Research Agency, Maxwell AFB, Alabama.

22. Wacław Jędrzejewicz, Janusz Cisek, *Kalendarium życia Józefa Piłsudskiego 1867–1935*, vol. 2, 1918–1926 (Rytm, Warszawa, 1998), pp. 82–96; Kenneth Malcolm Murray, "The Kościuszko Squadron," *Poland Magazine* (New York), February 1924, p. 74. Sterling Seagrave, *Soldiers of Fortune* (Alexandria, 1985), p. 35.

23. R. Karolevitz, R. Fenn, *Flight of Eagles*, p. 16. Krzysztof Dubiński, "Polska odyseja Kapitana Coopera. Amerykańscy piloci Eskadry Kościuszkowskiej," *Prawo i Życie* (Warsaw), no. 47 (1455), November 21, 1992.

24. M. Cooper to Flight-Lieutenant Bieńkowski, September 13, 1942, The Polish Institute and Sikorski Museum, London, Collection Lot A.V 49/34/5.

25. "American Flyers Plan to Join Polish Corps. Expect Germans to Oppose New Nations, and Are Eager to Face Old Foe Again," *The New York Times*, no. 22425, June 18, 1919.

26. *Gazeta Lwowska*, vol. CL (110), no. 212, Lwów September 17, 1920.

27. Capt. Zbigniew Orzechowski, Memoriał w sprawie nominacji ppłk Faunt-le-Roya na generała WP, Lwów 9 maja 1921 [Memo on the subject of promotion of Lt. Col. Fauntleroy to the rank of General], Central Military Archive, Records of Ministry of Military Affairs, no. 14429/21.

28. Kenneth M. Murray, *Wings Over Poland. The Story of the 7th (Kościuszko) Squadron of the Polish Air Service, 1919, 1920, 1921* (D. Appleton and Company New York 1932), p. 11.

29. Kenneth M. Murray, "The Kościuszko Squadron," *Poland Magazine* (New York), no. 2, February 1924, p. 74.

30. Mariusz Patelski, "Gwiaździsta eksadra," *Życie* (Warsaw), no. 61 (745), March 13–14, 1999.

31. Col. Tadeusz Kasprzycki, Piłsudski's Aide de camp to Capt. Merian Cooper, May 14, 1920, Merian Cooper Personal File, Central Military Archive, no. 5238. Jan Sęk, "Amerykański Kościuszko," *Tygodnik Solidarność* (Warsaw), no. 33 (100), August 17, 1990.

32. All documents from the Personal File of Capt. Merian Cooper, Central Military Archive, Warsaw, no. 5238.

33. Capt. Merian C. Cooper, Air Service to Commanding General, AEF in Paris, Warsaw, May 19, 1919, Merian C. Cooper Collection, Hoover Institution Archives, Appendix 1A.

34. Recommendation of Col. William R. Grove regarding Capt. Merian C. Cooper for Herbert Hoover, U.S. Food Administration, Warsaw, May 20, 1919, and following documentation from Merian C. Cooper Collection, Hoover Institution Archives.

35. Merian C. Cooper Collection, Hoover Institution Archives, Appendix 1A and 21C.

36. Merian C. Cooper Collection, Hoover Institution Archives, Appendix 17C.

37. Cedric Errol Fauntleroy, Personal File, Central Military Archive, Warsaw, no. 2743. C. Fauntleroy, Audio Interview, June 3, 1962, Hollywood Race Track, Hollywood Turf Club, Inglewood, CA, Collection of *The Cross & Cockade. The Society of World War I Aero Historians*, deposited now at the Oral History Program, Air Force Historical Research Agency, Maxwell AFB, Alabama. Edward V. Rickenbacker, *Fighting the Flying Circus* (Frederick A. Stokes Company, New York, 1919), pp. 354–357.

38. "Our Fliers to Aid Poles," *The New York Times*, no. 22496, August 28, 1919.

39. George Marter Crawford, Personal File, no. 4794, Central Military Archive, Warsaw.

40. Kenneth Shrewsbury, Personal File, Central Military Archive, Warsaw, no. 15175; Kenneth Shrewsbury papers in the collection of Dr. Tomasz Kopański, Warsaw. Zygmunt Kozak, "Udział lotników amerykańskich w wojnie polskosowieckiej," *Biuletyn Wojskowej Służby Archiwalnej* (Warsaw), no. 18, 1995, p. 91.

41. Edward C. Corsi, Personal File, no. 5240, Akta Krzyża Virtuti Militari [Documentation of the Cross of the "Virtuti Militari" decoration], no. 18-1092, Central Military Archive, Warsaw.

42. Clark C. Clark, Personal File, no. 5226; Akta Krzyża Virtuti Militari, no. 18-1094, Central Military Archive, Warsaw. Zygmunt Kozak, "Udział lotników amerykańskich w wojnie polsko-sowieckiej," *Biuletyn Wojskowej Służby Archiwalnej*, no. 18 (Warsaw, 1995), p. 91.

43. Edwin Lawrence Noble, Personal File, no. 585; Akta Krzyża Virtuti Militari, no. 18-1149, Central Military Archive, Warsaw. Some documents regarding E. Noble are now in the possession of Mr. Paul Konys, Rocky River, OH. Zygmunt Kozak, "Udział lotników amerykańskich w wojnie polsko-sowieckiej," *Biuletyn Wojskowej Służby Archiwalnej* (Warsaw), no. 18, 1995, p. 91.

44. Arthur H. Kelly, Personal File, no. 7185, Central Military Archive, Warsaw. Zygmunt Kozak, "Udział lotników amerykańskich w wojnie polsko-sowieckiej," *Biuletyn Wojskowej Służby Archiwalnej* (Warsaw), no. 18, 1995, p. 95.

45. Central Military Archive, Warsaw, Merian Cooper Personal File, no. 5238. See also: Kontrakty lotników amerykańskich, "Lotnicy amerykańscy dla Armii Polskiej" [Contracts of American Pilots — American Pilots for the Polish Army], Central Military Archive, Warsaw, I.301.7.16. Entire contract of Lt. Elliot Chess is reprinted in: Jerzy Rozwadowski, *Gwiaździsta Eskadra* (Sigma Press, Albany, 1976), pp. 26–27. Contract of Kenneth Shrewsbury is now in the collection of Dr. Tomasz Kopański in Warsaw. For comparison, see contracts and terms of service of American pilot-volunteers during the Spanish Civil War, in: John Carver Edwards, *Airmen Without Portfolio; U.S. Mercenaries in Civil War Spain* (Praeger, Westport, Connecticut, London, 1997). For terms of service of the Polish pilots in France and Great Britain during WWII, see: Micheal A. Peszke, *Battle for Warsaw 1939–1944* (East European Monographs, Boulder, 1995), Appendix 5, pp. 263–271.

46. U.S. Military Attache, American Legation, Warsaw to Director of Military Intelligence, Washington, November 11, 1919 (Gen. Sosnkowski's document

was issued September 15, 1999). Harmon Rorison Personal File, no. 4176, Central Military Archive, Warsaw.

47. Col. Stanislaw Haller, Chief of General Staff to Deputy Minister, Ministry of Military Affairs, Warsaw, September 3, 1919, no. 2721/I. Gen. K. Sosnkowski, Deputy Minister, Ministry of Military Affairs to the High Command, Warsaw, September 10, 1919, Central Military Archive, Inspectorate of the Air Forces, no. 4139.

48. Zygmunt Kozak, "Udział lotników amerykańskich w wojnie polskosowieckiej," *Biuletyn Wojskowej Służby Archiwalnej* (Warsaw), no. 18, 1995, p. 75.

Chapter 3

1. For correspondence of Kenneth Shrewsbury with the Polish Embassy in Washington, D.C. during WWII, see: papers of K. Shrewsbury now in the collection of Dr. Tomasz Kopański in Warsaw.

2. For pilots' comments on the financial conditions of service, see Cooper's letter addressed to "Dear Coryell," now in the Central Military Archive, Warsaw: "This Polish-Bolshevik show was a lot of fun and we had plenty of action for our money. In fact figuring it from the financial side the odds were greatly in favor of the action as I drew about 7 dollars a month as Captain." The letter was reprinted by T. Kopański in: "Ostatni lot bojowy kapitana Coopera," *Militaria* (Warsaw) vol. 3, no. 1/1997, p. 11.

3. Merian C. Cooper to Józef Piłsudski, April 29, 1919, Cooper File, Pilsudski Institute, New York.

4. Kenneth M. Murray, *Wings over Poland. The Story of the 7th (Kościuszko) Squadron of the Polish Air Service, 1919, 1920, 1921* (D. Appleton and Company New York, London, 1932), p. VII.

5. "Edmund Graves," *Kurier Lwowski* (Lwów), no. 232, November 25, 1919.

6. Edward Corsi, *Poland; Land of the White Eagle* (New York, 1932), passim.

7. Zygmunt Kozak, "Udział lotników amerykańskich w wojnie polskosowieckiej," *Biuletyn Wojskowej Służby Archiwalnej* (Warsaw), no. 18, 1995, pp. 78–79.

8. M.C. Cooper to Sen. Duncan U. Fletcher, undated, probably written in the spring of 1920, Merian C. Cooper Collection, Hoover Institution Archives, Appendix 1B.

9. "Services in Honor of Colonel Fauntleroy, Chicago, Sunday, November 14,1920," C. Fauntleroy File, Pilsudski Institute, New York.

10. "Services in Honor of Colonel Fauntleroy, Chicago, Sunday, November 14, 1920," C. Fauntleroy File, Pilsudski Institute, New York.

11. C. Fauntleroy, Memorandum to Col. E.M. House, New York, January 5, 1933, Col. House Papers, Sterling Library, Yale University.

12. "Services in Honor of Colonel Fauntleroy, Chicago, Sunday, November 14, 1920," Cedric Fauntleroy File, Pilsudski Institute, New York.

> *The Minister of Poland*
> *requests the honor of the presence of*
> *Miss Anassa E. Sterrett*
> *at the function of bestowing the distinguished decoration*
> *"Virtuti Militari"*
> *upon*
> *Captain Harmon Rorison*
> *and*
> *Lieutenant Kenneth Shrewsbury*
> *former officers of the United States Army, who later voluntarily served in the aviation corps of the Polish Army and rendered very valuable and noble services, for which the above mentioned decoration had been awarded them by the Commander-in-Chief of the Polish Army.*
> *The ceremony will take place at the Legation of Poland, 2640 Sixteenth Street, Washington, D.C. on March the fourteenth 1921, at 11 o'clock.*

Invitation letter for Ms. A.E. Sterrett from the Ambassador of Poland. (Courtesy of Dr. T. Kopański, Warsaw.

   13.   Raport Biura Prasowego Polskiego w Nowym Jorku z dnia 2 i 3 listopada 1920 [New York Polish Press Bureau Report for November 2, 3, 1920. Pilsudski Institute, New York, Adjutancy General of the Commander in Chief, vol. 71/1, p. 10.
   14.   Kenneth Malcolm Murray, *Wings over Poland* (New York, 1932), p. IX.
   15.   [M.C. Cooper], *Faunt-le-Roy i jego Eskadra w Polsce* (Chicago 1922), pp. 18, 58–61.
   16.   [M.C. Cooper], *Things Men Die For* (Putnam & Sons, New York, London, 1927). "*Cives Leopolis*" (Los Angeles), May 1973, p. 7.
   17.   Major E.H. Schelling to MID in Washington, Report no. 1381, February 3, 1919, National Archive, Washington, D.C. Record Group 165.
   18.   Major E.H. Schelling do MID in Washington, Report no. 2067-53, February 27, 1919, National Archive, Record Group 165.
   19.   Elbert Farman to War Department in Washington, Report no. 140, October 16, 1919, National Archive, Washington, Record Group 165.

20. Report of Lt. Col. Respaldiza, Polish Attache Militaire in Bucharest on the visit of Col. Yates to Lwów, June 27, 1919, Pilsudski Institute, New York, Adjutancy General of the Commander in Chief, vol. 110/1.

21. Elbert Farman to MID, January 10, 1920, National Archive, Washington, Record Group 165.

Chapter 4

1. Alfred E. Cornebise, *Typhus and Doughboys; The American Polish Typhus Relief Expedition 1919-1921* (University of Delaware Press, Newark, London, Toronto, 1982), pp. 38-40.

2. P. Simonenko, "Amerykanskije letcziki na Ukrainie, Wojna z Polszej, 1919-1920" [American pilots in the Ukraine, in: War against Poland], "*Wojenno-Istoriczeskij Żurnał,*" (Moscow), no.3/1992, pp. 48-52.

3. [Merian C. Cooper], *Faunt-le-Roy i jego Eskadra w Polsce* (Chicago, 1922), pp. 49-54. Kenneth Malcolm Murray, The Kościuszko Squadron, *Poland Magazine*, March 1924, pp. 153-155. R. Karolevitz, R. Fenn, *Flight of Eagles, Story of the American Kościuszko Squadron in the Polish-Russian War 1919-1920* (Sioux Falls, South Dakota, 1974), pp. 37-38.

4. *Gazeta Poranna*, no. 231 (2453) (Warsaw), August 24, 1919. S. Benedykt, "Pierwszy polski samolot," *TydzieńPolski*, no. 28 (167), London, July 15, 1967. W. Jędrzejewicz, Janusz Cisek, *Kalendarium życia Józefa Piłsudskiego 1867-1935*, vol. 2, 1918-1926 [Chronicle of Pilsudski's Life, vol. II, 1918-1926] (Warsaw, 1998), pp.124-125.

5. Teresa Garbacz, "Geneza i początki organizacji lotnictwa polskiego," in: *Lotnictwo Polskie w okresie międzywojennym (Materiały z sesji popularnonaukowej)* [Origins and beginnings of the organization of the Polish Air Force, in: Polish Air Force in the interwar period; Proceedings of the Conference in Suwałki] (Warsaw-Suwałki, 1993), p. 27.

6. Jerzy Cynk, *History of the Polish Air Force, 1918-1968* (Osprey Publishing Ltd., 1972), pp. 13-17. Andrzej Przedpełski, *Lotnictwo Wojska Polskiego 1918-1996. Zarys Historii* [Airforce of the Polish Army; Outline of History, 1918-1996]. (Bellona, Warszawa, 1997), p. 13 ff.

7. E. Farman to MID in Washington, May 29, 1919, Report no.1509, National Archive, Washington, Record Group 165.

8. Edmund Pike Graves, Personal File, Central Military Archive, Warsaw. Zygmunt Kozak, "Udział lotników amerykańskich w wojnie polsko-sowieckiej," *Biuletyn Wojskowej Służby Archiwalnej* (Warsaw), no. 18, 1995, p. 93.

9. Elliot Chess, Personal File, Central Military Archive, Warsaw, no. 4937; Kenneth Malcolm Murray, "The Kościuszko Squadron," *Poland Magazine* (New York), March, 1924, p. 155.

10. "Eskadra Kościuszkowska," *Skrzydła* (London), vol. XXV, no. 87/573, 1964. J. Pawlak, *Polskie Eskadry w latach 1918-1939* (Wydawnictwa Komunikacji i Łączności, Warsaw, 1989), pp. 54-56.

11. Tomasz Kopański, "Początek skrzydlatej epopeji," *Polska Zbrojna,"Magazyn Tygodniowy*, no. 45 (161), November 12-14, 1993. *"Obrona Lwowa 1-22 listopada 1918. Relacje Uczestników,"* vol. II (Lwów 1936), pp. 715-728. Teresa Garbacz, "Geneza i początki organizacji lotnictwa polskiego," in: *Lotnictwo Polskie w okresie miedzywojennym (Materiały z sesji popularnonaukowej* (Warsaw-Suwałki, 1993), p.31.

12. Order of the Chief of Aviaton to the C.O. of the 3rd Air Group in Lwów, L. Dz. 334, Warsaw, October 15th, 1919, requesting the C.O. of the 7th Squadron to relieve his duties and to transfer the unit to Maj. Fauntleroy. The transfer had to take place before October 24th 1919, Central Military Archive, Warsaw.

13. Ludomił Rayski, *Słowa prawdy o lotnictwie polskim* (London, 1948). Personal Files of the pilots, Central Military Archive, Warsaw.

14. Notatka Płk Juliana Stachiewicza, nr. 4990/III, Warszawa 31 października 1919 [Memo of Col. J. Stachiewicz, no. 4990/III, October 31, 1919], Central Military Archive, C. Fauntleroy File.

15. C. Fauntleroy to Chief of the Polish Aviation Service in Warsaw, Lwów, November 1, 1919, Central Military Archive, 1st Department, High Command of the Polish Army, I.301.7.34, doc.L.res.12/19.

16. C. Fauntleroy to First Deputy Minister of Military Affairs in Warsaw, Lwów, November 1st, 1919, Central Military Archive, Warsaw, C. Fauntleroy File, doc.L.Res.13-19.

17. Deputy CO of the Polish Air Force to Diplomatic Section of the 2nd Intelligence Bureau, High Command, Warsaw, November 6, 1919, Central Military Archive, I.301.7.34.

18. "War Chance for Aviators; Major Paul Baer Organizing Squadron for Service in Poland," *The New York Times*, no. 22569, November 9, 1919.

19. Paul Baer to Ignacy Paderewski, New York, January 2, 1920, Paderewski Collection, AAN, Warsaw, vol. 813, p. 53.

20. Col. H.S. Howland, American Attache to the Polish Military Mission in Paris to Mr. Jechalski at the Polish Embassy in Washington, Paris, December 28, 1919, Embassy in Washington, AAN, vol. 2305.

21. Kenneth Malcolm Murray, The Kościuszko Squadron, *Poland Magazine* (New York), April, 1924, pp. 220-221.

22. P. Simonenko, "Amerikanskije letcziki na Ukrainie," Wojna z Polszej, 1919-1920gg" [American Pilots in Ukraine *War against Poland, 1919-1920]*, "*Wojenno-Istoriczeskij Zurnal*" (Moscow), no. 3/1992, pp. 47-51.

23. Zygmunt Kozak, "Udział lotników amerykańskich w wojnie polskosowieckiej," *Biuletyn Wojskowej Służby Archiwalnej* (Warsaw), no. 18 (1995), pp. 77-78. For profiles of the Polish pilots of the Squadron, see, among other sources, the Report of U.S. Military Attache in Warsaw, S. Winslow (no. 3158), May 17, 1938, in which he characterized Rayski in the following way: "in any event most foreigners believe that he is the only general officer in the Army competent to handle the air forces in peace or war." L. Rayski, *Słowa prawdy o lotnictwie polskim* (London, 1948). L. Rayski, "Inż Aleksander Senkowski (Wspomnienie pośmiertne)," *"Skrzydła—Wiadomości ze Świata,"* vol. XXV, no. 87/573 (1964), London,

p. 28. Senkowski Aleksander, LOT Collection, Polish Museum and the Sikorski Institute, London. Zygmunt Kozak and Tomasz Matuszak, "Ludwik Idzikowski — bohater tragiczny," *"Przegląd Lotniczy—Aviation Revue"* (Warsaw) no. 8/99, pp. 12–13.

24. Gen. Józef Leśniewski do Inspektora Wojsk Lotniczych, L.13772/19/S.P.V, Warsaw, December 16th, 1919. Inspektorat Wojsk Lotniczych, Rozkaz Oficerski nr. 5 [Gen. J. Lesniewski to the Air Force Inspectorate. Inspectorate of the Air Forces, Officer's Order no. 5], Warsaw, December 31, 1919, Central Military Archive, Inspectorate of the Air Forces, 9736, December 24, 1919.

25. "Oficerowie amerykańscy dla chłopców polskich" [American officers for Polish boys], *Czas* (Cracow), no. 308, November 27, 1919.

26. [Merian C. Cooper], *Faunt-le-Roy i jego Eskadra w Polsce* (Chicago, 1922), pp. 72–74.

27. "Pożar Pałacu Potockich we Lwowie" [Fire at the Potocki Palace in Lwów], *Czas* (Cracow), no. 307, November 26, 1919.

28. Report of Capt. Bastyr, C.O., III Air Group to the Chief of Aviation in Warsaw, No. 580, Lwów, November 28, 1919, Central Military Archive, Warsaw, Naczelne Dowodztwo WP, Oddzial IIIb, L.Dz.7334/2389/III.

29. "Pogrzeb lotnika" [Funeral of a pilot], *Czas* (Cracow), no. 308, November 27, 1919.

30. Kenneth Malcolm Murray, The Kościuszko Squadron, *Poland Magazine* (New York), April 1924, p. 219.

31. Sumaryczny wykaz lotów bojowych [Summary of combat sorties], Central Military Archive, Warsaw, I 300.38.44.

32. "Sprawozdanie Szefostwa Lotnictwa z działalności za czas kwiecień-maj 1920 i projekt przeorganizowania" [Report of the Polish Air Force Command on Air Force activities in April and May, 1920 and proposal for reorganization], Żytomierz, May 7, 1920, Pilsudski Institute, New York, Adjutancy General of the Commander in Chief, vol. 8/2, pp. 45–55.

33. P. Simonenko, "Amerikanskije Letcziki na Ukrainie, Wojna z Polszej, 1919–1920gg," *Wojenno-Istoriczeskij Żurnał* (Moscow), no. 3/1992.

34. Robert Karolevitz, Ross S. Fenn, *Flight of Eagles; The Story of the American Kościuszko Squadron in the Polish-Russian War 1919–1920* (Sioux Falls, South Dakota, 1974), pp. 82–84.

35. Kenneth Malcom Murray, The Kościuszko Squadron, *Poland Magazine* (New York), April 1924, pp. 222–223.

36. [Merian C. Cooper], *Faunt-le-Roy i jego eskadra w Polsce* (Chicago, 1922), p.79.

37. "Sprawozdanie Szefostwa Lotnictwa z działalności za czas kwiecień-maj 1920 i projekt przeorganizowania," Żytomierz May 1920, Pilsudski Institute, New York, Adjutancy General of the Commander in Chief, vol. 8/2, pp. 45–55.

38. Tomasz Matuszczak, "Organizacja Szefostwa Lotnictwa Naczelnego Dowództwa WP w latach 1919–1920 w świetle akt Centralnego Archiwum Wojskowego" [Organization of the Command of the Polish Air Force in the light of records of the Central Military Archive], *Biuletyn Wojskowej Służby Archiwalnej*,

LEGATION OF POLAND
MILITARY AND NAVAL ATTACHE
WASHINGTON, D. C.
3147 SIXTEENTH STREET

No. 3091   Washington December 17th, 1 9 2 0.

Mr.Kenneth A.Shrewsburry,
Hotel Judson,
53 Washington Square,
New York City.

Dear Sir:

        I have the honor of informing you that you had been awarded the Polish Decoration "Virtuti Militari", for your bravery in action on the Polish-Bolshevik Front.

        The Polish Legation desires to decorate you and Captain Rorison with the crosses, and if you wish to come to Washington, I shall be glad to inform you of the date. On this occasion I would greatly appreciate your corroborating your address, which after extensive searching I have been able to locate.

        Yours very truly,

        Mach

        Major.
   Acting Military Attaché
        of. Poland.

Letter of the Polish Attache Militaire in Washington (Maj. Mach) inviting K. Shrewsbury to Washington for Virtuti Militari decoration ceremony. (Courtesy of Dr. Tomasz Kopański collection, Warsaw.)

no. 19 (Warsaw, 1996), pp. 43–45. Dominik Noskowski, "Naczelne władze lotnicze II Rzeczypospolitej" [Chief Authorities of the Polish Air Force in the Second Republic], in: *Lotnictwo Polskie w okresie międzywojennym Materiały z sesji popularnonaukowej)* (Warsaw, Suwałki, 1993), pp. 45–50.

    39. "Ordre de Bataille" Wojsk Lotniczych na Frontach Litewsko-Białoruskim, Wołyńskim, Podolskim, Pomorskim, Śląskim i Wielkopolskim z dnia 1 marca 1920 [Order of the Battle of the Polish Air Force on the Belorussian, Podolian, Pomeranian, Silesian and *Great Poland* (Wielkopolski) Fronts as of March 1, 1920], Pilsudski Institute, New York, Adjutancy General of the Commander in Chief,

vol. 89/4, pp. 53–56. Krzysztof Tarkowski, *Lotnictwo Polskie w wojnie z Rosją Sowiecką 1919–1920* (Wydawnictwa Komunikacji i Łączności, Warsaw, 1991), pp. 46–47.

40. "Wnioski i Perspektywy w Sprawie Technicznego Materiału i Warsztatów w Lotnictwie" [Conclusions and Perspectives on the issue of Technical Equipment and Repair Shops of the Aviation Service], August 11, 1920, Pilsudski Institute, New York, Adjutancy General of the Commander in Chief, vol. 9. Krzysztof Sandomirski, Polska Misja Wojskowa zakupów w Paryżu w latach 1919–1920, *Wojskowy Przegląd Historyczny*, vol. XXIII (1978), no. 4, pp. 64–98. Tomasz Kopański, *British WWI Aircraft in the Polish Air Service* (Mashroom Magazine Special, Wydawnictwo Diecezjalne Sandomierz, 1999).

41. "Kilka Słów o Lotnictwie w Polsce" [Few Words about Polish Aviation], Warsaw, March 18, 1920, Pilsudski Institute, New York, Adjutancy General of the Commander in Chief , vol. 7/3, pp. 20–28.

42. "Raport o stanie Niższej Szkoły Lotników w Warszawie" [Report on the School of Basic Aviation], Warsaw. May 17, 1920, Pilsudski Institute, New York, Adjutancy General of the Commander in Chief, vol. 9.

43. Elbert Farman to MID, Report no. 519, "Poland. Combat Factor," January 8, 1920, National Archive, Washington, DC, Record Group 165.

44. "Eskadra Kościuszkowska," *Skrzydła; Wiadomości ze Świata* (London), vol. XXV (1964), p. 7.

45. E. Farman to MID, Report no. 685, "Poland — Combat Factor. Aviation. Additional Information," undated, received in Washington on April 17, 1920, National Archive, Washington, DC, Record Group 165.

46. "Maj. Stachowski do Departamentu III (Żeglugi Powietrznej)" [Maj. Stachowski to the Department of Aerial Navigation], L.dz.706/20/D.Z., Warsaw, May 15, 1920, Pilsudski Institute, New York, Adjutancy General of the Commander in Chief, vol. T.8/3, p. 21.

47. Kenneth Malcom Murray, "The Kościuszko Squadron," *Poland Magazine* (New York), April 1924, p. 252, May 1924, p. 292.

48. Krzysztof Tarkowski, *Lotnictwo Polskie w wojnie z Rosją Sowiecką 1919–1920* (Wydawnictwa Komunikacji i Łączności, Warsaw, 1991), pp. 55–56.

49. Kenneth Malcom Murray, "The Kościuszko Squadron," *Poland Magazine* (New York), June 1924, p. 373.

50. Gen. Antoni Listowski, Dziennik [Diary], vol. III, pp. 144–146, Czartoryski Library, Cracow, manuscript XVII 2988.

51. Gen. Antoni Listowski, Dziennik [Diary], vol. III, p. 146, Czartoryski Library, Cracow, manuscript XVII 2988.

52. Kenneth Malcolm Murray, "The Kościuszko Squadron," *Poland Magazine* (New York), July 1924, pp. 19–48.

53. Krzysztof A. Tarkowski, *Lotnictwo Polskie w wojnie z Rosją sowiecką 1919–1920* (Wydawnictwa Komunikacji i Łączności, Warsaw, 1991), pp. 54–56. Jerzy B. Cynk, *History of the Polish Air Force 1918–1968* (Osprey Publishing Ltd, 1972), pp. 46–47. For military aspects of the Kiev expedition, see accounts of high ranking officers: Julian Stachiewicz, *Działania zaczepne 3 Armii na Ukrainie, Studia*

Operacyjne z historii wojen polskich 1918–21 (Warsaw, 1925). Tadeusz Kutrzeba, *Wyprawa Kijowska 1920 roku* (Gebethner i Wolf, Warsaw, 1937). For genesis of the Ukrainian-Polish alliance see: Michael Palij, *The Ukrainian-Polish Defensive Alliance: An Aspect of the Ukrainian Revolution* (Canadian Institute of Ukrainian Studies Press, Edmonton, Toronto, 1995).

Chapter 5

1. William Henry Chamberlin, *The Russian Revolution 1917–1921. vol. I, 1917–1918; From the Overthrow of the Tsar to the Assumption of Power by the Bolsheviks* (Princeton University Press, New Jersey, 1987), pp. 472–473. Halina Janowska, Tadeusz Jędruszczak, eds., *Powstanie II Rzeczypospolitej. Wybór Dokumentów 1866–1925* (Ludowa Spółdzielnia Wydawnicza, Warsaw, 1981), pp. 360–362.
2. Halina Janowska, Tadeusz Jędruszczak, eds., *Powstanie II Rzeczypospolitej. Wybór Dokumentów 1866–1925* (Ludowa Spółdzielnia Wydawnicza, Warsaw, 1981), pp. 364–365, 413–414.
3. Michael Palij, *The Ukrainian-Polish Defensive Alliance 1919–1921; An Aspect of the Ukrainian Revolution* (Canadian Institute of Ukrainian Studies Press, Edmonton, Toronto, 1995), p. 59 ff.
4. E. Farman to MID in Washington, Report no. 23, June 23, 1919, National Archive, Washington, DC, Record Group 165. Stanislaw Haller was at the time Chief of the General Staff of the Polish Army.
5. Janusz Cisek, *Sąsiedzi wobec wojny 1920 roku* (Polska Fundacja Kulturalna, Londyn, 1990), pp. 42–43.
6. Hugh Gibson to the Department of State, no. 2088, May 12, 1919, 860c.01/248 and 264, National Archive, Files of the Department of State, no. 2088, also: Zygmunt Gasiorowski, "Joseph Piłsudski in the Light of American Reports, 1919–1922," *The Slavonic and East European Review*, vol. XLIX, no. 116, 1971, pp. 419–420.
7. Hugh Gibson to the Department of State, no. 210, April 6, 1920, 760c.61/44, National Archive, Files of the Department of State, no. 2088, also: Zygmunt Gasiorowski, "Joseph Piłsudski in the Light of American Reports, 1919–1922," *The Slavonic and East European Review*, vol. XLIX, no. 116, 1971, pp. 420–421.
8. "Recent Developments in Polish Situation by Major H.S. Howland, Inf. American Representative to the Polish Military Mission in Paris," no. 2588-W, February 18, 1920, National Archive, Washington, DC, Record Group 165.
9. "Situation in Poland, by Maj. H.S. Howland, U.S.A., Chief of the Polish Mission in Paris," no. 2532, January 27, 1920, National Archive, Washington, DC, Record Group 165.
10. Piotr Wandycz, *The United States and Poland* (Harvard University Press, Massachusetts, 1980), pp. 144–145.
11. Piotr Wandycz, *The United States and Poland* (Harvard University Press,

Massachusetts, 1980), pp. 148–149; see also: Bogusław Winid, "After the Colby Note: The Wilson Administration and the Polish-Bolshevik War," *Presidential Studies Quarterly* (Washington, DC), vol. XXVI, no. 4, Fall 1996, pp. 1165–1168.

12. Bogusław Winid, "Polska w polityce zagranicznej prezydenta Woodow Wilsona w latach 1919–1920," *Teki Historyczne* (London), vol. XXII, 1999, pp. 186–189.

13. Bainbridge Colby to Baron Calillo Avezzano, August 10, 1920, in: *Foreign Relations of the United States 1920*, vol. 3 (Washington DC, 1935), pp. 463–468. P. Wandycz, *United States and Poland*, pp. 148–149.

Chapter 6

1. Kenneth Malcolm Murray, "The Kościuszko Squadron," *Poland Magazine* (New York), October, 1924, pp. 215–216.
2. Kenneth Malcolm Murray, "The Kościuszko Squadron," *Poland Magazine*, New York, October, 1924, pp. 241–242.
3. Kenneth Malcolm Murray, *Wings Over Poland* (D. Appleton and Company, New York-London, 1932), pp. 132–133.
4. Akta Krzyża "Virtuti Militari," Central Military Archive, Warsaw, no. 18-1094.
5. Akta Krzyża "Virtuti Militari," no. 19-1149, Personal File, no. 585, Central Military Archive, Warsaw. Kenneth Malcolm Murray, "The Kościuszko Squadron," *Poland Magazine*, November 1924, pp. 310–312.
6. Gen. Antoni Listowski, Diariusz [Diary], vol. III, p. 195, Czartoryski Library, Cracow, manuscript XVII, 2988.
7. E. Farman to MID, Washington, Report no. 301, May 1, 1920, National Archive, Washington, Record Group 165.
8. Gen. Antoni Listowski, Diariusz [Diary], vol. III, p. 204, Czartoryski Library, Cracow, manuscript XVII, 2988.
9. Kenneth Malcolm Murray, The Kościuszko Squadron, *Poland Magazine* (New York), January, 1925, pp. 21–22.
10. Ministerstwo Spraw Wojskowych, Dowództwo Lotnictwa [Ministry of Military Affairs, Department of Aviation], Central Military Archive, Warsaw, I.300.38.44.
11. E. Farman to MID in Washington, Report no. 314, May 11, 1920, National Archive, Washington, Record Group 165.
12. E. Farman to MID in Washington, Report no. 315, May 12, 1920, National Archive, Washington, Record Group 165.
13. E. Farman to MID in Washington, Report no. 330, May 18, 1920, National Archive, Washington, Record Group 165.
14. Kenneth Malcolm Murray, "The Kościuszko Squadron," *Poland Magazine* (New York), January 1925, p.48.
15. Gen. Antoni Listowski, Diariusz [Diary], vol. III, p. 223, Czartoryski Library, Cracow, manuscript XVII, 2988.

16. C. Fauntleroy, to Lt. Leopold Toruń, May 21, 1920, Leopold Toruń Papers, Warsaw.
17. [M. Cooper], *Faunt-le-Roy i jego Eskadra w Polsce* (Chicago, 1922).
18. Tomasz Jan Kopański, 3.Eskadra Wywiadowcza 1918–1920 (Wydawnictwo Fenix, Warsaw, 1999). Tomasz Kopański, "Krótka Historia 3 Eskadry Wywiadowczej" [Short History of the 3rd Reconnaissance Squadron], in: *Lotnictwo Polskie w okresie miedzywojennym (Materiały z sesji popularnonaukowej* (Warszawa, Suwałki, 1993), p. 71. Lt. Col. Pilot Tadeusz Prauss, "Kronika Wojenna 3-ciej Eskadry Lotniczej" [Chronicle of the 3rd Squadron], *"Przegląd Lotniczy* (Warsaw), vol. IV, no. 8–9, August-September, 1931, p. 624.
19. E. Farman to MID in Washington, Report no. 812, May 22, 1920, National Archive, Washington, Record Group 165.
20. Gen. Antoni Listowski, Diariusz [Diary], vol. III, p. 245, Czartoryski Library, Cracow, manuscript XVII, 2988.
21. Account of Crawford's action in: Akta Krzyża "Virtuti Militari" [Cross of the "Virtuti Militari" documentation], Central Military Archive, Warsaw, no. 19-1093. R. Karolevitz, R. Fenn, *Flight of Eagles*, pp. 122–123.
22. Gen. Antoni Listowski, Diariusz [Diary] vol. III, pp. 245–248, Czartoryski Library, Cracow, manuscript XVII, 2988.
23. Akta Krzyża "Virtuti Militari" [Cross of the "Virtuti Militari" documentation], Central Military Archive, Warsaw.
24. "Sumaryczny wykaz lotów bojowych" [Summary of combat sorties], Central Military Archive, Warsaw, I.300.38.44.
25. Tomasz Kopański, "Krótka historia 3 Eskadry wywiadowczej 1918–1920," in: *Lotnictwo Polskie w okresie miedzywojennym (Materiały z sesji popularnonaukowej* (Warsaw, Suwałki, 1993), p. 72.
26. Lt. Col. Edward Lewandowski, Lotnictwo w walce z Armią Konną Budiennego [Air Force in combat with the Budenny's *"Konarmia"*] *Przegląd Lotniczy* (Warsaw), vol. V, no. 1–2, January-February, 1932, pp. 28–29.
27. Dowództwo 6 Armii, Rozkaz nr 46, Główna Poczta Polowa [H.Q of the 6th Army, Order no. 46, Main Military Field Post Office] no. VI, May 9, 1921, Central Military Archive, Warsaw, Records of the 6 Army, I.311.6.1.
28. E. Farman to MID in Washington, Report no. 1005, "Cavalry Operations," October 26, 1920, National Archive, Washington, Record Group 165.
29. Tadeusz Kutrzeba, *Wyprawa Kijowska 1920 roku* (Gebethner i Wolff, Warsaw, 1937), pp. 160–176.
30. Ministerstwo Spraw Wojskowych, Dowództwo Lotnictwa [Ministry of Military Affairs, Command of the Air Force], Central Military Archive, Warsaw, I.300.38.44.
31. Sumaryczny wykaz lotów bojowych [Summary of combat sorties], Central Military Archive, Warsaw, I.300.38.44. Merian C. Cooper, *Fauntleroy i jego Eskadra w Polsce* (Chicago, 1922), pp. 168–169.
32. Tomasz Kopański, *3.Eskadra Wywiadowcza 1918–1920* (Wydawnictwo Fenix, Warszawa 1999), p. 82ff.
33. Tomasz Kopański, Krótka historia 3 Eskadry wywiadowczej 1918–1920,

in: *Lotnictwo Polskie w okresie miedzywojennym (Materiały z sesji popularno naukowej)* (Warszawa-Suwałki, 1993), p. 73. M. Cooper, *Faunt-le-Roy i jego Eskadra w Polsce* (Chicago, 1922). "Sumaryczny wykaz lotów bojowych," I.300.38.44 [Summary of combat sorties]. Akta Krzyża "Virtuti Militari," Central Military Archive, Warsaw, no. 18-1092, 1094.

34. Kenneth Malcom Murray, "The Kościuszko Squadron," *Poland Magazine* (New York), June 1925, p. 372.

35. Central Military Archive, Warsaw, I.300.38.44; Akta Krzyża "Virtuti Militari," no. 1078, Central Military Archive, Warsaw. R. Karolevitz, R. Fenn, *Flight of Eagles*, pp. 149–152.

36. "*Czyn Zbrojny Wychodźstwa Polskiego w Ameryce. Zbiór Dokumentów i Materiałów* Historycznych (Wydawnictwo Stowarzyszenia Armii Polskiej w Ameryce, New York, Chicago 1957), p. 761. Central Military Archive, Warsaw, I.300.38.44. [M. Cooper], *Fauntleroy i jego Eskadra w Polsce* (Chicago 1922), pp. 180–187. Kenneth M. Murray, *Wings over Poland*, pp. 222–228.

37. [Merian C. Cooper], *Fauntleroy i jego Eskadra w Polsce* (Chicago, 1922), p. 188.

38. "*Czyn Zbrojny Wychodzstwa Polskiego w Ameryce. Zbiór Dokumentów i Materialów Historycznych* (Wydawnictwo Stowarzyszenia Armii Polskiej w Ameryce (New York, Chicago, 1957), pp. 750–751.

39. Kenneth Malcolm Murray, *Wings over Poland: The Story of the 7th (Kościuszko) Squadron of the Polish Air Service, 1919, 1920, 1921* (D. Appleton and Company, New York, London, 1932), p.229.

40. "*Czyn Zbrojny Wychodźstwa Polskiego w Ameryce. Zbiór Dokumentów i Materiałów Historycznych* (Wydawnictwo Stowarzyszenia Armii Polskiej w Ameryce, New York, Chicago 1957), p. 771.

41. Gen. Antoni Listowski, Diariusz [Diary], vol. III, p. 292, Czartoryski Library, Cracow, manuscript XVII, 2988.

42. Sumaryczny wykaz lotów bojowych [Summary of combat sorties], Central Military Archive, Warsaw, I.300.38.44.

43. R. Karolevitz, R. Fenn, *Flight of Eagles*, pp. 156–158.

44. Gen. Antoni Listowski, Diariusz [Diary], vol. III, p. 302, Czartoryski Library, Cracow, manuscript XVII, 2988.

45. Gen. Antoni Listowski, Diariusz [Diary], vol. III, p. 306, Czartoryski Library, Cracow, manuscript XVII, 2988.

46. Gen. Antoni Listowski, Diariusz [Diary], vol. III, p. 313, Czartoryski Library, Cracow, manuscript XVII, 2988.

47. "Employment of Aviation in the Polish-Bolshevik War," OD to MID in Washington, Report no. 870, July 3, 1920, National Archive, Washington, Record Group 165.

48. Tomasz Kopański, Ostatni lot kapitana Coopera, *Militaria* (Warsaw), vol. 3, no. 1/1997, pp. 6–12.

49. Oddzial I NDWP [Department I, High Command of the Polish Army], Central Military Archive, Warsaw, I.301.7.34. Kenneth Malcolm Murray, *Wings over Poland: The Story of the 7th (Kościuszko) Squadron of the Polish Air Service,*

1919, 1920, 1921 (D. Appleton and Company, New York, London, 1932), pp. 304–305.

50. Sumaryczny wykaz lotów [Summary of combat sorties] Central Military Archive, Warsaw, I.300.38.44. Kenneth Malcolm Murray, *Wings over Poland: The Story of the 7th (Kościuszko) Squadron of the Polish Air Service, 1919, 1920, 1921* (D. Appleton and Company, New York, London, 1932), pp. 307–309.

51. R. Karolevitz, R. Fenn, *Flight of Eagles*, pp. 186–188. Kenneth Malcolm Murray, *Wings over Poland*, pp. 319–322.

52. Sumaryczny wykaz lotów [Summary of combat sorties], Central Military Archive, Warsaw, I. 300.38.44.

53. Sumaryczny wykaz lotów, Central Military Archive, Warsaw, I.300.38.44.

Chapter 7

1. Władysław Ścibor-Rylski, *Obrona Państwa w 1920 roku. Księga Sprawozdawczo-Pamiątkowa Generalnego Inspektoratu Armii Ochotniczej i Obywatelskich Komitetów Obrony Państwa* [Defense of the State in 1920; Report and Memorial Book of the Inspectorate General of the Volunteer Army and Regional Committees for Defense of the State] (Nakładem Obywatelskiego Komitetu Obrony Państwa, Warsaw, 1923).

2. Notatka dla Pana Ministra Spraw Zagranicznych "W sprawie ochotników cudzoziemskich" [Memo for the Minister of Foreign Affairs "About foreign volunteers"], July 20, 1920, Pilsudski Institute, New York, Adjutancy General of the Commander in Chief, vol. 67b/2, p. 68.

3. Attache Wojskowy z Londynu do Naczelnego Dowództwa WP w Warszawie, no. 1458 [Attache Militaire of Poland in London to the High Command in Warsaw], July 1, 1920, Pilsudski Institute, New York, Adjutancy General of the Commander in Chief, vol. 67b/1, p. 60.

4. Attache Militaire of Poland in London to the High Command in Warsaw, no. 1525, July 12, 1920; Odpowiedź Szefa Sztabu Generalnego [Reply of the Chief of Staff of the Polish Army], Pilsudski Institute, New York, Adjutancy General of the Commander in Chief, vol. 67b/1, pp. 88–89.

5. Janusz Cisek, *Sąsiedzi wobec wojny 1920 roku* (Polska Fundacja Kulturalna, Londyn 1990), pp. 92–117.

6. Notatka dla Pana Ministra Spraw Zagranicznych "W sprawie ochotników cudzoziemskich" [Memo for the Minister of Foreign Affairs "About the foreign volunteers"], July 20, 1920, Pilsudski Institute, New York, Adjutancy General of the Commander in Chief, vol. 67b/2, p. 68.

7. Mieczyslaw B. Biskupski, "Kościuszko, We Are Here?: American Volunteers for Poland and the Polish-Russian War, 1918–1920," in: Stanislaus Blejwas, Mieczyslaw Biskupski, eds., *Pastor of the Poles. Polish-American Essays Presented to Right Reverend Monsignor John P. Wodarski in Honor of the Fiftieth Anniversary of His Ordination* (Polish Studies Program Monograph, Central Connecticut State College, New Britain, CT, 1982), p. 196.

8. "*Sprawozdanie z działalności Amerykańskiego Komitetu dla Obrony Polski. Centrala na Stany Wschodnie*" (Nakładem Amerykańskiego Komitetu dla Obrony Polski, New York, 1920).

9. Gen. Brynk to the High Command of the Polish Armed Forces, no. 764, May 10, 1920, Pilsudski Institute, New York, Adjutancy General of the Commander in Chief, vol. 67a/2, pp. 67–70.

10. K. Lubomirski, to the Ministry of Foreign Affairs in Warsaw, no. 132, May 27th, 1920, Pilsudski Institute, New York, Adjutancy General of the Commander in Chief, vol. 67a/1, p. 75.

11. K. Lubomirski to Foreign Ministry in Warsaw, no. 132, May 27, 1920, Pilsudski Institute, New York, Adjutancy General of the Commander in Chief, vol. 67a/2, p. 90.

12. H.H. Fisher, *America and the New Poland* (Macmillan Company, New York, 1928), p. 261.

13. Pilsudski Institute, New York, Adjutancy General of the Commander in Chief, vol. 67b/1, p. 86.

14. K. Lubomirski to Foreign Ministry in Warsaw, no. 170, July 18, 1920, Pilsudski Institute, New York, Adjutancy General of the Commander in Chief, vol. 67b/2.

15. K. Lubomirski to Foreign Ministry in Warsaw, no. 180, August 9, 1920, Pilsudski Institute, New York, Adjutancy General of the Commander in Chief, vol. 68a/3.

16. E. Farman to MID, no. 437, August 5, 1920, National Archive, Washington, Record Group 165.

17. Foreign Minister E. Sapieha to K. Lubomirski in Washington, D.C., no. 160, August 6, 1920, Ambasada RP w Waszyngtonie [Embassy of Poland in Washington, DC], AAN, vol. 226, p. 99.

18. Depesza Naczelnego Dowództwa Wojska Polskiego do Attache Wojskowego w Waszyngtonie [Dispatch of the High Command of the Polish Army to the Polish Attache Militaire in Washington, DC], no. 31148, August 6, 1920, Ambasada RP w Waszyngtonie, AAN, Warsaw, vol. 2305.

19. Gen. Sosnkowski and Foreign Minister Sapieha to Gen. Brynk in Washington, DC, no. 159, August 8, 1920, Ambasada RP w Waszyngtonie, AAN vol. 226, p. 100; Lubomir Zyblikiewicz, "Stany Zjednoczone a Polska w latach 1920–1921 (Stosunki dyplomatyczne — wybrane zagadnienia)" [United States and Poland, 1920–1921, selected issues], in: *Ameryka Północna; Studia* (Państwowe Wydawnictwo Naukowe, Warszawa, 1975), pp. 232–234.

20. Col. Harry Howland to K. Lubomirski, August 10, 1920, Ambasada RP w Waszyngtonie, vol. 226, pp. 106–108. Richard Ulrich, General Tadeusz Rozwadowski and the Attempt to Establish a Volunteer American Legion Within the Polish Army, 1919–1920, *The Polish Review* (New York), vol. XXXVII, no. 1, 1992, pp. 107–109.

21. Bainbridge Colby to Baron Camillo Avezzano, August 10, 1920, in: *Foreign Relations of the United States 1920*, vol. 3 (Washington DC, 1935), pp. 463–468.

22. *Wiadomości Codzienne* (Cleveland, OH), August 19, 1920. "*Sprawozdanie z działalności Amerykańskiego Komiteteu dla Obrony Polski. Centrala na Stany Wschodnie"* (Nakładem Amerykańskiego Komitetu dla Obrony Polski, New York, 1920), p. 10ff.

23. K. Lubomirski to B. Colby, August 14, 1920, Ambasada w Waszyngtonie, AAN, vol. 226; Lubomir Zyblikiewicz, "Stany Zjednoczone a Polska w latach 1920–1921 (Stosunki dyplomatyczne — wybrane zagadnienia)," in: *Ameryka Północna Studia* (Warsaw, 1975), pp. 238–239.

24. Mieczysław B. Biskupski, "Kościuszko, We Are Here?": American Volunteers for Poland and the Polish-Russian War, 1918–1920, in: Stanislaus Blejwas, Mieczysław Biskupski, eds., *Pastor of the Poles. Polish-American Essays Presented to Right Reverend Monsignor John P. Wodarski in honor of the Fiftieth Anniversary of His Ordination* (Polish Studies Program Monograph, Central Connecticut State College, New Britain, CT, 1982), pp. 200–202.

25. "Przegląd prasy anglo-amerykańskiej z dnia 9 i 10 lipca 1920" [Review of the American and British press from July 9–10, 1920], Pilsudski Institute, New York, Adjutancy General of the Commander in Chief vol. 68a/3, p. 9. "Raport Biura Prasowego Polskiego w Nowym Jorku z 4, 5, 6 września 1920" [Report of the Polish Press Bureau in New York City for September 4, 5, 6, 1920], Pilsudski Institute, New York, Adjutancy General of the Commander in Chief, vol. 69a.

26. Gutzon Borglum to K. Lubomirski, August 18, 1920, Ambasada R.P. w Waszyngtonie, AAN, vol. 2305.

27. Mieczysław B. Biskupski, "*Kościuszko, We Are Here?": American Volunteers for Poland and the Polish-Russian War, 1918–1920,* pp. 199–202.

28. R. Karolevitz, R. Fenn, *Flight of Eagles,* pp. 190–191.

29. "Przegląd prasy amerykańskiej z dnia 9, 10 lipca 1920" [Review of the American press from July 9–10, 1920), Pilsudski Institute, New York, Adjutancy General of the Commander in Chief, vol. 68a/3.

Chapter 8

1. "Raport Biura Prasowego Polskiego w Nowym Jorku z dnia 10 i 11 sierpnia, 1920" [Report of the Polish Press Bureau in New York City for August 10, 11, 1920], Pilsudski Institute, New York, Adjutancy General of the Commander in Chief, vol. 69b/3.

2. On the origins of the plan for the Battle of Warsaw and the role of Gen. M. Weygand see: Zdzisław Musialik, *General Weygand and the Battle of the Vistula 1920* (Pilsudski Institute, London 1987), 57ff. Piotr Wandycz, "General Weygand and the Battle of Warsaw of 1920," *Journal of Central European Affairs,* vol. XIX, no. IV, January 1960, pp. 357–365. Janusz Cisek, *Sąsiedzi wobec wojny 1920 roku* (London, 1990).

3. Edgar V. d'Abernon, *The Eighteenth Decisive Battle of the World: Warsaw 1920* (Hodder & Stoughton, London 1931). J.F.C. Fuller, The Battle of Warsaw, in: J.F.C. *Decisive Battles of the Western World and Their Influence Upon History*

(London, 1979). Norman Davies, *White Eagle Red Star. The Polish-Soviet War 1919–1920* (Orbis Books, Ltd., London, 1983). M.K. Dziewanowski, Joseph Pilsudski, the Bolshevik Revolution and Eastern Europe, in: *Essays on Poland's Foreign Policy, 1918–1939* (Pilsudski Institute, New York, 1970).

4. Krzysztof Tarkowski, *Lotnictwo Polskie w wojnie z Rosją Sowiecką 1919–1920* (Wydawnictwa Komunikacji i Łączności, Warsaw, 1991), pp. 92–100. K. Tarkowski, Działania lotnictwa polskiego w Bitwie Warszawskiej w sierpniu 1920r. [Polish Air Force in the Battle of Warsaw, August, 1920], *Wojskowy Przegląd Historyczny* (Warsaw), vol. XXXV, no. 1–2 (131–132), 1990, pp. 56–59. Jerzy B. Cynk, *History of the Polish Air Force 1918–1968* (Osprey Publishing Ltd, 1972), p.56.

5. K. Tarkowski, "Działania lotnictwa polskiego w Bitwie Warszawskiej w sierpniu 1920r.," *Wojskowy Przegląd Historyczny* (Warsaw), vol. XXXV, no. 1–2 (131–132), 1990, pp. 56–59.

6. Maj. Władysław Madejski, Lotnictwo w Bitwie pod Lwowem w sierpniu 1920 roku, *Przegląd Lotniczy* (Warsaw), vol. X, no. 4, 1937, pp. 456–464.

7. Rozkaz Szefa Lotnictwa Naczelnego Dowództwa WP [Order of the Chief of Aviation of the High Command of the Polish Army], L.Dz.2532/ Lot. Pf., Warsaw, August 18, 1920, Pilsudski Institute, New York, Adjutancy General of the Commander in Chief vol. 11/3. pp. 52–53. Cedric Fauntleroy, Personal File, Central Military Archive, Warsaw, no. 2743. U.S. Military Attache in Warsaw to MID in Washington, Report no. 972, "Poland Combat Factor. Aviation Monograph," September 21st, 1920, National Archive, Washington, DC, Record Group 165.

8. George Crawford, Personal File, Central Military Archive, Warsaw, no. 4794.

9. Sumaryczny wykaz lotów bojowych [Summary of combat sorties], Central Military Archive, Warsaw, I.300.38.44.

10. Sumaryczny wykaz lotów bojowych, Central Military Archive, Warsaw, I.300.38.44. Lt. Col. Edward Lewandowski, "Lotnictwo w walce z Armią Konną Budennego" [Aviation in combat with the Budenny's "Konarmia"], *Przegląd Lotniczy* (Warsaw), vol. V, no. 1–2, January–February 1932), p. 30.

11. Maj. Władysław Madcjski, "Lotnictwo w Bitwie pod Lwowem w sierpniu 1920 roku" [Aviation in the battle for Lwów, August, 1920], *Przegląd Lotniczy*, (Warsaw), vol. X, no. 4, April 1937, pp. 464–467. Lt. S. Turbiak, "Walki III Dywizjonu Lotniczego z Konną Armią Budennego pod Lwowem (Wspomnienia i uwagi)" [Combat of the 3rd Air *Dyon* with Budenny's "Konarmia" near Lwów; Recollections and remarks], *Bellona* (Warsaw), vol. V, no. 1, January 1922, pp. 123–126.

12. Sumaryczny wykaz lotów bojowych [Summary of combat sorties], Central Military Archive, Warsaw, I.300.38.44.

13. Sumaryczny wykaz lotów bojowych, Central Military Archive, Warsaw, I.300.38.44. Lt. Col. Edward Lewandowski, Lotnictwo w walce z Armią Konną Budennego, *Przegląd Lotniczy* (Warsaw), vol. V, no. 1–2, January–February, 1932, p. 32.

14. Jerzy Rozwadowski, *Gwiaździsta Eskadra* (Sigma Press, Albany, NY, 1976), p. 18.

15. Sumaryczny wykaz lotów bojowych [Summary of combat sorties], Central Military Archive, Warsaw, I.300.38.44.

16. Lt. S. Turbiak, Walki III Dywizjonu Lotniczego z Konną Armią Budiennego pod Lwowem (Wspomnienia i uwagi) [Combat of the 3rd Air *Dyon* with Budenny's "Konarmia" near Lwów; Recollections and remarks], *Bellona* (Warsaw), vol. V, no. 1, January 1922, pp. 126–128.

17. Maj. Władysław Madejski, "Lotnictwo w Bitwie pod Lwowem w sierpniu 1920 roku," *Przegląd Lotniczy* (Warsaw), vol. X, no. 4, April 1937, pp. 471–474.

18. Seweryn Faliński, *Rycerze Zadwórzańscy* [Warriors of Zadworze], wstęp Józef Białynia-Chołodecki (Nakładem Małopolskiej Straży Obywatelskiej, Lwów, 1927), p. 22. Jerzy Pogonowski, *Bój o Lwów (Z walk Armii Ochotniczej z 1920 roku)* [Battle for Lwów, from the battles of the Volunteer Army] (Lotos, Gdańsk, 1921), p. 32 ff.

19. Krzysztof Tarkowski, *Lotnictwo Polskie w wojnie z Rosją Sowiecką 1919–1920* [Polish Air Force in the 1919–1920 war against Soviet Russia] (Wydawnictwa Komunikacji i Łączności, Warsaw, 1991), pp. 100–101. Maj. Władysław Madejski, Lotnictwo w Bitwie pod Lwowem w sierpniu 1920 roku, *Przegląd Lotniczy* (Warsaw), vol. X, no. 4, April 1937, pp. 475–477. Lt. S. Turbiak, Walki III Dywizjonu Lotniczego z Konną Armią Budiennego pod Lwowem (Wspomnienia i uwagi) *Bellona* (Warsaw), vol. V, no. 1, January 1922, pp. 128–129. Lt. Col. Pilot Edward Lewandowski, Lotnictwo w walce z Armi1 Konn1 Budennego, *Przegląd Lotniczy* (Warsaw), vol. V, no. 1–2, January–February 1932, p. 32.

20. Seweryn Faliński, *Rycerze Zadwórzańscy*, wstęp Józef Białynia-Chołodecki, (Nakładem Małopolskiej Straży Obywatelskiej, Lwów 1927), p. 22.

21. [Merian C. Cooper], *Faunt-le-Roy i jego Eskadra w Polsce* (Chicago, 1922), pp. 233–234.

22. Translation of the Budenny's dispatch, intercepted by the Polish intelligence in: Pilsudski Institute, New York, Adjutancy General of the Commander in Chief, vol. 27/2, pp. 125–126.

23. Izaak Babel, *Dziennik 1920* [Diary, 1920] (Czytelnik, Warsaw, 1990), p. 133.

24. Lt. Col. Farman to MID in Washington, Report no. 870, "Employment of Aviation in the Polish-Bolshevik War," July 3, 1920.

25. Sumaryczny wykaz lotów bojowych [Summary of combat sorties], Central Military Archive, Warsaw I.300.38.44.

26. Lt. Col. Pilot Edward Lewandowski, Lotnictwo w walce z Armią Konną Budenego, *Przegląd Lotniczy* (Warsaw), vol. V, no. 1–2, January–February, 1932, p. 32. Jerzy Rozwadowski, *Gwiaździsta Eskadra* (Sigma Press, Albany, NY, 1976), p. 18.

27. Maj. Władysław Madejski, Lotnictwo w Bitwie pod Lwowem w sierpniu 1920 roku, *Przegląd Lotniczy*, vol. X, no. 4, Warsaw, April 1937, pp. 478–480.

28. Izaak Babel, *Dziennik 1920* [Diary, 1920] (Czytelnik, Warsaw, 1990), p. 147.

29. Norman Davies, *White Eagle Red Star the Polish-Soviet War 1919–20* (Orbis Books, London, 1983), p. 129.

30. Raport Biura Prasowego Polskiego w Nowym Jorku z dnia 29 i 30 sierpnia 1920 [Report of the Polish Press Bureau in New York City for August 29, 30, 1920], Pilsudski Institute, New York, Adjutancy General of the Commander in Chief vol. 69b/3, p. 51. Raport Biura Prasowego Polskiego w Nowym Jorku z dnia 4, 5, 6 września 1920 [Report of the Polish Press Bureau in New York City for September 4, 5, 6, 1920], Pilsudski Institute, New York, Adjutancy General of the Commander in Chief, vol. 69a, p. 46.

31. Dowództwo 6 Armii, Rozkaz Nr.74, Główna poczta polowa, Nr.VI, dnia 17 września 1920, L.p.792 — Rozkaz pochwalny dla III Dyonu Lotniczego [Commendation order of the 6th Army for the 3rd Air *Dyon,* Main Field Post Office, September 17, 1920].

32. Sumaryczny wykaz lotów bojowych [Summary of combat sorties], Centralne Military Archive, Warsaw, I.300.38.44. Krzysztof Tarkowski, *Lotnictwo Polskie w wojnie z Rosją Sowiecką 1919–1920* (Wydawnictwa Komunikacji i Łączności, Warsaw, 1991), p. 106.

33. Personal File, no. 4672 Central Military Archive, Warsaw; R. Karolevitz, R.S. Fenn, *Flight of Eagles,* p. 206ff.

34. Raport Biura Prasowego Polskiego w Nowym Jorku z dnia 4, 5, 6, września 1920, Raport Biura Prasowego Polskiego w Nowym Jorku z dnia 7, 8, września [Report of the Polish Press Bureau in New York City, September 4, 5, 6, 1920. Report of the Polish Press Bureau in New York City for September 7, 8, 1920], Adjutancy General of the Commander in Chief, Pilsudski Institute, vol. 69a, pp. 47, 49.

35. Personal File of Lt. Thomas H. Garlich, Central Military Archive, Warsaw, no. 6868.

36. Personal File of Lt. Inglis Maitland, Central Military Archive, Warsaw, no. 9305.

37. Personal File of Lt. John Speaks, Central Military Archive, Warsaw, no. 13127.

38. Kenneth Malcolm Murray, "The Kościuszko Squadron," *Poland Magazine* (New York), November 1925, p. 692.

39. Kenneth M. Murray, "The Kościuszko Squadron," *Poland Magazine* (New York), November, 1925, p. 692.

40. OD to MID in Washington, no. 972, "Poland. Combat Factor. Aviation Monograph," September 21, 1920, National Archive, Washington, DC.

Chapter 9

1. Walter Ciszek, Daniel L. Flaherty, *With God in Russia* (McGraw-Hill Company, New York, Toronto, London, The America Press, New York, 1964).

2. OD to MID, no. 972, September 21, 1920, "Poland Combat Factor, Aviation Monograph." Raport Biura Prasowego Polskiego w Nowym Jorku z dnia 7, 8 września 1920 [Report of the Polish Press Bureau in New York, September 7, 8, 1920], Pilsudski Institute, Adjutancy General of the Commander in Chief, vol. 69a, p. 48; vol. 69b/3, p. 76.

Notes — Chapter 9

3. Maj. Cedric Fauntleroy to John C. Cooper in Florida, Merian C. Cooper Collection, Hoover Institution Archives, Appendix 23.

4. Raport C. Fauntleroya oraz protokoły przesłuchań świadków, Szefostwo Lotnictwa 6 Armii, L.675/pf, Lwów, September 24, 1920 [Report by Fauntleroy and witness testimonies, Air Force Command, 6th Army], Central Military Archive, Personal File, 7185.

5. R.G. Simonenko, "Amerikanskije letcziki na Ukrainie, Wojna z Polszej 1919–1920gg." *Wojenno-Istoriczeskij Żurnał* (Moscow), no. 3/1992, p. 54.

6. Merian Cooper to Marek Mażyński in Pasadena, May 24, 1972, Pilsudski Institute, New York, Marek Mażyński File. On conditions in Bolshevik prisons and help provided to Cooper as well as his later escape from Russia, see: Marguerite Harrison, *There's Always Tomorrow: The Story of a Checkered Life* (Farrar and Rinehart, New York, 1935) pp. 346–350.

7. [Merian Cooper], *Things Men Die For, by "C"* (Putnam & Sons, New York, London, 1927), pp. 59–62.

8. M. Cooper to the Chief of Aviation, Warsaw, May 12, 1921, 1285, Central Military Archive, Warsaw. Report is quoted in full in: T. Kopański, Ostatni lot bojowy kapitana Coopera, *Militaria* (Warsaw), vol. 3, no. 1/1997, p. 10.

9. Ryan to Paris, Riga, April 28, 1921, Merian C. Cooper Collection, Hoover Institution Archives.

10. No. 164-334 (File N.), Telegram no. 201 from Riga, April 28, 1921, National Archive, Washington, Record Group 165.

11. No. 164-334, 85–87, Riga, July 13, 1921, National Archive, Washington, Record Group 165.

12. M. Cooper to Herbert Hoover, Secretary of Commerce in Washington, Warsaw June 7, 1921, Merian C. Cooper Collection, Hoover Institution Archives.

13. R. Simonenko, "Amerikanskie letcziki na Ukraine, Wojna z Polszej, 1919–1920gg," *Wojenno-Istoriczeskij Żurnał* (Moscow), no. 3/1992, p. 57.

14. Rozkaz nr. 46 Dowództwa 6 Armii. Główna Poczta Polowa, Nr. VI, dnia 9 maja 1921 [Order of the 6th Army HQ, no.46, May 9th, 1921], Central Military Archive, Records of the 6th Army, I.311.6.1. Wacław Jędrzejewicz, Janusz Cisek, *Kalendarium życia Józefa Piłsudskiego 1867–1935*, vol. II (1918–1926) (Rytm, Warszawa, 1998), p. 320.

15. Miecislaus Haiman, *Kościuszko; Leader and Exile* (The Kosciuszko Foundation & The Polish Institute of Arts and Sciences, New York, 1977), pp. 75–80. R. Karolevitz, R. Fenn, *Flight of Eagles*, p. 233.

16. Sterling Seagrave, *Soldiers of Fortune* (Time-Life Books, Alexandria, Virginia, 1985) p. 235. Jerzy Rozwadowski, *Gwiaździsta Eskadra* (Signa Press, Albany, NY 1976), pp. 21–23.

17. Zbigniew Orzechowski, Memoriał w sprawie nominacji ppłk Faunt-le-Roy'a na generała WP [Memo on the issue of promotion of Lt. Col. Fauntleroy to the rank of General], Lwów, May 9th, 1921, Ministry of Military Affairs, 14429/21, Central Military Archive, Warsaw.

Chapter 10

1. Tadeusz Krząstck, "Związki lotnictwa wojskowego Francji i Polski, Waldemar Wójcik, Wojskowe szkolnictwo lotnicze (1919–1920)," in: *Lotnictwo Polskie w okresie miedzywojennym* (Warsaw-Suwałki, 1993), pp. 29, 53–60, 153–158.
2. "*Wykład o Lotnictwie Wojskowym*" (Nakładem Generalnego Inspektoratu Artylerii [Lecture on Military Aviation, Printed by the Inspectorate of Artillery] (Warsaw, 1919), pp. 5–6.
3. Tomasz Kopański, *British WWI Aircraft in the Polish Air Force* (Mashroom Magazine Special, Sandomierz, 1999).
4. OD to MID, no. 972, September 21, 1920, "Poland. Combat Factor. Aviation Monograph," National Archive, Washington, Record Group 165.
5. OD to MID, no. 972, September 21, 1920, "Poland. Combat Factor. Aviation Monograph," National Archive, Washington, Record Group 165.
6. Raport Biura Prasowego Polskiego w Nowym Jorku z dnia 22 i 23 listopada 1920 roku [Report of the Polish Press Bureau in New York, November 22, 23, 1920], Pilsudski Institute, Adjutancy General of the Commander in Chief, vol. 72a/1, p. 124.
7. "Employment of Aviation in the Polish-Bolshevik War," OD to MID in Washington, no. 870, July 3, 1920, National Archive, Washington, Record Group 165.
8. Elbert F. Farman, "The Polish-Bolshevik Cavalry Campaign of 1920," *Cavalry Journal*, vol. 30 (1921), July, pp. 223–239.
9. [M. Cooper], *Faunt-le-Roy i jego Eskadra w Polsce*, pp. 159–160.
10. [M. Cooper], *Faunt-le-Roy i jego Eskadra w Polsce*, pp. 178–179.
11. Kenneth Malcolm Murray, "The Kościuszko Squadron," *Poland Magazine* (New York), April 1925, p. 248.
12. Ppłk pil. Tadeusz Prauss, "Kronika wojenna 3-ciej Eskadry Lotniczej," *Przegląd Lotniczy* (Warsaw), vol. IV, no. 8–9, August–September, 1931, p. 624.
13. Ppłk pil. Edward Lewandowski, "Lotnictwo w walce z Armią Konną Budiennego," *Przegląd Lotniczy*, vol. V, no. 1–2, January–February, 1932, p. 34.
14. Lt. S. Turbiak, "Walki III Dywizjonu Lotniczego z konną armią Budiennego pod Lwowem (Wspomnienia i uwagi)," *Bellona* (Warsaw), vol. V, no. 1, January 1922, p. 131.
15. "Nasze Lotnictwo i Jego Działalność. Uwagi zebrane na podstawie operacji wojennych 6-tej, 3-ej i 2-ej Armii w czasie od kwietnia do września 1920 r" [Our Aviation and its Activities. Notes collected on the basis of combat operations of the 6th, 3rd and 2nd Army in the period from April to September, 1920], Central Military Archive, Warsaw, 400.1084.
16. "Nasze Lotnictwo i Jego Działalność. Uwagi zebrane na podstawie operacji wojennych 6-tej, 3-ej I 2-ej Armii w czasie od kwietnia do września 1920 r." Central Military Archive, Warsaw, 400.1084.
17. "Nasze Lotnictwo i Jego Działalność. Uwagi zebrane na podstawie operacji wojennych 6-tej, 3-ej i 2-ej Armii w czasie od kwietnia do września 1920 r." Central Military Archive, Warsaw, 400.1084.

18. Maj. Władysław Madejski, "Lotnictwo w Bitwie pod Lwowem w sierpniu 1920 roku" [Aviation in the battle of Lwów, August, 1920], *Przegląd Lotniczy* (Warsaw), vol. X, no. 4, April, 1937, p. 484.
19. Maj. Marian Romeyko, "Doświadczenia lotnicze z wojny polsko-sowieckiej" [Air Force experience during the Polish-Soviet War], *Bellona* (Warsaw), vol. XXIV, 1926.
20. Maj. Marian Romeyko, "Doświadczenia lotnicze z wojny polsko-sowieckiej," *Bellona* (Warsaw), vol. XXIV, 1926, pp. 251–255.
21. David T. Zabecki, "Hollywood's Merian C. Cooper did more than film adventure in the air—he lived it as well," *Aviation History*, vol. 7, no. 4, March 1997, p. 12ff.

Chapter 11

1. Carl Molesworth, Gabby; *A Fighter Pilots Life as Told to C. Molesworth* (Orion Books, New York, 1991), p. 55ff. "Lt. Col. F.S. Gabreski, Polish-American Ace," *The Polish Review* (New York), vol. V, no. 21, June 28, 1945. Flint O. DuPre, *U.S. Air Force; Biographical Dictionary* (Franklin Watts, Inc., New York, 1965), p. 81.
2. Z. Burzyński, "*Kościuszko" nad Ameryką* [Kościuszko Balloon over America] (Wydawnictwo Aeroklubu R.P., Warsaw 1934), pp. 129–137. "*American Polish Participation, New York World's Fair 1939. Polish Week, October 10 to 15, 1939*" (New York, 1939).
3. Exchange of correspondence between Polish Attache Militaire in Washington and the General Staff in Warsaw, in: Polish Museum and Sikorski Institute, LOT Collection, AI.2/16.
4. "Col. Fauntleroy Offers to Fight for Poles Again," *The New York Herald Tribune* (New York) vol. XCIX, no. 33887, August 27, 1939.
5. Jerzy B. Cynk, *The Polish Air Force at War. The Official History. 1939–1945* (Shiffer Military History, Atglen PA, 1998). Jerzy B. Cynk, "Osiemdziesiąte urodziny" (part 2), *Tydzień Polski* (London), no. 48 (273), November 14, 1998. Jerzy Pawlak, *Polskie Eskadry w latach 1918–1939* (Wydawnictwa Komunikacji i Łączności, Warsaw 1989), pp. 58–69. Jerzy Rozwadowski, Gwiaździsta Eskadra (Sigma Press, Albany, 1976), pp. 28–42.
6. *"It Speaks for Itself. What British War Leaders Said About the Polish Armed Forces, 1939–1946," Selection form communiques, speeches, messages and Press reports* (London, 1946), p. 23.
7. "Poland's Part in the Air (1939–1945)," *The Aeroplane* (London), vol. LXXIII, no. 1892–1893, September 19, 1947. "*The Battle of Britain, August–October 1940*," *An Air Ministry Account of the Great Days from 8 August to 31 October 1940*" (His Majesty Stationary Office, London 1941), D. Brobiński, "Zanim się wojna skończy, panie poruczniku. O Dywizjonie 303 inaczej" [Before the war is over. The 303 Squadron from a different perspective], *Skrzydła, Wiadomości ze Świata* (London), vol. XXXVIII (1968), no. 95/581, June 1968, pp. 16–17. Jan

Koniarek, *Polish Air Force 1939–1945* (Squadron/Signal Publications Carrolton), pp. 29–31.

    8. "Poland's Circus Master," Interview [with Gen.Stanisław Skalski] by Jon Guttman, *Aviation History*, vol. 10, no. 2, September 1999, pp. 34–40.

    9. "Poland's Circus Master," Interview [with Gen. Stanisław Skalski] by Jon Guttman, *Aviation History*, September 1999, p. 40.

    10. Wolfgang Saxon, "Gen. Witold Urbanowicz, 88, Polish Fighter Ace in World War II," *The New York Times* (New York), August 20, 1996.

    11. "Orzeł z Forest Hills" (Rozmowa z płk.Wojciechem H.Kołaczkowskim b. dowódcą Dywizjonu 303 i Skrzydeł Myśliwskich nr 1 i 2), *Przegląd Polski—Nowy Dziennik* (New York), March 29, 1990, Wojciech Kołaczkowski (1908–2001). Nie chciał zwyciężać za każdą cenę *Nowy Dziennik*, New York, August 17, 2001. Dowóldca Dywizjonu 303 nie żyje, *Rzeczpospolita* no. 177 (5950) July 31, 2001.

    12. For a visit of C. Fauntleroy at Brooklyn's Polish National Union see: Stefan Lenartowicz, *Złota Księga Zjednoczenia Narodowego Polskiego na Brooklynie, 1903–1953* (New York 1953), p. 50. Merian Cooper's membership in the "Polish Veterans of World War I" as of April 20, 1937, is documented in the records of the Archive of the Association of Polish Veterans of WWI in New York City.

    13. C.E. Fauntleroy, M.C. Cooper to Officers of the Kościuszko Squadron 303 in London, March 9, 1942, The Polish Institute and Sikorski Museum, London, LOT Collection, A.V.49/34/5.

    14. Lt. Zygmunt Bieńkowski to Merian Cooper, London May 30, 1942, Merian C. Cooper Collection, Hoover Institution Archives, Appendix 27.

    15. M.C. Cooper, Headquarters China Air Task Force, Office of the Commanding General, Peishiyi, China, September 13, 1942, to Flight-Lieutenant Bieńkowski, Polish Institute and Sikorski Museum, London, LOT Collection, A.V.49/34/5.

    16. "Dekoracja Amerykanów" [Military Decorations for Americans], Polish Institute and Sikorski Museum, London, LOT Collection, A.V.49/34/5.

    17. Dorothy Cooper to Flight-Lieutenant Bieńkowski, October 2, 1943, Polish Institute and Sikorski Museum, London, LOT Collection, A.V.49/65.

    18. Leonard Maltin's *Movie Encyclopedia* (A Dutton Book, New York, 1994), pp. 170–171.

    19. Marek Mażyński, "Osobiste wspomnienia o Eskadrze Kościuszkowskiej oraz jej założycielu ś.p.M.Cooperze" [My personal recollections on the Kościuszko Squadron and its founder, the Late M. Cooper], *Biuletyn Koła Lwowian* (London), vol. XIV, no. 28, June 1975, pp. 17–19.

    20. "Wzruszający gest Amerykańskiego Generała" [A touching gesture of American General], *Dziennik Polski Dziennik Żołnierza* (London), no. 176, July 26, 1965.

    21. M.J. Mażyński, "Millenijne historyczne spotkanie" [Historical reunion], *Nowy Świat* (New York), vol. LXIX, no. 33, February 9, 1966. "Niezwykła uroczystość; Bankiet na cześć gen. Meriana Coopera b. dowódcy Mysliwskiej Eskadry im. T. Kościuszki" [Extraordinary celebration. A Banquet in honor of Gen. M. Cooper, CO of the Kościuszko Squadron], *Weteran* (New York), no. 542, August 1966.

Chapter 12

1. The idea of a separate place of burial for the war heroes was first introduced in December 1918, see: Stanislaw S. Nicieja, *Cmentarz Obrońców Lwowa* (Ossolineum, Wrocław, 1990), pp. 66 ff. "Straż Mogił," *Gazeta Lwowska* (Lwów), vol. CX (110), no. 209, September 14, 1920. St. Sł. Nicieja, A. Przewoźnik, K. Hejke, *Tam gdzie Lwowskie śpią Orlęta* (Warsaw 2002), pp. vi–xix.
2. Stanisław S. Nicieja, *Cmentarz Obrońców Lwowa* (Ossolineum, Wrocław 1990), pp. 211–218.
3. Progress in the work on the memorial was reported by U.S. Military Attaches in Warsaw, see: Maj. Charles B. Moore to MID in Washington, Warsaw, May 7, 1923, no. 2084, National Archive, Washington, DC, Record Group 165.
4. English translation of Piniński's speech in: Merian C. Cooper Collection, Hoover Institution Archives, Appendix 26B.
5. McKinney to MID in Washington, Warsaw June 1, 1928, no. 604, National Archive, Washington, DC, Record Group 165, Photographic documentation from the Memorial Day and other celebrations at the cemetery is available at the Archive of Mechanical Documentation in Warsaw, see: Jan Boniecki, *Kresy Wschodnie II Rzeczypospolitej w fotografii; Katalog fotografii z Archiwum Dokumentacji Mechanicznej w Warszawie (1919–1939)* [Eastern Borderlands of the Second Republic in the photographs of the Archive of Mechanical Documentation, 1919–1939] (Wydawnictwo DiG, Warsaw, 1996), pp. 15–55.
6. Col. Albert Gilmor, Military Attache in Warsaw to Military Intelligence Division in Washington, June 26, 1935, National Archive, Washington, DC, Record Group 165.
7. Jerzy Pawlak, *Polskie Eskadry w latach 1918–1939* (Wydawnictwo Komunikacji i Łączności, Warszawa 1939), p. 66. Jerzy Rozwadowski, Gwiaździsta Eskadra (Sigma Press, Albany, 1976), pp. 30–31.
8. Wiktor Trościanko, "Profanation in Lwów," *East Europe; An International Magazine* (New York), vol. 21, no. 5, May 1972, pp. 28–30.
9. Wiesław Domaniewski, "A Letter of Protest," *East Europe; An International Magazine* (New York), vol. 21, no. 5, May 1972, pp. 29–30.
10. Honorable John D. Dingell, in: Congressional Record, Proceedings and Debates of the 92nd Congress 2nd Session, March 1, 1972, p. 6451.
11. Andrzej Kaczyński, "Cmentarz Orląt. Zgoda na Odbudowę." Andrzej Kościński, "Przyszłość cmentarza zależy od wyborów," *Rzeczpospolita* (Warsaw) no. 23, January 22, 1998.
12. Piotr Kościński, "Wizy, cmentarz, rurociąg," *Rzeczpospolita* (Warsaw), no. 11, January 14, 1999.
13. "Tablica usunięta, *Rzeczpospolita* (Warsaw), no. 121, Warsaw, May 15–16, 1999.
14. "Zażegnany kryzys: Energopol wraca na Cmentarz Orląt," *Nowy Dziennik* (New York), August 16, 1999; "Spór wokół Cmentarza Orlat," *Rzeczpospolita* (Warsaw), September 7, 2000. "Lwowscy deputowani uważają, że w sprawie Cmentarza Orląt poszli na daleko idący kompromis. Nie wystarczy kawaleryjski atak," *Rzeczpospolita*, no. 116 (6193), May 20, 2002.

Resources

Archival Collections

Air Force History Research Program, Maxwell AFB
Cedric Fauntleroy audiotape interview, 1962, from the collection of *The Cross & Cockade. The Society of World War I Aero Historians.*

Archiwum Akt Nowych, Warsaw
Embassy of the Republic of Poland in Washington, DC
Ignacy Jan Paderewski Archive

Butler Library, Columbia University, New York
Boris Bahmetiev Archive

Central Military Archive, Warsaw
Akta Orderu Wojennego "Virtuti Militari"
Akta Szefostwa Lotnictwa Naczelnego Dowództwa Wojska Polskiego
Personal Files

Czartoryski Library, Cracow
General Antoni Listowski Diary, 1919–1920

Hoover Institution on War, Revolution and Peace, Stanford, CA
Merian C. Cooper Collection, 1917–1958 (1964)
Hugh Simons Gibson Collection
Polish Embassy in Washington, DC, 1919–1935
Ludomił Rayski Collection

Library of Congress, Washington, DC
Gen. John J. Pershing Collection

National Archive, Washington, DC
Records of the War Department General and Special Staffs (Military Intelligence Division), Documents in Record Group 165; Reports of the United States Military Attaches in Poland.

Pilsudski Institute for Research in the Modern History of Poland, New York
Adiutantura Generalna Naczelnego Wodza 1918–1922 (Adjutancy General of the Commander in Chief, Polish Armed Forces, 1918–1922)
Teki Gen. T. Rozwadowskiego (Gen. T. Rozwadowski Files)
Michał Mościcki Archive
Gen. Janusz Beaurain File
Lt. Col. Merian Cooper File
Col. Cedric Fauntleroy File
Elbert Farman File (Parts of notes kept by Lt. Col. Elbert E. Farman, U.S. Military Attache in Poland, Spring 1919–June 1923)
Col. Francis Gabreski File
Capt. Marek Mażyński File

Polish Institute and General Sikorski Museum, London
Collection LOT

Polish Army Veterans of World War I, New York
General Archive

Sterling Library, Yale University
Col. Edward D. House Papers, Box 42, folder 1339; Cedric Fauntleroy, Memorandum to Col. E.M. House, New York, January 5, 1933

Private Collections
Kenneth Shrewsbury Papers (in the collection of Dr. Tomasz Kopański, Warsaw)
Edwin Noble Papers (in the collection of Paul Konys, Rocky River, OH)
Leopold Toruń Papers (in the hands of his family in Warsaw)
Collection of Małgorzata "Daisy" Słomczyńska

Periodicals

The Aeroplane, London; *Aviation History*, *Bellona*, Warsaw-London; *Biuletyn Koła Lwowian*, London; *Biuletyn Wojskowej Służby Archiwalnej*, Warsaw; *Cavalry Journal; Czas*, Cracow; *Dziennik Polski i Dziennik Żołnierza*, London; *East Europe*, New York; *Free Poland*, Chicago; *Gazeta Lwowska*, Lwów; *Gazeta Polska*, Warsaw; *Kurier Lwowski*, Lwów; *Military Quarterly; Militaria*, Warsaw; *The New York Times*, New York; *Nowy Dziennik*, New York; *Nowy Świat*, New York; *Panorama Polonii*, Los Angeles; *Poland Magazine*, New York; *Polska Zbrojna*, Warsaw; *Przegląd Lotniczy-Aviation Revue*, Warsaw; *Slavonic and East-European Review*; *Skrzydła*, London; *Tygodnik Solidarność*, Warsaw; *Weteran*, New York; *Wojenno-Istoriczeskij Żurnał*, Moscow, *Wojkowy Przegląd Historyczny*, Warsaw; *Zycie*, Warsaw.

Geographical Index

Adamówka 97
Annapolis (U.S. Naval Academy) 18, 26, 168
Antonów 122
Atlantic Ocean 135
Archangel 34

Baliatycze 156
Bar 85
Bastille 34
Belvedere Palace, Warsaw 54, 201
Bełż 158
Berchtesgaden 187
Berdyczew 83, 85, 86, 96, 97, 98, 100, 102, 103, 104, 105, 108, 123, 157, 180, 202, 204, 205, 207
Beresteczko 127, 143, 145, 146
Bereświca 80
Bereza Kartuska 88
Beverly Hills, CA 191
Biała Cerkiew 104, 105, 106, 108, 110, 112, 116
Białowieża 91
Biel 142
Bielówka 122, 123
Birmingham 37
Blackpool 186
Bóbrka 155
Borszczowice 155, 156
Borynicze 155
Boryspol 110
Boston 193
Brest Litovsk 140
Bristol, PA 36

Brody 127, 143, 157
Bron 185
Browar 110
Brzozdowicze 155
Brzuchowice 146
Bucharest 49
Bug River 129, 146, 147, 148, 149, 152
Burkacze 145
Busk 143, 148, 152, 157

Cazaux 69
Charleston, MA 38
Chicago 193
Chołojów 143, 148
Chreniów 156
Christianówka 103, 116
Churchill, Mississippi 35
Coblenz 52, 53
Columbus, OH 163
Compiegne 21
Cracow 55, 56, 57, 113
Cwietkowo 103,
Czarnuszowice 156
Czerkassy 108, 111, 112, 114, 203
Czudnów 81, 96, 97, 100

Dalnicz 156
Darnica 111
Dęblin 188
Derewlana 147
Didycze 166, 201
Dniepr River 7, 93, 103, 107, 108, 110, 111, 114, 117, 118, 179, 203, 204, 205
Dniestr River 156

Geographical Index

Don River (cossacks) 121
Dubna 157
Dun-sur-Meuse 20
Dvina River 93
Dymirki 110, 118
Dziedziców 149
Dzionka 122

El Paso, TX 57, 163

Fastov 102, 116, 119, 123, 124
Fort Worth, TX 57

Gdańsk (Danzig) 7, 51
Gievres 34
Gołodka River 96
Grand Duchy of Lithuania 92
Grudziądz 140

Hethel 187
Hołoby 127, 128, 129, 165
Horne 190
Horyń River 128
Hrubieszów 129, 158, 159
Human 112, 114

Issoudon 20, 35, 36, 37, 69

Jabłonówka 149
Jacksonville, FL 18, 166
Jakiniów 149

Kalenkowicze 95
Kamieniec Podolski 72, 73
Kamienny Bród 83
Kamionka Strumiłowa 143, 147, 149, 157
Kaniów 108
Kansas City 163
Kędzierzawice 151
Kiev 47, 53, 58, 81, 85, 89, 91, 93, 94, 95, 102, 108, 109, 110, 117, 118, 177, 199, 201
Kiev Offensive 70, 75, 77, 96ff, 176. 199, 202
Kirton 187
Kolonia Mytnica 145
Komarów 158, 159
Kopczynka 73
Korczów 158
Korosteń 106

Korownica 96
Korsuń 108, 112, 206
Kovel 102
Kovno 131
Koziatyń 95, 115, 116, 117, 118, 119, 120, 122, 123, 157, 177, 201, 206
Kozin 143
Kozłów 149
Krasne 149, 152
Krzemieniec 157
Kuban (cossacks) 121
Kulikowo 179
Kupcze 151
Kurne 97

Ławica (airfield near Poznań?) 79
Lewandówka (airfield) 57, 58, 59, 60, 61, 64, 69, 70, 72, 73, 78, 128, 142, 144
Lindsay 187
Lipki 102
Lipowiec 105, 119, 206
Lisko 149
London 30, 131, 186, 191
Łopatyń 146
Lublin 79, 103
Łuck 104, 105, 127, 128, 166, 193, 200
Łuków 142,
Lwów 3, 22, 23, 24, 25, 28, 32, 47, 48, 49, 51, 55, 56, 57, 58, 59, 64, 65, 67, 69, 72, 73, 76, 85, 88, 121, 127, 128, 141, 142, 147, 148, 149, 150, 152, 153, 154, 156, 157, 158, 159, 160, 180, 191, 192, 193, 194, 195, 197, 198, 199
Lyon 185

Majdan Nowy 145
Małkinia 142
Markowa 102
Medwin 112
Memphis 163
Meuse-Argonne 20
Michajlenki 96
Międzyrzec 142
Mikaszewicze 91
Mikołajów 155
Mikulińce 80
Milatyn 149, 151
Mineola Field, LI 36, 37, 38, 69
Mińsk Mazowiecki 141
Miropol 97

Miroszyn 149
Mohylów 86,
Mokotów (airfield) 184,
Monastyrki 145
Morozowka 121
Moscow 53, 168, 187
Mozyrz 95
Murowana 121

Napadowka 119
Neuilly 21
New York 67, 163, 188
New York's World Fair of 1939 184
Newburyport, Mass. 56
Niemiłów 145
Niesłuchów 149
Northolt 186
Nowochwastow 206
Nowogród Wołyński 98, 123
Nowosiołki 152

Ober-Ost 86
Ohladów 145
Okuninowo 118
Olechowicze 155
Olszanica 116, 206
Ołyka 202
Orza 93
Ostryjka 106,

Pacific Palisades, CA 190
Paris 7, 51, 52, 59, 62, 63, 102, 165, 200, 201, 207,
Pedosy 119
Philadephia 161
Piatek River 96, 98, 100
Piatigory 108
Pittsburgh 138
Plattsburg (Cadet School) 36
Płoskirów 81, 86
Poburzana 147, 149
Podwołczyska 157
Pohrebyszcze 119
Pole Mokotowskie (airfield) 53, 171, 183, 184
Połonne 81, 85, 86, 97, 98, 102, 105, 124, 157
Post Wołyński (airfield) 110
Powołocz 106
Poznań 55, 79, 176
Przemyśl 49, 155, 157

Przemyślany 155
Puławy 141
Pulin 97

Raczki 96, 97, 98
Radostawka River 145
Radziechów 143
Radzymin 141
Rajki 98
Rakobuty 149
Rakowice (airfield) 57
Remenów 155
Richmond, Virginia 193
Riga 7, 171, 202,
Rome 180
Romorantin 69
Roś (rail station) 119
Roś River 115
Rouen 186
Rovne 80, 86, 166
Rozdoły 155
Rużyn 122, 123
Rzepniów 149, 151
Rżyszczew 114

St. Mihiel 20
Salt Lake City 190
Samhorodek 95, 115, 122
Sankt Petersburg 87
Savannah 61
Sebin 145
Serbinówka 98
Siedlce 142
Silesia 11, 13, 14, 45, 51, 52
Skwira 104, 105, 122
Śmielna 108
Sob River 115
Sobolewka 102
Sokal 146, 157
Sołomianki 110
Sotnik 108
Środopolce 145
Stanisławczyk 143
Starokonstantynów 81, 85, 86
Stawiszcze 113
Stojanów 143
Stoczek Łukowski 142
Stołpów 98
Streptów 149
Stryj 157
Strypa River 146, 149

Sulejów 83
Szajelki 83
Szczurowice 143
Szepietówka 86, 98, 157

Talnoje 113, 203
Taraszcze 116, 206
Tarnopol 73, 74, 75, 76, 157
Targowica 127
Teterew River 96
Toporów 143
Toronto 57, 162
Toruń 7, 176
Tripolje 117, 202, 204, 205
Tyszowiec 158

Ukraine 23
Ukrainian Peoples Republic 88
Upavon Wilts 37
Uściług 129, 158, 159
Uwina 145

Vienna 58
Vilnius 92
Vistula River 7, 32, 132, 141
Vitebsk 93

Wapniarka 179
Warsaw 2, 23, 51, 55, 59, 88, 102, 124, 130, 132, 141, 146, 153, 155, 171, 176, 180, 183, 184, 202

Washington, D.C. 132, 134, 135, 140, 163, 191, 208
Waterloo 19
Werbkowice 158
West Ukrainian Peoples Republic 88
Wielkie Łuki 168
Wieprz River 141, 153
Wierzblany 149
Winnica 95, 103, 105
Witaczów 117
Włodarpa 108
Włodzimierz Wołyński 141, 156
Worthy Down 37
Wrocław (Breslau) 21, 45
Wygoda 145

Zabłotów 145
Zadwórze 149, 152
Zamość 141, 156, 158, 159
Zbrucz River 9, 89, 90
Żelechów 142, 149
Zieleńce 199
Żmerynka 105
Żółtańce 155
Żurawno 156
Zwiahel 203, 204, 205, 206, 208
Żytomierz 81, 83, 95, 123, 124, 207, 208

General Index

Abraham, Roman, Gen. 195
Abżółtowski, Sergiusz, Col. 75, 182
AEG (aircraft) 127
Albatros B. II (aircraft) 142
Albatros D. III (aircraft) 65, 66, 71, 72, 79, 82, 85, 142
Alexander the Great 19
Allen, Richard 163
American Air Squadrons (in France): 20 Aero Squadron 20; 22 Aero Squadron 69; 49 Aero Squadron 163; 94 Air Force Division (U.S.) 187; 94 "Hat-in-the Ring" Squadron 35; 96 Bomber Squadron 38; 119 Aero Squadron 162; 200 Aero Squadron 20; 201 Aero Squadron 20; U.S. 14 Army, Air Force, China 188
"American Airlines" 188
American Committee for the Defense of Poland 136
American Expeditionary Force (AEF) 1, 6, 7, 9, 10, 11, 12, 13, 14, 16, 29, 32, 34, 40, 53
American Flying Club (New York) 62, 63, 64, 138
American Food Administration (U.S. Food Administration) 21, 23, 24, 34, 36
American Relief Administration (ARA) 26, 31, 36, 48, 50
American Typhus Relief (American Polish Typhus Relief Expedition/American-Polish Relief Expedition) 52
Antosz, Andrzej, Corp. 166

Appleton, Daniel, Gen. 138
Aristotle 18
Arnold, Henry, H., Gen. 10

Babel, Isaac 154, 156, 157
Baczyński, Włodzimierz 76
Baer, Paul, Maj. 42, 62, 63, 138
Baker, Newton, D. 7, 72
Bakhmietieff, Boris 94
Balilla (Ansaldo A1 Balilla [aircraft]) 82, 85, 103, 104, 105, 109, 111, 125, 126, 127, 142, 144, 145, 147, 150, 160, 175
Baltimore Sun 137
Bartkowiak, Sec. Lt. 149, 158, 159
Bastyr, Stefan, Capt. 58, 76, 121, 143, 192
Battle of Britain 185, 186, 187
Battle of Warsaw (Battle of the Vistula, 1920) 32, 140–142
Beaurain, Janusz, Lt.-Gen. 55, 58
Belin, Gen. 16
Bessoneau (hangar) 75
Bieńkowski, Witomir, Lt. 30, 189, 190
Bjornstad, Alfred, W., Gen. 9, 15, 16, 18, 136
Bliss, Tasker, H., Gen 16
Blitzkrieg 183
Booth, Ewing, D., Gen. 53
Borglum, John, Gutzon 138
Boruta-Spiechowicz, Mieczysław, Gen. 195
Brandenburg (aircraft) 57, 72
Breguet (aircraft) 110, 118
Brewster, Paul, Capt. 61, 69

Brynk, Zygmunt, Gen 133, 134, 136, 137
Brzechwa-Ajdukiewicz, Adam, Maj. 180
Buczkowski, Leonard 184
Budenny, Semion 95, 108, 114, 115, 120, 121, 122, 125, 126, 129, 142, 143, 146, 148, 151, 153, 156, 158, 159, 178, 179
Bułak-Bałachowicz, Stanisław, Gen. 5
Burzyński, Lt. 184

Caesar, Julius 19
Castle, Benjamin, Col. 63, 64, 72, 138, 139, 163, 167
Central Flying School, Upavon, Wilts 37
Central Military Archive, Warsaw 27, 39, 68
Chess, Elliot W., Lt. 56, 57, 64, 65, 67, 73, 75, 104, 105, 116, 119, 121, 122, 123, 129, 147, 158, 159, 162, 173, 184, 206
Churchill, Winston, S. 186
Chwila (Lwów) 24
Ciechanowski, Jan 9
Ciecierski, Stefan, Capt. 128, 166
Ciszek, Walter 165
Clark, Carl, C., Capt. 37, 38, 64, 75, 76, 83, 98, 100, 103, 104, 105, 108, 110, 112, 113, 117, 118, 127, 173, 204, 205
Colby, Bainbridge 94, 136
Committee of National Defense (KON), Chicago 132
"Congressional Medal of Honor" 199
Cooper, John 18, 19, 61, 165
Cooper, Merian, Lt. Col. 13, 18, 19, 20, 21, 23, 24, 24, 25, 26, 27, 28, 29, 30, 31, 32, 33, 34, 36, 38, 40, 41, 43, 45, 46, 48, 56, 61, 64, 66, 70, 71, 73, 75, 78, 81, 82, 83, 85, 94, 96, 100, 102, 110, 112, 117, 118, 121, 122, 123, 127, 164, 165, 166, 167, 168, 169, 170, 171, 172, 173, 177, 182, 183, 184, 184, 187, 188, 189, 190, 191, 196, 201, 202
Cooper, Richard, Capt. 191
cordon sanitaire 7
Corsi, Edward, C., Capt. 37, 45, 67, 73, 74, 83, 105, 108, 110, 112, 117, 118, 121, 122, 123, 125, 126, 128, 129, 146, 147, 150, 152, 154, 158, 159, 162, 173, 184, 204

Crawford, George, M., Maj. 36, 48, 64, 81, 104, 108, 111, 112, 113, 114, 116, 123, 128, 129, 143, 147, 159, 162, 163, 173, 203, 204
"Cross of Polish Soldiers from America" 205, 206, 208
"Cross of Valor" 200, 201, 203, 204, 205, 206, 208
Crozier, Gen. 131
Cummings, Thomas, J., Maj. 190

Darwin, Charles 18
Denikin, Anton, Gen. 46, 65, 73, 90, 107
Dewey, Charles 194
Dingell, John, D. 196
"Distinguished Service Cross" 21, 30
Dmowski, Roman 7, 88
Dornier DO.17 (aircraft) 186
Dowbor-Muśnicki, Józef, Gen. 56
Drogoń, Józef, Lt. 195
Duke of Kent 186
Dziembowski, Lt. 149, 151, 153, 155
"Dziennik Polski Dziennik Żołnierza" (London) 191

Eastern Airlines 188
Embick, Stanley, D. 16
"Energopol" (Company) 197, 198
Escadrille Spad 77 37
Evans, Earl, F. 161, 162, 163, 173
Evening Mail 137
Evening Post 175
Evening Telegram 138

Farman (aircraft) 111
Farman, Elbert, Lt. Col 25, 42, 49, 50, 56, 77, 78, 79, 89, 90, 106, 107, 125, 126, 154, 175, 176, 177
Fauntleroy, Cedric, Col. 29, 31, 32, 35, 36, 38, 43, 46, 47, 48, 52, 54, 59, 60, 61, 62, 64, 66, 67, 69, 70, 71, 72, 74, 75, 80, 81, 82, 96, 103, 104, 105, 106, 109, 110, 112, 114, 116, 118, 119, 120, 121, 122, 123, 124, 125, 126, 127, 128, 138, 143, 146, 148, 149, 151, 153, 156, 157, 158, 163, 165, 166, 167, 173, 189, 193, 194, 195, 196, 200, 201, 203, 206, 207
Fenn, Ross 190
Ferić, Mirosław 187

Fletcher, Duncan, U., Sen. 45
Foch, Ferdinand, Marshal 93, 202
Fokker D. VII (aircraft) 142, 149, 192
Fronczak, Franciszek, Col. 132, 136

Gabreski, Francis, Col. 183
Gałecki, Kazimierz 67
Garlich, Thomas, H. 161, 162, 173
Gazeta Lwowska (Lwów) 31
George VI, king of Great Britain 186
Gibson, Hugh, U.S. Envoy in Warsaw 50, 69, 91, 94
Goodyear, Anson, C., Col. 51
Gordon Benett Cup 184
Gotha (aircraft) 65, 142
Grand Armee (Napoleon's, 1812) 199
Graves, Edmund, P., Lt. 45, 56, 57, 67, 68, 85, 161, 192, 193, 195
Gretzyngier, Robert 85
Gromyko, Andriej 197
Grove, William, R., Col. 24, 34
Gwynn, William, N. 193

Haller, Józef, Gen. 6, 7, 13, 56, 114, 171, 172
Haller, Stanisław, Col. 13, 89, 131
Haller's Army (Blue Army) 6, 7, 8, 30, 51, 52, 55, 56, 132, 160
Halpin, Robert, J., Col. 10
Harbord, James, G., Gen. 14
Harris, Walter 19
Harvard University 37, 57
Haviland DH.9 (aircraft) 142
Hays, Charles, E., Lt. 163, 176
Head Office of the State Archives, Warsaw 97
Hendricks, Józef, Lt. 147, 155, 158
Hennenberg, Zdzisław 187
Hitler, Adolf 187
Holmes, Maj. 72
Hoover, Herbert 18, 21, 22, 34
House, Edward, M. 8, 34
Howland, Harry, Col. 9, 11, 12, 14, 15, 16, 18, 31, 52, 63, 92, 135, 136
Huntington, Prof. 18
Hynek, Franciszek, Capt. 184

Idzikowski, Ludwik, Lt. 59, 64, 67
Iwaszkiewicz, Wacław, Gen. 86, 142

Jabłoński, Jerzy, Sec. Lt. 146

Jakir 142, 156, 158
Jakubowski, Stanisław, Sec. Lt. 166
Jasiński, Stanisław, Maj. 31, 173, 200
Jesionowski, Kazimierz, Capt. 54
Jomini, Henri, Gen. 19

Karolewitz, Robert 190
Kasprzycki, Tadeusz, Col. 32, 33
Kauffman, S.T. 163.
Kędzierski, Mariusz 113, 179
Kellog, Vernon 21, 22
Kelly, Arthur, H., Capt. 64, 74, 127, 164, 165, 166, 193
Kesserling, Rudolf 68
Kierenski, Alexander 94
Klim, Jan, Lt. Col. 33
Kłoczkowski, Wacław, Rear Admiral 159, 188
Knights of Columbus 63
Kolczak, Alexander 46
Konarmia (Budenny's) 108, 114, 115, 141, 142, 143, 145, 153, 154, 155, 157, 158, 159, 166
Konopka, Władysław, Lt. 64, 67, 96, 98, 100, 104, 125, 127, 128, 129, 159, 162, 193
Konys, Paul 41, 52, 98
Kopański, Tomasz 23, 26, 35, 37, 58, 60, 66, 70, 72, 74, 76, 78, 80, 101, 103, 104, 105, 107, 109, 111, 117, 126, 144, 145, 147, 150, 160, 161, 162, 170, 172, 216, 220
Kościuszko (balloon) 184
Kościuszko (ocean liner) 184
Kościuszko, Tadeusz (Thaddeus), Gen. 2, 3, 30, 43, 44, 45, 65; Insurection of 1794 133, 196, 199
Kościuszko Squadron 1, 2, 3, 5, 13, 17, 30, 36, 38, 43, 45, 46, 48, 57, 58, 59, 64, 66, 67, 70, 71, 72, 74, 75, 76, 77, 78, 79, 80, 81, 83, 86, 96 100, 102, 103, 104, 105, 108, 110, 112, 114, 117, 118, 120, 121, 122, 124, 125, 127, 128, 129, 133, 139, 140, 143, 146, 148, 149, 151, 152, 153, 154, 155, 157, 158, 159, 163, 173, 177, 180, 181, 182, 183, 184, 188, 189, 200, 201, 203, 204, 206, 207
Kossowski, Jerzy, Maj. 110, 117, 118, 124
Krasnodębski, Zdzisław, Maj. 185, 188, 190

Krassin, Leonid 131
Kryska-Karski, Tadeusz 200
Kubala, Kazimierz, Lt. 121, 143, 146, 158
Kubijda, Vasil 197
Kuchma Leonid 198
Kurcjusz, Tadeusz, Lt. Col. 120

Lafayette Escadrille 30, 138, 163
Lansing, Robert 9, 11, 15, 16, 17, 94
Lawrencis College, Birmingham 37
League of Nations 132
Lehigh University 36
Lenin, V.I. 2, 90, 91
Leonard, Edmond, C., Lt. 20
Leśniewski, Józef, Gen. 64
Lewandowski, Edward, Lt. Col. 114, 149, 152, 159
Listowski, Antoni, Gen. 82, 86, 98, 100, 102, 103, 105, 106, 108, 110, 115, 120, 122, 124, 125
Livickij, Andrij 89
Łokuciewski, Witold, Maj. 187
Łossowski, Hipolit, Lt. Col. 33
Lubomirski, Casimir 53, 133, 134, 135, 136, 138
Luftwaffe 174, 182, 185
Lusitania 35

Macewicz, Gustaw, Gen. 64
Mach, Maj. 220
Mahan, Alfred, T., Admiral 19
Maitland, John, I., Lt. 161, 162, 173
Mażyński, Marek 167, 190
McCallum, John, Stanley, Capt. 159, 160, 161, 193
Meissner, Janusz 146
Merejkovskij, Dimitr 131
Messerschmitt Me109, Me110 (aircraft) 185
Moltke, Helmuth, K., Gen. 19
Mosher, Frank 167
Murray, James 20
Murray, Kenneth, M., Lt. 32, 44, 161, 162, 163, 173, 178

Napoleon Bonaparte 19, 199
National Defense Council, Warsaw 130, 132
National Guard 19
Nelson, Horatio, Admiral 19

New York Times 30, 31, 36, 45, 62
New York Herald Tribune 184
Nicholas I, Tsar of Russia 130
Nixon, Richard 197
Noble, Edwin, L., Lt. 38, 41, 64, 73, 74, 83, 98, 99, 100, 101, 102, 165, 207, 208
North Atlantic Treaty Organization (NATO) 2

Ohio State University 69
Orzechowski, Zbigniew, Capt. 31, 67, 162, 173

Paderewski, Ignacy J. 6, 7, 8, 9, 11, 15, 42, 52, 62, 62, 138, 206
Paerson, U.S. Ambassador to Poland 194
Palludan, Capt. 131
Pancho Villa 19
Paqualen, Col. 115
Paszkiewicz, Ludwik, Lt. 186
Patrick, Mason, M., Gen. 13, 47
Pavlenko (Omelianovich-Pavlenko), M., Col. 79, 142
Perrini, Camillo, Capt. 56, 83, 86, 143, 175
Pershing, John, Gen. 11, 12, 14, 206
Peter, Franciszek, Lt. 109
Petlura, Semen, Ataman 5, 88, 89, 107
Petrushevich, Evhen 88
Philips, Charles, Maj. 102
Piątkowski, Sergeant. 148
Pichon, Stephen 12, 13
Piłsudski, Józef 6, 9, 13, 25, 26, 27, 28, 29, 30, 31, 32, 33, 44, 47, 54, 55, 56, 70, 74, 86, 87, 88, 89, 90, 91, 95, 96, 98, 100, 108, 124, 131, 135, 140, 141, 142, 171
Piłsudski Institute (New York) 196
Piłsudski's Legion (1914–1917) 6
Piniński, Leon 194
Plato 18
Platowski, Zygmunt, Maj. 40
Poland Magazine (New York) 31
Polish Air Force 31, 53, 55, 61, 64, 75, 160, 163, 203, 204, 208; 2 Air Group (*Dyon*) 85, 86, 102; 2 Technical Park 109; 3 Air Group (*Dyon*) 67, 76, 86, 142, 143, 146, 151, 152, 154, 155, 157, 158, 200; 3 Technical Park 108, 109; 5

General Index

Air Wing 117, 118, 124; 5 *Dyon* 86; 2 Squadron 86; 3 Squadron 57, 71, 86, 110, 114; 4 Squadron 57; 5 Squadron 76, 86, 147, 151, 153, 180; 6 Squadron 57, 71, 76, 86, 109, 147, 151, 153, 180; 8 Squadron 159; 9 Squadron 86, 124, 159; 12 Squadron 153, 155; 14 Squadron 159; 15 Squadron 142, 143, 147, 148, 149, 151, 153, 155, 157, 159, 179, 180, 181; 16 Squadron 86; 17 Squadron 86; 21 Squadron 86, 127; 111 Squadron 183, 185, 186, 188, 195; 112 Squadron 186; 121 Squadron 183, 195; 303 Squadron (WWII – RAF) 167, 186, 187, 188, 189, 190; 316 Squadron (WWII – RAF) 187; 317 Squadron (WWII – RAF) 183, 187; *see also* Kościuszko Squadron; Polish-American Air Group
"Polish-American Air Group" 45, 59, 61, 63, 64, 200
Polish Legion (Piłsudski's) 5, 55
Polish Military (W.P.): 2 Army 82, 86, 94, 96, 97, 106, 108, 110, 112, 125, 180, 205, 207; 3 Army 86, 94, 102, 110, 117, 125; 6 Army 86, 94, 114, 115, 142, 153, 154, 157, 180; 25 Infantry Brigade 119; 26 Infantry Brigade 119; 1 Infantry Division (Legionnaires) 141; 3 Infantry Division (Legionnaires) 141; 5 Infantry Division 76, 149; 6 Infantry Division 142, 146, 149, 152; 7 Infantry Division 115; 12 Infantry Division 76, 142, 149, 154, 155; 13 Infantry Division 82, 83, 114, 115, 118, 119, 120, 122, 142, 149, 154, 155, 201; 14 Infantry Division ("Wielkopolska") 141; 15 Infantry Division 146; 21 Infantry Division 141; 5 Infantry Regiment 65; 19 Infantry Regiment 120; 38 Infantry Regiment 146; C-in-C *see* Piłsudski, Józef; Gen. Romer Cavalry Division 125; Gen. Rómmel Cavalry Group 143, 146, 155; Gen. Szylling Operational Group 118, 144; Gen. Szymań-ski Operational Group 143, 146, 155; High Command 12, 13, 14, 25, 31, 61, 96, 97, 105, 115, 127, 140, 142, 143, 148, 153, 159, 203; Ministry of Military Affairs 33, 40, 61, 173, 207; Podolski Front 76; Southern Front 141, 148, 141, 155

Polish Military Organization 5, 171
Polish National Committee (Paris) 6, 7
Polk, Frank, L. 63
Pollit, Allen, W., Maj. 16
Pomiankowski, Józef, Gen. 9
Poniatowski, Józef, Marshal 199
Poray 138
Potocki, Jerzy 207
Poznański, Antoni 162
Prauss, Tadeusz, Lt. Col. 178
Prosiński, Capt. 159
Przewoźnik, Andrzej 187
Pulaski, Casimir, Gen. 1, 18, 26, 43, 44, 45, 59, 61, 133, 196

Rakovski, Christian 88
Rayski, Ludomił, Gen. 65, 127, 172, 184, 191
Red Army 185; 3 Army 141; 4 Army 141; 6 Cavalry Division 154, 166; 6 Infantry Division 154; 8 Cavalry Division 156, 157; 11 Army 142; 12 Army 95, 196; 14 Army 95, 142; 15 Army 141; 16 Army 141; 21 Air Regiment 110; Air Force 65, 86; HQ 153 156; Jakir Group 142, 156; Mozyr Group 141; *see also Konarmia*
Red Cross (U.S.) 50, 63, 65
Reptki, Lt. 127
Republic Aviation (U.S. airlines) 188
Richards, H.H.C., Capt. 20
Rodichev, Fiodor 131
Roland CLII (aircraft) 54
Roland, Eugeniusz 58
Romei, Longhena, Gen. 175
Romer, Jan, Gen. 9, 32, 82, 83, 86, 96, 115, 125, 200
Romeyko, Marian, Maj. 181, 182
Rómmel, Juliusz, Gen. 143, 146, 147, 155
Rorison, Harmon, Ch., Capt. 69, 73, 74, 75, 81, 82, 96, 104, 106, 108, 111, 112, 119, 121, 123, 125, 126, 127, 128, 173, 205, 206
Roussin, C., Capt. 85
Royal Air Force (RAF) 162, 163, 183, 186, 187; Squadrons 303, 316, 317; *see also* Polish Air Force
Rozmarek 147, 158
Rozwadowski, Tadeusz, Gen. 9, 10, 11, 12, 13, 14, 16, 18, 25, 26, 28, 29, 31, 32, 36, 39, 42, 53, 61,, 93, 140

Różycki, Józef 193
Rzeczpospolita (Kingdom of Poland, Republic of Poland) 45, 87

Sapieha, Eustachy 134
Savinkov, Boris 131
Schelling, Earnest, H., Maj. 48
School of Aerial Gunnery, Forth Worth, TX 57
SE5 (aircraft) 128
Senkowski, Aleksander, Lt. 59, 64, 75, 81, 104, 105, 108, 111, 112, 113, 116, 129, 143, 146, 154, 158, 159, 162
Serednicki, Aleksander, Lt. Col. 75
Shrewsbury, Kenneth, Lt. 37, 96, 98, 102, 105, 106, 113, 116, 121, 123, 124, 127, 173
Simonenko, P. 53, 64, 171
Skalski, Stanisław, Col. 187, 188
Skarżyński, Józef 193
Skarżyński, Stanisław, Lt. 127, 128
Skoropadski, Pavlo, Hetman of Ukraine 88
Słowik, Karol, Lt. 54
Śmigły-Rydz, Edward, Gen. 86, 110, 124, 125
Smulski, John 7, 11, 16, 132
Sokołowski, Stanisław, Lt. 168, 170
Solidarity (labor movement) 197
Sopwith F.1 Camel (aircraft) 163
Sosnkowski, Kazimierz, Gen. 42, 61, 134, 207
SPAD S.VII (aircraft) 65
"Spartakus" (German workers movement) 6
Speaks, John, C., Lt. 162, 163, 173
Spinoza, Baruch 18
Stabile, Maj. 175
Stalin, Josif 43, 195
Stec, Stefan, Maj. 55, 58, 193
Strahm, V.H., Gen. 190
Strojev, M. 148
Szylling, Antoni, Maj. 118
Szymański, Paweł, Gen. 143, 146, 147, 155

Tachanki 146
Third Reich 183

Timoshenko, Semion, K., Marshal 167
Toruń, Leopold, Lt.Col. 55, 109, 193
Townsend, Gen. 15
Trotsky, Leon 2, 90
Trunov 157
Tumulty, Joseph 136
Turbiak, S., Lt. 158, 179
Tysler, Paweł, Lt. 143, 146

Ujejski, Stanisław, Gen. 184
Ukraine: Army 79, 154; Ukrainian Peoples Republic 5, 88; West Ukrainian Peoples Republic 48, 88
United States Naval Academy, Annapolis 18, 26, 168
Universal News Service 140
University of Texas 163
Urbanowicz, Witold, Gen. 185, 186, 188, 190

Vergnette, de, Lt. Col. 144
Viard, Gen. 82
"Victoria Cross" 199
"Virtuti Militari" 154, 171, 199, 200, 201, 202, 204, 205, 206, 207, 208

Wallace 63
Washington, George 133
Weber, Jerzy 59, 64, 85, 102, 106, 110, 112, 113, 116, 117, 123, 124, 125, 128, 129, 147, 149, 152, 153, 158, 159, 162, 183, 193
Wellington, Arthur, W. 19
Weygand, Maxime, Gen. 140, 141
White Ingineering Corporation, NY 69
Wilson, Woodrow 6, 7, 8, 9, 17, 138
Wrangel, Peter, Gen 64, 90, 107, 114, 131
Wronowski, Jan, Corporal 65

Yale University 18, 38
Yates, Col. 49

Zalewski, Stanisław, Corporal 168, 170
Zumbach, Jan, Capt. 187, 190

www.ingramcontent.com/pod-product-compliance
Ingram Content Group UK Ltd.
Pitfield, Milton Keynes, MK11 3LW, UK
UKHW041937140426
5217IPUK00014B/519